DIESEL & ELECTRIC LOCOMOTIVE REGISTER

Alan Sugden

Published by Platform 5 Publishing Ltd., 15 Abbeydale Park Rise, Sheffield S17 3PB.

Printed by Heanor Gate Printing Co., Delves Road, Heanor, Derbyshire.

ISBN 0 906579 40 6

CONTENTS

1. INTRODUCTION

GENERAL

The purpose of this publication is to provide the enthusiast with a reference book to record sighting dates, mileages or any other information for personal use. All of the non-steam locomotives which have operated on British Railways or constituent companies are included. For detailed information on coversion dates, fittings, liveries, etc., the reader is recommended to study "Locomotive Directory" by D.C. Strickland which is published by the Diesel and Electric Group. This book is available from the Platform 5 Mail Order Department.

FORMAT OF BOOK

Each class has a heading which is made up of a combination of the following:-

A   CLASS
    The latest B.R. classification is used where possible, but any classes which were disposed of before this came into effect have been referred to as "UNCLASSIFIED" or their former classification is used.

B   BUILDER/ENGINE MAKE/ELECTRICAL EQUIPMENT
    Where each of the sections is the same, the manufacturer is shown once only.
    A.E.I.   Associated Electrical Industries
    B.R.   British Railways
    B.T.H.   British Thomson Houston
    C.P.   Crompton Parkinson
    G.E.C.   General Electric Co.
    G.W.R.   Great Western Railway
    L.M.S.   London, Midland & Scottish Railway
    L.N.E.R.   London & North Eastern Railway
    M.A.N.   Maschinenfabric Augsburg-Nürnberg
    Met.Vic.   Metropolitan Vickers
    M.R.   Motor Rail & Tram Co.
    N.B.L.   North British Locomotive Co.
    S.L.M.   Schweiz. Lokomotive und Maschinenfabric, Winterthür
    S.R.   Southern Railway
    Y.E.C.   Yorkshire Engine Co.

C   TYPE
    Main line locomotives were give type codes in the range 1 to 5 during the early stages of the Modernisation Programme, most where identified in this manner.

D   HORSEPOWER

E   TRANSMISSION TYPE
    BE   Battery electric
    DE   Diesel electric
    DM   Diesel mechanical
    DH   Diesel hydraulic

DX	Diesel mechanical & electric
ED	Electro diesel
EE	Electric
GE	Gas turbine electric
GM	Gas turbine mechanical
OE	Overhead electric
PM	Petrol mechanical
RE	3rd Rail electric

F   WHEEL ARRANGEMENT

LOCOMOTIVE DETAILS

1   LOCO. NUMBER   The first two or three columns show the locomotive numbers carried to-date, the first column being the earliest number.

2   DATE WITHDRAWN   Month and year of withdrawal from service.

3   BRAKE   Type of train brake currently fitted or fitted at the time of withdrawal. See inside back cover.

4   TRAIN HEATING   Where fitted, the type of train heating is shown (This does not apply to shunters). See inside back cover.

5   HOW DISPOSED

C	Cut up
D	Departmental
E	Exported
F	Further use
R	Re-built
P	Preserved
W	War department
Z	Destroyed in tests

6   WHERE DISPOSED   Where a withdrawn locomotive was cut-up, sold to for further use or the present location.

Abbreviations used:

A.P.C.M.	Associated Portland Cement Manufacturers Ltd.
B.S.C.	British Steel Corporation
B.I.S.	British Industrial Sand
C.E.G.B.	Central Electricity Generating Board
D.P.	Disposal point
I.C.I.	Imperial Chemical Industries
L.C.P.	Lunt Comley & Pitt
N.C.B.	National Coal Board
N.C.B.O.E.	National Coal Board Opencast Executive
N.S.F.	National Smokeless Fuels
P.D.	Powell Duffryn
U.S.S.R.	Union of Soviet Socialist Republics

7   DISPOSAL   C Indicates cut-up together with month and year.
    E Exported date.

Most diesel locomotives were numbered with a D prefix, which was eliminated when steam duplications ceased to exist. Similarly, electric locomotives had a E prefix. Re-numbering reference has been omitted for this change. In conclusion, a list of names officially carried by locomotives is printed for reference.

I would like to thank those who have rendered assistance in providing and checking the information contained in this book. If there are any comments or errors detected in the information, due consideration will be given to making any necessary amendments in a future issue.

ALAN SUGDEN
1984

2. B.R. DIESEL & ELECTRIC LOCO NUMBERING

NUMBERING SYSTEMS

Three numbering sustems for diesel and electric locomotives have been used on B.R. as follows:

(1)   The 1948 number series. Diesel locos. were allocated numbers between 10000 and 19999 (actually up to 15236) and electric locos between 20000 and 29999 (actually 20001-27006).

(2)   The 1957 number series was a four figure series with diesel locos. having a "D" prefix (which was dropped after all steam locos had been withdrawn in 1968) and electric locos having an "E" prefix. Existing electric locos in the 2xxxx series retained their existing numbers with the addition of an E prefix.

(3)   From 11/71 for electric locos and 3/73 for diesel locos the TOPS series was introduced with the class number followed by a serial number.

ORDER OF CLASSES

B.R. Locomotives are listed generally in order of their 1957 number, since almost all locos carried such a number. Locos which carried only a TOPS number (classes 56, 58 and 87) are listed at the end of their sections. For the convenience of younger readers, a list of TOPS class numbers with their 1957 number and the page on which the class starts is listed below:

TOPS CLASS	NO. SERIES	PAGE	TOPS CLASS	NO. SERIES	PAGE
01	D2953	47	33	D6500	85
02	D2850	47	35	D7000	93
03	D2000, D2372	36, 42	37	D6600, 6700	87
04	D2200	39	40	D200	16
05	D2400	42	42	D800, D866	21, 23
	D2550	44	43	D833	22
06	D2410	43	44	D1	12
07	D2985	48	45	D11	12
08	D3xxx	48	46	D138	15
09	D3xxx	61	47	D1100, D1500	26
10	D3xxx	51	48	D1702	30
11	12033*	8	50	D400	20
12	15211*	11	52	D1000	24
13	D4500	70	53	D1200	26
14	D9500	106	55	D9000	105
15	D8200	102	56	No 1957 number	107
16	D8400	103	58	No 1957 number	110
17	D8500	103	70	20001	114
20	D8000, D8300	98, 102	71	E5000	121
21	D6100	83	73	E6001	122
22	D6300	84	74	E6101	123
23	D5900	83	76	26000 (later E26000)*	114
24	D5000	70	77	27000 (later E27000)*	116
25	D5151, D7500	73, 95	81	E3001, D3096	116, 118
26	D5300	76	82	E3046	117
27	D5347	76	83	E3024, E3098	117, 118
28	D5700	81	84	E3036	117
29	D6100	83	85	E3056	118
30	D5500, D5800	78, 82	86	E3101	119
31	D5500, D5800	78, 82	87	No 1957 number	123

* — These are 1948 numbers.

3. L.M.S. & EARLY B.R. MAIN-LINE DIESELS

These locos were never renumbered in the 1957 series.

LMS/ENGLISH ELECTRIC/ENGLISH ELECTRIC   1600 h.p. DE   Co-Co
Built 1947-1948

10000	12/63	vb	C	J. Cashmore, Great Bridge	(C04/68)	
10001	03/66	vb	C	Cox & Danks, North Acton	(C12/66)	

B.R./PAXMAN/FELL 2040 h.p. DM   2-D-2
Built 1952 for L.M. Region

10100	11/58	vb	C	B.R. Derby Works	(C07/60)	

B.R./ENGLISH ELECTRIC/ENGLISH ELECTRIC 1750 h.p. DE   1 Co-Co 1
Built 1950-1951 for Southern Region

10201	12/63	vb	C	J. Cashmore, Great Bridge	(C01/68)	
10202	12/63	vb	C	J. Cashmore, Great Bridge	(C05/68)	

B.R./ENGLISH ELECTRIC/ENGLISH ELECTRIC 2000 h.p. DE   1 Co-Co 1
Built 1954 for Southern Region

10203	12/63	vb	C	J. Cashmore, Great Bridge	(C03/68)	

N.B.L./PAXMAN/B.T.H. 827 h.p. DE   Bo-Bo
Built 1950 for L.M. Region

10800	08/59	vb	F	Brush, Loughborough	(C /76)	

B.R./PAXMAN/POWERLOW 500 h.p. DM   0-6-0
Built 1950 for Southern Region

11001	08/59	n	C	B.R. Ashford Works	(C12/59)	

4. PRE-NATIONALISATION SHUNTERS

L.M.S. DIESEL SHUNTERS

ARMSTRONG WHITWORTH/SAURER 90 h.p. DE   0-4-0
Built 1934

34		10/49	n		A. Young	(	)	

L.M.S./PAXMAN/HASLAM & NEWTON 400 h.p. DM   0-6-0
Built 1932 on chassis of Midland Railway "1F" 0-6-0

1831		09/39	v	D	MPU3	(	)	

DREWRY/ALLEN/WILSON 160 h.p. DM   0-4-0
Built 1934

	7050	03/43	n	P	National Railway Museum, York		

HUNSLET/M.A.N./HUNSLET 150 h.p. DM   0-6-0
Built 1932

7401	7051	12/45	n	P	National Railway Museum, York		

HUNSLET/McLAREN/HUNSLET 150 h.p. DM   0-6-0
Built 1934

7402	7052	12/43	n	W	Admiralty, Maryport	(C	/69)	

HUNSLET/BROTHERHOOD/DAVID BROWN 150 h.p. DM   0-6-0
Built 1934

7403	7053	12/42	n	F	Hunslet Engine Co., Leeds	(C	/54)	

HUNSLET/PAXMAN/HUNSLET 180 h.p. DM   0-6-0
Built 1934

	7054	05/43	n	F	N.C.B. Hickleton Colliery	(C10/74)	

HUDSWELL CLARKE/MIRRLESS/BOSTOCK-BRAMLEY 150 h.p. DM   0-6-0
Built 1935

	7055	04/39	n	D	MPU1	(	)	
	7056	05/39	n	D	MPU2	(	)	

HARLAND & WOLFF/BURMEISTER/S.L.M. 175 h.p. DM   0-6-0
Built 1934

	7057	01/44	n	F	Ulster Transport Authority	(C	/65)	

ARMSTRONG WHITWORTH/SULZER/LAURENCE SCOTT 250 h.p. DE   0-6-0
Built 1934

7408	7058	12/49	n	C	B.R. Derby Works	(	)	

ARMSTRONG WHITWORTH/SULZER/C.P. 350 h.p. DE   0-6-0
Built 1936

7059		11/44	n	F	Belgian Railways	(C03/58)	
7060		12/42	n	W	War Dept.	(C /51)	
7061		11/44	n	F	Belgian Railways	(C02/65)	
7062		11/44	n	F	Germany	( )	
7063		11/44	n	F	C.E.G.B., Hams Hall, Birmingham	(C02/67)	
7064		11/44	n	F	Belgian Railways	(C05/61)	
7065		12/42	n	F	Egypt	( )	
7066		12/42	n	W	War Dept.	(C /51)	
7067		11/44	n	F	Belgian Railways	(C01/66)	
7068		12/42	n	F	Egypt	( )	

HAWTHORN LESLIE/E.E./E.E. 350 h.p. DE   0-6-0
Built 1936

7069		04/40	n	W		(L /40)	
7070		01/40	n	W		(L /40)	
7071		04/40	n	W		(L /40)	
7072		04/40	n	W		(L /40)	
7073		01/40	n	W		(L 40)	
7074	12000	04/61	n	C	B.R. Derby Works	(C06/62)	
7075		01/40	n	W		(L /49)	
7076	12001	02/62	n	C	B.R. Horwich Works	(C04/62)	
7077		01/40	n	W		(L /40)	
7078		01/40	n	W		(L /40)	

HAWTHORN LESLIE/E.E./E.E. 350 h.p. DE   0-6-0
Built 1934

7079	12002	06/56	v	C	B.R. Derby Works	(C09/56)	

L.M.S./E.E./E.E. 350 h.p. DE   0-6-0
Built 1939-1942

7080	12003	11/67	n	C	Slag Reduction Co., Ickles	(C08/68)	
7081	12004	12/67	n	C	J. Cashmore, Great Bridge	(C05/68)	
7082	12005	09/67	n	C	C.F. Booth, Rotherham	(C04/68)	
7083	12006	09/67	n	C	Slag Reduction Co., Ickles	(C06/68)	
7084	12007	10/67	n	C	Slag Reduction Co., Ickles	(C04/68)	
7085	12008	07/67	n	C	C.F. Booth, Rotherham	(C02/68)	
7086	12009	09/67	n	C	Slag Reduction Co., Ickles	(C09/68)	
7087	12010	09/67	n	C	Slag Reduction Co., Ickles	(C09/68)	
7088	12011	03/66	n	C	B.R. Derby Works	(C05/66)	
7089	12012	12/67	n	C	W. Hatton Ltd, at Bolton Depot	(C07/68)	
7090	12013	11/67	n	C	Slag Reduction Co., Ickles	(C08/68)	
7091	12014	10/67	n	C	Slag Reduction Co., Ickles	(C04/68)	
7092	12015	10/67	n	C	Slag Reduction Co., Ickles	(C04/68)	
7093	12016	09/67	n	C	Slag Reduction Co., Ickles	(C10/68)	
7094	12017	10/67	n	C	Slag Reduction Co., Ickles	(C04/68)	
7095	12018	10/67	n	C	Slag Reduction Co., Ickles	(C04/68)	
7096	12019	10/67	n	C	Slag Reduction Co., Ickles	(C04/68)	
7097	12020	11/67	n	C	Slag Reduction Co., Ickles	(C08/68)	
7098	12021	10/67	n	C	Slag Reduction Co., Ickles	(C04/68)	
7099	12022	11/66	n	C	J. Cashmore, Great Bridge	(C08/67)	
7100		12/42	n	W	M.E.F. 11	( )	

7101		12/42	n	W	M.E.F. 12	( )	
7102		12/42	n	W	M.E.F. 17	( )	
7103		12/42	n	W	M.E.F. 13	( )	
7104		12/42	n	W	M.E.F. 14	( )	
7105		12/42	n	W	M.E.F. 18	( )	
7106		12/42	n	W	Italy	( )	
7107		12/42	n	W	M.E.F. 16	( )	
7108		12/42	n	W	M.E.F. 15	( )	
7109		12/42	n	W	North Africa	( )	
7110	12023	12/67	n	C	W. Hatton Ltd, at Bolton Depot	(C07/68)	
7111	12024	12/67	n	C	J. Cashmore, Great Bridge	(C03/68)	
7112	12025	11/67	n	C	Slag Reduction Co., Ickles	(C10/68)	
7113	12026	10/67	n	C	Slag Reduction Co., Ickles	(C04/68)	
7114	12027	10/67	n	C	Slag Reduction Co., Ickles	(C04/68)	
7115	12028	06/67	n	C	C.F. Booth, Rotherham	(C04/68)	
7116	12029	05/66	n	C	B.R. Derby Works	(C07/66)	
7117	12030	08/64	n	C	B.R. Derby Works	(C08/67)	
7118	12031	12/67	n	C	J. Cashmore, Great Bridge	(C07/68)	
7119	12032	12/67	n	C	J. Cashmore, Great Bridge	(C07/68)	

CLASS 11   L.M.S./ENGLISH ELECTRIC/ENGLISH ELECTRIC 350 h.p. DE   0-6-0
Built 1945-1953

7120	12033	01/69	n	C	J. Cashmore, Great Bridge	(C08/70)	
7121	12034	11/68	n	C	J. McWilliams, Shettleston	(C09/69)	
7122	12035	11/68	n	C	J. McWilliams, Shettleston	(C09/69)	
7123	12036	11/68	n	C	J. Cashmore, Great Bridge	(C08/70)	
7124	12037	10/68	n	C	J. Cashmore, Great Bridge	(C07/70)	
7125	12038	01/69	n	C	G. Cohen, Kettering	(C07/71)	
7126	12039	10/68	n	C	J. Cashmore, Great Bridge at Bescot Depot	(C01/70)	
7127	12040	10/68	n	C	J. Cashmore, Great Bridge	(C02/70)	
7128	12041	10/68	n	C	B.R. Swindon Works	(C09/69)	
7129	12042	10/68	n	C	J. Cashmore, Newport	(C11/69)	
7130	12043	10/68	n	C	J. Cashmore, Great Bridge	(C11/69)	
7131	12044	10/68	n	C	J. Cashmore, Great Bridge	(C11/69)	
	12045	01/69	n	C	J. Cashmore, Great Bridge	(C11/69)	
	12046	01/69	n	C	G. Cohen, Kettering at Bletchley Depot	(C12/69)	
	12047	01/69	n	C	J. Cashmore, Great Bridge	(C12/69)	
	12048	01/69	n	C	J. Cashmore, Great Bridge	(C08/70)	
	12049	10/71	n	F	Day & Sons, Brentford Town Goods Depot		
	12050	07/70	n	F	N.C.B., Philadelphia Loco Depot	(C12/71)	
	12051	10/71	n	C	J. Cashmore, Great Bridge	(C12/73)	
	12052	06/71	n	F	Derek Crouch, Widdrington D.P.		
	12053	04/71	n	C	Birds Comml. Motors, Long Marston	(C11/71)	
	12054	07/70	n	F	A.R. Adams, Newport		
	12055	07/71	n	C	C.F. Booth, Rotherham	(C08/72)	
	12056	10/71	n	C	G. Cohen, Kettering	(C05/73)	
	12057	01/69	n	C	J. Cashmore, Great Bridge	(C02/70)	
	12058	04/71	n	C	J. Cashmore, Newport	(C02/73)	
	12059	01/69	n	C	J. Cashmore, Newport	(C01/70)	
	12060	02/71	n	F	N.C.B., Philadelphia Loco Depot		
	12061	10/71	n	F	N.C.B., Nantgarw Coking Plant		
	12062	04/70	n	C	B.R. Derby Works	(C12/71)	
	12063	01/72	n	F	N.C.B., Nantgarw Coking Plant		
	12064	03/69	n	C	J. Cashmore, Great Bridge	(C01/70)	
	12065	05/71	n	C	J. Cashmore, Great Bridge	(C08/72)	
	12066	03/69	n	C	J. Cashmore, Great Bridge	(C02/70)	

12067	01/69	n	C	G. Cohen, Kettering	(C02/70)	
12068	12/67	n	C	G. Cohen, Kettering	(C07/68)	
12069	03/71	n	C	Birds Comml. Motors, Long Marston	(C03/72)	
12070	10/69	n	C	C.F. Booth, Rotherham	(C08/70)	
12071	10/71	n	F	N.C.B., Nantgarw Coking Plant		
12072	12/68	n	C	G. Cohen, Kettering	(C02/70)	
12073	11/71	n	C	C.F. Booth, Rotherham	(C08/72)	
12074	01/72	n	F	Johnsons, Swalwell D.P.		
12075	11/71	n	C	G. Cohen, Kettering	(C07/73)	
12076	12/71	n	C	G. Cohen, Kettering	(C07/73)	
12077	10/71	n	P	Midland Railway Centre, Butterley		
12078	01/71	n	C	G. Cohen, Kettering	(C11/71)	
12079	09/71	n	C	C.F. Booth, Rotherham	(C08/72)	
12080	04/71	n	C	B.R. Doncaster Works	(C11/71)	
12081	06/70	n	C	C.F. Booth, Rotherham	(C08/72)	
12082	10/71	n	F	UK Fertilisers Ltd., Ince Marshes		
12083	10/71	n	F	Tilcon Construction Ltd., Grassington		
12084	05/71	n	F	N.C.B., Philadelphia Loco Depot		
12085	05/71	n	F	T.W. Ward, Barrow	(C04/75)	
12086	07/69	n	C	J. Cashmore, Great Bridge	(C02/70)	
12087	07/71	n	C	G. Cohen, Kettering	(C05/73)	
12088	05/71	n	F	Johnsons, Swalwell D.P.		
12089	09/70	n	C	B.R. Derby Works	(C12/71)	
12090	07/71	n	C	C.F. Booth, Rotherham	(C08/72)	
12091	06/70	n	C	B.R. Derby Works	(C12/71)	
12092	03/69	n	C	J. Cashmore, Great Bridge	(C01/70)	
12093	05/71	n	F	Derek Crouch, Widdrington D.P.		
12094	10/71	n	C	C.F. Booth, Rotherham	(C08/72)	
12095	03/69	n	C	J. Cashmore, Great Bridge	(C08/70)	
12096	01/69	n	C	G. Cohen, Kettering	(C02/70)	
12097	03/71	n	C	B.R. Doncaster Works	(C11/71)	
12098	02/71	n	F	N.C.B., Philadelphia Loco Depot		
12099	07/71	n	F	Hargreaves Ltd., Astley, West Yorks.		
12100	02/69	n	C	J. Cashmore, Great Bridge	(C01/70)	
12101	08/70	n	C	G. Cohen, Kettering	(C08/71)	
12102	01/71	n	C	G. Cohen, Kettering	(C10/71)	
12103	06/72	n	C	J. Cashmore, Newport	(C03/73)	
12104	05/67	n	C	G. Cohen, Canning Town at Stratford Depot	(C10/67)	
12105	01/71	n	C	Steelbreaking & Dismantling, Chesterfield	(C06/72)	
12106	07/70	n	C	C.F. Booth, Rotherham	(C01/71)	
12107	12/67	n	C	J. McWilliams, Shettleston	(C09/68)	
12108	12/71	n	C	T.W. Ward, Beighton	(C03/78)	
12109	11/72	n	C	Marple & Gillott, Attercliffe	(C08/73)	
12110	11/72	n	C	Marple & Gillott, Attercliffe	(C09/73)	
12111	05/71	n	C	Steelbreaking & Dismantling, Chesterfield	(C09/72)	
12112	10/69	n	C	C.F. Booth, Rotherham	(C09/70)	
12113	03/71	n	C	G. Cohen, Kettering	(C08/71)	
12114	10/70	n	C	Steelbreaking & Dismantling, Chesterfield	(C09/72)	
12115	10/70	n	C	Steelbreaking & Dismantling, Chesterfield	(C07/72)	
12116	08/69	n	C	G. Cohen, Kettering	(C01/70)	
12117	01/69	n	C	A. Young, Rotherham	(C10/69)	
12118	04/71	n	C	G. Cohen, Kettering	(C09/71)	
12119	11/68	n	F	N.C.B., Philadelphia Loco Depot		
12120	12/68	n	F	N.C.B., Lambton Engine Works	(C03/80)	
12121	07/71	n	C	C.F. Booth, Rotherham	(C04/72)	
12122	07/71	n	F	Hargreaves Ltd., Crigglestone	(C10/75)	
12123	06/67	n	C	T.W. Ward, Beighton	(C03/68)	

12124	11/68	n	C	G. Cohen, Kettering	(C07/69)	
12125	06/69	n	C	J. McWilliams, Shettleston	(C09/69)	
12126	11/68	n	C	A. Young, Rotherham	(C08/69)	
12127	10/72	n	C	B.R. Doncaster Works	(C04/75)	
12128	07/70	n	C	C.F. Booth, Rotherham	(C11/71)	
12129	09/67	n	C	Steelbreaking & Dismantling, Chesterfield	(C02/68)	
12130	07/72	n	C	J. Cashmore, Newport	(C04/73)	
12131	03/69	n	P	North Norfolk Railway, Sheringham		
12132	06/72	n	C	J. Cashmore, Newport	(C03/73)	
12133	01/69	n	F	N.C.B., Philadelphia Loco Depot		
12134	11/72	n	C	G. Cohen, Kettering	(C04/73)	
12135	06/69	n	C	J. McWilliams, Shettleston	(C09/69)	
12136	12/71	n	C	T.W. Ward, Beighton	(C03/77)	
12137	11/68	n	C	J.E. McMurray, Greenford at Stratford Dep.	(C11/69)	
12138	11/68	n	C	G. Cohen, Kettering	(C10/69)	

L.N.E.R. DIESEL & PETROL SHUNTERS

CLASS DES 1   L.N.E.R./E.E./E.E. 350 h.p. DE   0-6-0
Built 1944-5 for L.N.E.R.

LNER	BR						
8000	15000	08/67	b	C	R.A. King, Norwich	(C08/68)	
8001	15001	04/67	v	C	J. Cashmore, Great Bridge	(C08/67)	
8002	15002	08/67	v	C	R.A. King, Norwich	(C08/68)	
8003	15003	05/67	b	C	Slag Reduction Co., Ickles	(C08/68)	
8004					Frames used for 15004		

CLASS DES2   B.R./PETTER/BRUSH 350 h.p. DE   0-6-0
Built 1949 for E.R.

	15004	10/62	b	C	B.R. Doncaster Works	(C10/62)	

CLASS Y11   M.R. 'SIMPLEX' 40 h.p. PM   4w
Built 1919-22 for L.N.E.R., G.E.R., N.B.R., respectively.

LNER	LNER	BR		
L4		15097	C	
8430	8188	15098*	C	
8431	8189	15009*	C	

Also caried 68188/9 for a time.

G.W.R. DIESEL SHUNTERS

HAWTHORN-LESLIE/E.E./E.E. 350 h.p. DE   0-6-0
Built 1936 for G.W.R.

GWR	BR						
2	15100	04/65	n	C	G. Cohen, Kettering	(C07/65)	

HAWTHORN-LESLIE/E.E./E.E. 350 h.p.
Built 1949 for W.R.

0-6-0

15101	08/67	n	C	G. Cohen, Kettering	(C01/70)	
15102	07/67	n	C	Steelbreaking & Dismantling, Chesterfield	(C09/68)	
15103	09/67	n	C	Steelbreaking & Dismantling, Chesterfield	(C09/68)	
15104	07/67	n	C	Steelbreaking & Dismantling, Chesterfield	(C09/68)	
15105	09/67	n	C	G. Cohen, Kettering	(C01/70)	
15106	09/67	n	C	G. Cohen, Kettering	(C09/69)	

B.R./PETTER/BRUSH 350 h.p. DE
Built 1949 for W.R.

0-6-0

15107	06/58	n	C	B.R. Swindon Works	(C07/58)	

S.R. DIESEL SHUNTERS

S.R./E.E./E.E. 350 h.p. DE
Built 1937 for S.R.

0-6-0

SR	BR						
1	15201	11/64	n	C	G. Cohen, Morriston	(C03/72)	
2	15202	11/64	n	C	J. Cashmore, Newport	(C05/66)	
3	15203	12/64	n	C	J. Cashmore, Newport	(C04/66)	

CLASS 12   B.R./E.E./E.E. 350 h.p. DE
Built 1949-52

0-6-0

15211	12/71	n	C	J. Cashmore, Newport	(C11/72)	
15212	12/71	n	C	J. Cashmore, Newport	(C11/72)	
15213	11/68	n	C	B.R. Hither Green Depot	(C12/69)	
15214	10/71	n	C	J. Cashmore, Newport	(C05/72)	
15215	03/68	n	C	B.R. Swindon Works	(C08/68)	
15216	03/69	n	C	B.R. Swindon Works	(C09/69)	
15217	08/70	n	C	B.R. Selhurst Depot	(C07/71)	
15218	01/70	n	C	C.F. Booth, Rotherham	(C08/70)	
15219	10/71	n	C	J. Cashmore, Newport	(C07/72)	
15220	10/71	n	C	J. Cashmore, Newport	(C11/72)	
15221	10/71	n	C	J. Cashmore, Newport	(C07/72)	
15222	10/71	n	F	John Williams Ltd., Kidwelly	(C09/78)	
15223	06/69	n	C	J. Cashmore, Newport	(C07/70)	
15224	10/71	n	P	Brighton Loco Works		
15225	10/71	n	C	J. Cashmore, Newport	(C05/72)	
15226	04/69	n	C	J. Cashmore, Newport	(C12/69)	
15227	04/70	n	C	B.R. Eastleigh Works	(C05/70)	
15228	02/69	n	C	B.R. Swindon Works	(C07/69)	
15229	10/71	n	C	J. Cashmore, Newport	(C05/72)	
15230	10/71	n	C	J. Cashmore, Newport	(C11/72)	
15231	10/71	n	F	Tilcon Construction Ltd., Grassington	(C05/84)	
15232	04/71	n	C	B.R. Swindon Works	(C04/72)	
15233	05/69	n	C	J. Cashmore, Newport	(C12/69)	
15234	12/68	n	C	B.R. Swindon Works	(C07/69)	
15235	05/71	n	C	J. Cashmore, Newport	(C11/72)	
15236	12/68	n	C	B.R. Swindon Works	(C10/69)	

5. B.R. DIESEL LOCOMOTIVES

CLASS 44   B.R./SULZER/C.P. TYPE 4 2300 h.p. DE   1 Co-Co 1
Built 1959 - 1960 PEAK CLASS

D1	44001	10/76	vr	C	B.R. Derby Works	(C02/77)
D2	44002	02/79	vr	C	B.R. Derby Works	(C12/79)
D3	44003	07/76	vr	C	B.R. Derby Works	(C07/76)
D4	44004	11/80	vr	P	Midland Railway Centre, Butterley	
D5	44005	04/78	vr	C	B.R. Derby Works	(C12/78)
D6	44006	01/77	vr	C	B.R. Derby Works	(C02/77)
D7	44007	11/80	vr	C	B.R. Derby Works	(C10/81)
D8	44008	11/80	vr	P	Strathspey Railway, Aviemore	
D9	44009	03/79	vr	C	B.R. Derby Works	(C02/80)
D10	44010	05/77	vr	C	B.R. Derby Works	(C07/78)

Names:

44001 SCAFELL PIKE	44006 WHERNSIDE
44002 HELVELLYN	44007 INGLEBOROUGH
44003 SKIDDAW	44008 PENYGHENT
44004 GREAT GABLE	44009 SNOWDON
44005 CROSS FELL	44010 TRYFAN

CLASS 45   B.R./SULZER/C.P. TYPE 4 2500 h.p. DE   1 Co-Co 1
Built 1960 - 1963

D11	45122		xe			
D12	45011	05/81	xb	C	B.R. Derby Works	(C09/81)
D13	45001		xb			
D14	45015		xb			
D15	45018	01/81	xi	C	B.R. Swindon Works	(C11/82)
D16	45016		xi			
D17	45024	10/80	xb	C	B.R. Swindon Works	(C08/83)
D18	45121		xe			
D19	45025	05/81	xb	C	B.R. Derby Works	(C11/81)
D20	45013		xb			
D21	45026		xb			
D22	45132		xe			
D23	45017		xb			
D24	45027	05/81	xb	C	B.R. Swindon Works	(C09/83)
D25	45021	12/80	xb	C	B.R. Swindon Works	(C04/83)
D26	45020		xi			
D27	45028	01/81	xi	C	B.R. Swindon Works	(C04/83)
D28	45124		xe			
D29	45002	10/84	xb			
D30	45029		xi			
D31	45030	11/80	xb	C	B.R. Derby Works	(C06/81)
D32	45126		xe			
D33	45019		xb			
D34	45119		xe			
D35	45117		xe			
D36	45031	05/81	xi	C	B.R. Derby Works	(C11/81)
D37	45009		xi			
D38	45032	12/80	xb	C	B.R. Swindon Works	(C09/83)

D39	45033		xb			
D40	45133		xe			
D41	45147		xe			
D42	45034		xi			
D43	45107		xe			
D44	45035	05/81	xb	C	B.R. Derby Works	(C11/81)
D45	45036		xi			
D46	45037		xi			
D47	45116		xe			
D48	45038		xb			
D49	45039	10/80	xb	C	B.R. Swindon Works	(C05/83)
D50	45040		xi			
D51	45102		xe			
D52	45123		xe			
D53	45041		xi			
D54	45023	09/84	xb			
D55	45144		xe			
D56	45137		xe			
D57	45042		xb			
D58	45043	09/84	xi			
D59	45104		xe			
D60	45022		xb			
D61	45112		xe			
D62	45143		xe			
D63	45044		xi			
D64	45045	05/83	xi			
D65	45111		xe			
D66	45146		xe			
D67	45118		xe			
D68	45046		xb			
D69	45047	08/80	xb	C	B.R. Derby Works	(C04/81)
D70	45048		xb			
D71	45049		xi			
D72	45050	09/84	xb			
D73	45110		xe			
D74	45051		xb			
D75	45052		xi			
D76	45053	11/83	xb			
D77	45004		xi			
D78	45054	45150	xe			
D79	45005		xb			
D80	45113		xe			
D81	45115		xe			
D82	45141		xe			
D83	45142		xe			
D84	45055		xb			
D85	45109		xe			
D86	45105		xe			
D87	45127		xe			
D88	45136		xe			
D89	45006		xb			
D90	45008	12/80	xb	C	B.R. Swindon Works	(C09/83)
D91	45056		xi			
D92	45138		xo			
D93	45057		xb			
D94	45114		xe			
D95	45054		xb			

D96	45101		xe				
D97	45058		xi				
D98	45059		xb				
D99	45135		xe				
D100	45060		xb				
D101	45061	08/81	xb	C	B.R. Swindon Works	(C05/82)	
D102	45140		xe				
D103	45062		xi				
D104	45063		xb				
D105	45064		xb				
D106	45106		xe				
D107	45120		xe				
D108	45012		xb				
D109	45139		xe				
D110	45065		xb				
D111	45129		xe				
D112	45010		xi				
D113	45128		xe				
D114	45066		xi				
D115	45067	07/77	xb	C	B.R. Derby Works	(C08/77)	
D116	45103		xe				
D117	45130		xe				
D118	45068		xi				
D119	45007		xi				
D120	45108		xe				
D121	45069		xb				
D122	45070		xb				
D123	45125		xe				
D124	45131		xe				
D125	45071	07/81	xb	C	B.R. Swindon Works	(C08/83)	
D126	45134		xe				
D127	45072		xi				
D128	45145		xe				
D129	45073	10/81	xb	C	B.R. Derby Works	(C05/82)	
D130	45148		xe				
D131	45074		xb				
D132	45075		xb				
D133	45003		xi				
D134	45076		xb				
D135	45149		xe				
D136	45077		xb				
D137	45014		xb				

Names:

45004	ROYAL IRISH FUSILIER
45006	HONOURABLE ARTILLERY COMPANY
45014	THE CHESHIRE REGIMENT
45022	LYTHAM ST. ANNES
45023	THE ROYAL PIONEER CORPS.
45039	THE MANCHESTER REGIMENT
45040	THE KING'S SHROPSHIRE LIGHT INFANTRY
45041	ROYAL TANK REGIMENT
45053	THE KING'S OWN ROYAL BORDER REGIMENT
45044	ROYAL INNISKILLING FUSILIER
45045	COLDSTREAM GUARDSMAN
45046	ROYAL FUSILIER
45049	THE ROYAL MARINES

45049	THE STAFFORDSHIRE REGIMENT (THE PRINCE OF WALES'S)
45055	ROYAL CORPS OF TRANSPORT
45059	ROYAL ENGINEER
45060	SHERWOOD FORESTER
45104	THE ROYAL WARWICKSHIRE FUSILIERS
45111	GRENADIER GUARDSMAN
45112	THE ROYAL ARMY ORDNANCE CORPS
45118	THE ROYAL ARTILLERYMAN
45122	THE LANCASHIRE FUSILIER
45135	3rd CARABINIER
45137	THE BEDFORDSHIRE AND HERTFORDSHIRE REGIMENT (T.A.)
45143	5th ROYAL INNISKILLING DRAGOON GUARDS
45144	ROYAL SIGNALS

CLASS 46 B.R./SULZER/BRUSH TYPE 4 2500 h.p. DE 1 Co-Co 1

Built 1961 - 1963

D138	46001	12/81	xb	C	B.R. Swindon Works	(C08/82)	
D139	46002	09/81	xb				
D140	46003	10/78	xb	C	B.R. Derby Works	(C04/80)	
D141	46004	06/83	xi				
D142	46005	12/77	xb	C	B.R. Derby Works	(C03/78)	
D143	46006	01/82	xb				
D144	46007	02/82	xb				
D145	46008	10/81	xb	C	B.R. Swindon Works	(C12/82)	
D146	46009	10/83	xb	D	(97401) Destroyed during tests	(Z07/84)	
D147	46010		xb				
D148	46011		xi				
D149	46012	07/80	xb	C	B.R. Swindon Works	(C10/80)	
D150	46013	08/80	xb				
D151	46014	05/84	xb				
D152	46015	12/80	xb				
D153	46016	12/83	xb	C	B.R. Swindon Works	(C09/84)	
D154	46017	04/84	xi				
D155	46018	12/83	xb				
D156	46019	12/80	xb	C	B.R. Swindon Works	(C08/83)	
D157	46020	12/80	xb				
D158	46021	01/83	xi				
D159	46022	03/82	xb	C	B.R. Swindon Works	(C10/83)	
D160	46023	12/83	xi	D	(97402)		
D161	46024	04/78	xb	C	B.R. Derby Works	(C10/78)	
D162	46025		xb				
D163	46026		xb				
D164	46027		xi				
D165	46028	05/84	xi				
D166	46029	01/83	xb				
D167	46030	10/80	xb	C	B.R. Swindon Works	(C11/82)	
D168	46031	04/83	xi	C	B.R. Swindon Works	(C08/83)	
D169	46032	04/84	xb				
D170	46033	06/83	xi				
D171	46034	11/80	xb	C	B.R. Swindon Works	(C11/82)	
D172	46035		xi				
D173	46036	05/82	xb	C	B.R. Swindon Works	(C01/83)	
D174	46037	06/84	xb				
D175	46038	03/82	xb				
D176	46039	10/83	xb				
D177	46040	10/80	xb	C	B.R. Derby Works	(C04/82)	
D178	46041	10/80	xb	C	B.R. Swindon Works	(C08/83)	

D179	46042	10/80	xb	C	B.R. Derby Works	(C12/82)	
D180	46043	11/80	xb	C	B.R. Swindon Works	(C05/84)	
D181	46044	04/84	xb				
D182	46045		xb				
D183	46046	05/84	xi				
D184	46047	09/84	xb				
D185	46048	09/81	xi	C	B.R. Swindon Works	(C09/83)	
D186	46049	12/82	xb				
D187	46050	10/82	xb				
D188	46051	12/83	xb	C	B.R. Swindon Works	C04/84)	
D189	46052	10/84	xb				
D190	46053	02/81	xb	C	B.R. Derby Works	(C09/81)	
D191	46054	01/82	xb	C	B.R. Swindon Works	(C08/83)	
D192	46055	10/82	xb				
D193	46056	10/82	xb				

Name:
46026   LEICESTERSHIRE AND DERBYSHIRE YEOMANRY

CLASS 40   ENGLISH ELECTRIC TYPE 4 2000 h.p. DE   1 Co-Co 1
Built 1958 - 1962

D200	40122		xb				
D201	40001	07/84	xr				
D202	40002	05/84	xr				
D203	40003	09/82	vi	C	B.R. Doncaster Works	(C01/84)	
D204	40004		xr				
D205	40005	01/76	vb	C	B.R. Crewe Works	(C02/77)	
D206	40006	03/83	xi				
D207	40007	02/83	xi	C	B.R. Doncaster Works	(C01/84)	
D208	40008	11/82	vr				
D209	40009		vr				
D210	40010	07/81	vr	C	B.R. Swindon Works	(C07/83)	
D211	40011	10/80	vi	C	B.R. Swindon Works	(C11/80)	
D212	40012		xb				
D213	40013		xb				
D214	40014	11/81	xi	C	B.R. Swindon Works	(C12/83)	
D215	40015		xb				
D216	40016	05/81	vb	C	B.R. Swindon Works	(C11/83)	
D217	40017	02/81	vi	C	B.R. Swindon Works	(C08/81)	
D218	40018	09/81	vb	C	B.R. Crewe Works	(C08/83)	
D219	40019	12/81	vb	C	B.R. Doncaster Works	(C02/84)	
D220	40020	08/82	vr				
D221	40021	07/76	vb	C	B.R. Crewe Works	(C05/77)	
D222	40022	03/84	xr				
D223	40023	05/81	vb				
D224	40024	06/84	xb				
D225	40025	10/82	vb				
D226	40026	08/80	vi	C	B.R. Swindon Works	(C09/83)	
D227	40027	04/83	xb	C	B.R. Crewe Works	(C04/84)	
D228	40028		xb				
D229	40029	04/84	xb				
D230	40030	05/83	xi	C	B.R. Crewe Works	(C04/84)	
D231	40031	05/81	vi	C	B.R. Crewe Works	(C05/83)	
D232	40032	02/81	vb	C	B.R. Swindon Works	(C05/82)	
D233	40033	09/84	xb				
D234	40034	01/84	xb	C	B.R. Doncaster Works	(C03/84)	

D235	40035	08/84	xb				
D236	40036	01/82	vr	C	B.R. Swindon Works	(C10/82)	
D237	40037	08/81	vr	C	B.R. Swindon Works	(C11/83)	
D238	40038	12/80	xr	C	B.R. Swindon Works	(C03/82)	
D239	40039	01/76	vb	C	B.R. Crewe Works	(C08/76)	
D240	40040	07/80	vr	C	B.R. Doncaster Works	(C12/80)	
D241	40041	07/76	vb	C	B.R. Crewe Works	(C12/78)	
D242	40042	12/80	vi	C	B.R. Derby Works	(C06/81)	
D243	40043	01/76	vb	C	B.R. Crewe Works	(C04/77)	
D244	40044		xb				
D245	40045	08/76	vb	C	B.R. Derby Works	(C03/77)	
D246	40046	02/83	vr	W	M.O.D.		
D247	40047		xi				
D248	40048	10/77	vi	C	B.R. Crewe Works	(C07/80)	
D249	40049	01/83	vi				
D250	40050	08/83	xb	C	B.R. Doncaster Works	(C11/83)	
D251	40051	01/78	vb	C	B.R. Doncaster Works	(C10/78)	
D252	40052	06/83	xb	C	B.R. Crewe Works	(C07/84)	
D253	40053	08/76	xb	C	B.R. Crewe Works	(C11/76)	
D254	40054	12/77	xb	C	B.R. Crewe Works	(C09/78)	
D255	40055	11/82	xh	C	B.R. Doncaster Works	(C05/83)	
D256	40056	08/84	xi				
D257	40057	07/84	xb				
D258	40058	09/84	xi				
D259	40059	08/77	vb	C	B.R. Doncaster Works	(C10/78)	
D260	40060		xi				
D261	40061	06/83	xi	C	B.R. Crewe Works	(C04/84)	
D262	40062	11/81	vi	C	B.R. Swindon Works	(C06/83)	
D263	40063	04/84	xi				
D264	40064	04/82	xi	C	B.R. Crewe Works	(C07/83)	
D265	40065	11/81	vi				
D266	40066	04/81	xb	C	B.R. Swindon Works	(C10/81)	
D267	40067	07/81	xb	C	B.R. Doncaster Works	(C06/82)	
D268	40068	07/83	xb	C	B.R. Doncaster Works	(C10/83)	
D269	40069	09/83	xi	C	B.R. Doncaster Works	(C06/84)	
D270	40070	06/81	vb	C	B.R. Doncaster Works	(C03/82)	
D271	40071	09/80	xi	C	B.R. Swindon Works	(C10/81)	
D272	40072	08/77	vb	C	B.R. Glasgow Works	(C06/78)	
D273	40073	06/83	xr				
D274	40074	03/84	xi				
D275	40075	12/81	vb				
D276	40076	04/83	xi	C	B.R. Doncaster Works	(C11/83)	
D277	40077	06/83	xb	C	B.R. Doncaster Works	(C04/84)	
D278	40078	08/81	xb	C	B.R. Doncaster Works	(C10/83)	
D279	40079		xr				
D280	40080	09/83	xi	C	B.R. Doncaster Works	(C08/84)	
D281	40081	02/83	xb	C	B.R. Doncaster Works	(C09/83)	
D282	40082		xr				
D283	40083	11/81	xb				
D284	40084	05/83	xb	C	B.R. Crewe Works	(C06/84)	
D285	40085	03/84	xi				
D286	40086		xb				
D287	40087	08/82	vi				
D288	40088	02/82	vr				
D289	40089	07/76	vi	C	B.R. Crewe Works	(C12/78)	
D290	40090	11/83	xi				
D291	40091	09/84	xr				

D292	40092	12/82	vi			
D293	40093	12/83	xi	C	B.R. Doncaster Works	(C06/84)
D294	40094	10/82	vr			
D295	40095	09/81	vi	C	B.R. Swindon Works	(C10/83)
D296	40096	12/83	xi	C	B.R. Doncaster Works	(C06/84)
D297	40097	06/83	xi	C	B.R. Doncaster Works	(C03/84)
D298	40098	04/81	xi	C	B.R. Swindon Works	(C04/83)
D299	40099		xr			
D300	40100	10/80	vi	C	B.R. Swindon Works	(C06/81)
D301	40101	08/82	vi			
D302	40102	01/76	vb	C	B.R. Crewe Works	(C01/77)
D303	40103	02/82	vi	C	B.R. Crewe Works	(C01/84)
D304	40104		xi			
D305	40105	12/80	vi	C	B.R. Swindon Works	(C03/81)
D306	40106	04/83	vb	P	Great Central Railway	
D307	40107	12/81	vb			
D308	40108	08/80	vb	C	B.R. Swindon Works	(C12/80)
D309	40109	12/80	vb	C	B.R. Swindon Works	(C03/84)
D310	40110	12/80	xi	C	B.R. Swindon Works	(C10/83)
D311	40111	05/81	xb	C	B.R. Swindon Works	(C02/82)
D312	40112	12/80	vb			
D313	40113	11/81	xb	C	B.R. Swindon Works	(C01/84)
D314	40114	10/80	vi	C	B.R. Swindon Works	(C08/82)
D315	40115	03/82	vr			
D316	40116	02/81	vb	C	B.R. Swindon Works	(C07/81)
D317	40117	09/81	xb	C	B.R. Swindon Works	(C11/83)
D318	40118		xb			
D319	40119	12/80	xb	C	B.R. Swindon Works	(C10/82)
D320	40120	05/81	vb	C	B.R. Swindon Works	(C10/83)
D321	40121	03/83	vi	C	B.R. Crewe Works	(C07/84)
D322		10/67	vb	C	B.R. Crewe Works	(C09/67)
D323	40123	07/80	vb	C	B.R. Crewe Works	(C01/83)
D324	40124	01/84	xi	C	B.R. Doncaster Works	(C03/84)
D325	40125	05/81	vi	C	B.R. Swindon Works	(C12/83)
D326	40126	02/84	xi	C	B.R. Doncaster Works	(C04/84)
D327	40127	02/82	xi	C	B.R. Swindon Works	(C11/83)
D328	40128	09/82	xi	C	B.R. Doncaster Works	(C08/83)
D329	40129	05/84	xi	C	B.R. Doncaster Works	(C08/84)
D330	40130	03/82	xr	C	B.R. Swindon Works	(C05/83)
D331	40131	10/83	xi			
D332	40132	03/82	xi			
D333	40133	01/84	xi	C	B.R. Doncaster Works	(C03/84)
D334	40134	05/81	xi	C	B.R. Swindon Works	(C11/83)
D335	40135		xi			
D336	40136	05/82	xi	C	B.R. Crewe Works	(C10/83)
D337	40137	01/81	xr	C	B.R. Swindon Works	(C12/81)
D338	40138	08/82	vr	C	B.R. Crewe Works	(C02/84)
D339	40139	02/82	vr			
D340	40140	03/82	xr	C	B.R. Crewe Works	(C08/83)
D341	40141	10/83	xi	C	B.R. Doncaster Works	(C08/84)
D342	40142	04/80	vb	C	B.R. Crewe Works	(C09/83)
D343	40143		xi			
D344	40144	05/81	vi	C	B.R. Swindon Works	(C10/83)
D345	40145	06/83	xi	P	Bury Transport Museum	
D346	40146	10/80	xi	C	B.R. Swindon Works	(C12/83)
D347	40147	09/80	xi	C	B.R. Swindon Works	(C08/83)
D348	40148	08/82	vi			

D349	40149	08/81	xi				
D350	40150		xi				
D351	40151	02/81	xb	C	B.R. Swindon Works	(C09/82)	
D352	40152		xr				
D353	40153	09/83	xr	C	B.R. Crewe Works	(C05/84)	
D354	40154	01/82	xi				
D355	40155		xi				
D356	40156	07/80	vi	C	B.R. Swindon Works	(C12/80)	
D357	40157	07/83	xi	C	B.R. Doncaster Works	(C10/83)	
D358	40158	12/83	xi				
D359	40159	03/82	xi	C	B.R. Swindon Works	(C03/84)	
D360	40160		xi				
D361	40161	12/80	vb	C	B.R. Swindon Works	(C06/81)	
D362	40162	12/82	xi				
D363	40163	06/82	xi				
D364	40164	07/83	xi	C	B.R. Doncaster Works	(C12/83)	
D365	40165	07/81	xb	C	B.R. Doncaster Works	(C06/83)	
D366	40166	02/82	xi	C	B.R. Crewe Works	(C05/83)	
D367	40167	02/84	xi	C	B.R. Doncaster Works	(C05/84)	
D368	40168		xi				
D369	40169	12/83	xi				
D370	40170	12/83	xr				
D371	40171	12/81	xi	C	B.R. Swindon Works	(C11/82)	
D372	40172	09/83	xi	C	B.R. Doncaster Works	(C02/84)	
D373	40173	08/81	vb				
D374	40174	05/84	xi				
D375	40175	05/81	vi	C	B.R. Swindon Works	(C03/83)	
D376	40176	08/81	xi				
D377	40177	07/84	xr				
D378	40178	06/81	xr	C	B.R. Swindon Works	(C10/83)	
D379	40179	02/81	vi	C	B.R. Swindon Works	(C03/82)	
D380	40180	05/83	xi	C	B.R. Crewe Works	(C01/84)	
D381	40181		xi				
D382	40182	06/82	xi	C	B.R. Crewe Works	(C02/84)	
D383	40183	05/83	vi				
D384	40184	12/82	vi	C	B.R. Doncaster Works	(C12/83)	
D385	40185	08/83	xi	C	B.R. Doncaster Works	(C12/83)	
D386	40186	12/82	xi	C	B.R. Doncaster Works	(C03/83)	
D387	40187	08/82	vi				
D388	40188	08/83	xr	C	B.R. Crewe Works	(C06/84)	
D389	40189	01/76	vi	C	B.R. Crewe Works	(C04/76)	
D390	40190	01/76	vr	C	B.R. Crewe Works	(C05/76)	
D391	40191	09/83	xi	C	B.R. Crewe Works	(C08/84)	
D392	40192		xr				
D393	40193	10/81	xr				
D394	40194		xr				
D395	40195	06/84	xr				
D396	40196	05/84	xr				
D397	40197	09/83	xi	C	B.R. Doncaster Works	(C06/84)	
D398	40198	01/83	vi	C	B.R. Doncaster Works	(C02/84)	
D399	40199	06/82	xr	C	B.R. Doncaster Works	(C05/83)	

Names:

40010	EMPRESS OF BRITAIN	40013	ANDANIA	40016	CAMPANIA
40011	MAURETANIA	40014	ANTONIA	40017	CARINTHIA
40012	AUREOL	40015	AQUITANIA	40018	CARMANIA

40019	CARONIA	40025	LUSITANIA	40031	SYLVANIA	
40020	FRANCONIA	40027	PARTHIA	40032	EMPRESS OF CANADA	
40021	IVERNIA	40028	SAMARIA	40033	EMPRESS OF ENGLAND	
40022	LACONIA	40029	SAXONIA	40034	ACCRA	
40023	LANCASTRIA	40030	SCYTHIA	40035	APAPA	
40024	LUCANIA					

CLASS 50   ENGLISH ELECTRIC TYPE 4 2700 h.p. DE   Co-Co
Built 1967 - 1968

D400	50050	xk
D401	50001	xk
D402	50002	xk
D403	50003	xk
D404	50004	xk
D405	50005	xk
D406	50006	xk
D407	50007	xk
D408	50008	xk
D409	50009	xk
D410	50010	xk
D411	50011	xk
D412	50012	xk
D413	50013	xk
D414	50014	xk
D415	50015	xk
D416	50016	xk
D417	50017	xk
D418	50018	xk
D419	50019	xk
D420	50020	xk
D421	50021	xk
D422	50022	xk
D423	50023	xk
D424	50024	xk
D425	50025	xk
D426	50026	xk
D427	50027	xk
D428	50028	xk
D429	50029	xk
D430	50030	xk
D431	50031	xk
D432	50032	xk
D433	50033	xk
D434	50034	xk
D435	50035	xk
D436	50036	xk
D437	50037	xk
D438	50038	xk
D439	50039	xk
D440	50040	xk
D441	50041	xk
D442	50042	xk
D443	50043	xk
D444	50044	xk
D445	50045	xk
D446	50046	xk

D447	50047	xk	
D448	50048	xk	
D449	50049	xk	

Names:

50001	Dreadnought	50026	Indomitable
50002	Superb	50027	Lion
50003	Temeraire	50028	Tiger
50004	St. Vincent	50029	Renown
50005	Collingwood	50030	Repulse
50006	Neptune	50031	Hood
50007	Hercules (to 2/84)	50032	Courageous
	SIR EDWARD ELGAR (from 2/84)	50033	Glorious
50008	Thunderer	50034	Furious
50009	Conqueror	50035	Ark Royal
50010	Monarch	50036	Victorious
50011	Centurion	50037	Illustrious
50012	Benbow	50038	Formidable
50013	Agincourt	50039	Implacable
50014	Warspite	50040	Leviathan
50015	Valiant	50041	Bulwark
50016	Barham	50042	Triumph
50017	Royal Oak	50043	Eagle
50018	Resolution	50044	Exeter
50019	Ramillies	50045	Achilles
50020	Revenge	50046	Ajax
50021	Rodney	50047	Swiftsure
50022	Anson	50048	Dauntless
50023	Howe	50049	Defiance
50024	Vanguard	50050	Fearless
50025	Invincible		

UNCLASSIFIED N.B.L./M.A.N./VOITH TYPE 4 2000 h.p. DH A1A-A1A
Built 1958 - 1959. Original "Warship" Class

D600	12/67	vb	C	D. Woodham, Barry	(C03/70)
D601	12/67	vb	C	D. Woodham, Barry	(C06/80)
D602	12/67	vb	C	J. Cashmore, Newport	(C10/68)
D603	12/67	vb	C	J. Cashmore, Newport	(C10/68)
D604	12/67	vb	C	J. Cashmore, Newport	(C08/68)

Names:

D600	ACTIVE	D602	BULLDOG	D604	COSSACK
D601	ARK ROYAL	D603	CONQUEST		

CLASS 42   B.R./MAYBACH/MEKYDRO TYPE 4 2100 h.p. DH   B-B
Built 1958 - 1961. Warship Class. D830 had Paxman engines.

D800	10/68	vb	C	J. Cashmore, Newport	(C03/70)
D801	08/68	vb	C	B.R. Swindon Works	(C10/70)
D802	10/68	vb	C	B.R. Swindon Works	(C10/70)
D803	01/72	vb	C	B.R. Swindon Works	(C10/72)
D804	10/71	vb	C	B.R. Swindon Works	(C03/72)
D805	10/72	vb	C	B.R. Swindon Works	(C05/73)
D806	11/72	vb	C	B.R. Swindon Works	(C05/75)
D807	09/72	vb	C	B.R. Swindon Works	(C11/72)

D808	10/71	vb	C	B.R. Swindon Works	(C02/72)	
D809	10/71	vb	C	B.R. Swindon Works	(C10/72)	
D810	12/72	vb	C	B.R. Swindon Works	(C09/73)	
D811	01/72	vb	C	B.R. Swindon Works	(C10/72)	
D812	11/72	vb	C	B.R. Swindon Works	(C07/73)	
D813	01/72	vb	C	B.R. Swindon Works	(C09/72)	
D814	11/72	vb	C	B.R. Swindon Works	(C02/74)	
D815	10/71	vb	C	B.R. Swindon Works	(C10/72)	
D816	01/72	vb	C	B.R. Swindon Works	(C09/72)	
D817	10/71	vb	C	B.R. Swindon Works	(C03/72)	
D818	11/72	vb	P	B.R., Swindon		
D819	10/71	vb	C	B.R. Swindon Works	(C03/72)	
D820	11/72	vb	C	B.R. Swindon Works	(C08/73)	
D821	12/72	vb	P	North Yorkshire Moors Railway		
D822	10/71	vb	C	B.R. Swindon Works	(C02/72)	
D823	10/71	vb	C	B.R. Swindon Works	(C05/72)	
D824	12/72	vb	C	B.R. Swindon Works	(C06/75)	
D825	08/72	vb	C	B.R. Swindon Works	(C10/72)	
D826	10/71	vb	C	B.R. Swindon Works	(C01/72)	
D827	01/72	vb	C	B.R. Swindon Works	(C10/72)	
D828	05/71	vb	C	B.R. Swindon Works	(C04/72)	
D829	08/72	vb	C	B.R. Swindon Works	(C01/74)	
D830	03/69	vb	C	B.R. Swindon Works	(C10/71)	
D831	10/71	vb	C	B.R. Swindon Works	(C06/72)	
D832	12/72	vb	P	Bury Transport Museum		

Names:

D800	SIR BRIAN ROBERTSON	D816	ECLIPSE
D801	VANGUARD	D817	FOXHOUND
D802	FORMIDABLE	D818	GLORY
D803	ALBION	D819	GOLIATH
D804	AVENGER	D820	GRENVILLE
D805	BENBOW	D821	GREYHOUND
D806	CAMBRIAN	D822	HERCULES
D807	CARADOC	D823	HERMES
D808	CENTAUR	D824	HIGHFLYER
D809	CHAMPION	D825	INTREPID
D810	COCKADE	D826	JUPITER
D811	DARING	D827	KELLY
D812	THE ROYAL NAVAL RESERVE	D828	MAGNIFICENT
	1859-1959	D829	MAGPIE
D813	DIADEM	D830	MAJESTIC
D814	DRAGON	D831	MONARCH
D815	DRUID	D832	ONSLAUGHT

Class continued with D866

CLASS 43   N.B.L./M.A.N./VOITH TYPE 4 2200 h.p. DH   B-B
Built 1960-1962. Warship Class.

D833	10/71	vb	C	B.R. Swindon Works	(C02/72)	
D834	10/71	vb	C	B.R. Swindon Works	(C02/72)	
D835	10/71	vb	C	B.R. Swindon Works	(C12/71)	
D836	05/71	vb	C	B.R. Swindon Works	(C03/72)	
D837	05/71	vb	C	B.R. Swindon Works	(C06/72)	
D838	03/71	vb	C	B.R. Swindon Works	(C07/72)	
D839	10/71	vb	C	B.R. Swindon Works	(C08/72)	

D840	04/69	vb	C	B.R. Swindon Works	(C07/70)	
D841	10/71	vb	C	B.R. Swindon Works	(C02/72)	
D842	10/71	vb	C	B.R. Swindon Works	(C03/72)	
D843	05/71	vb	C	B.R. Swindon Works	(C04/72)	
D844	10/71	vb	C	B.R. Swindon Works	(C05/72)	
D845	10/71	vb	C	B.R. Swindon Works	(C05/72)	
D846	05/71	vb	C	B.R. Swindon Works	(C12/71)	
D847	03/71	vb	C	B.R. Swindon Works	(C03/72)	
D848	03/69	vb	C	B.R. Swindon Works	(C08/70)	
D849	05/71	vb	C	B.R. Swindon Works	(C07/72)	
D850	05/71	vb	C	B.R. Swindon Works	(C03/72)	
D851	05/71	vb	C	B.R. Swindon Works	(C06/72)	
D852	10/71	vb	C	B.R. Swindon Works	(C06/72)	
D853	10/71	vb	C	B.R. Swindon Works	(C06/72)	
D854	10/71	vb	C	B.R. Swindon Works	(C05/72)	
D855	10/71	vb	C	B.R. Swindon Works	(C04/72)	
D856	05/71	vb	C	B.R. Swindon Works	(C01/72)	
D857	10/71	vb	C	B.R. Swindon Works	(C04/72)	
D858	10/71	vb	C	B.R. Swindon Works	(C06/72)	
D859	03/71	vb	C	B.R. Swindon Works	(C06/72)	
D860	03/71	vb	C	B.R. Swindon Works	(C12/71)	
D861	10/71	vb	C	B.R. Swindon Works	(C07/72)	
D862	10/71	vb	C	B.R. Swindon Works	(C05/72)	
D863	03/69	vb	C	J. Cashmore, Newport	(C08/72)	
D864	03/71	vb	C	B.R. Swindon Works	(C11/71)	
D865	05/71	vb	C	B.R. Swindon Works	(C06/72)	

Names:

D833	PANTHER		D850	SWIFT
D834	PATHFINDER		D851	TEMERAIRE
D835	PEGASUS		D852	TENACIOUS
D836	POWERFUL		D853	THRUSTER
D837	RAMILLIES		D854	TIGER
D838	RAPID		D855	TRIUMPH
D839	RELENTLESS		D856	TROJAN
D840	RESISTANCE		D857	UNDAUNTED
D841	ROEBUCK		D858	VALOROUS
D842	ROYAL OAK		D859	VANQUISHER
D843	SHARPSHOOTER		D860	VICTORIOUS
D844	SPARTAN		D861	VIGILANT
D845	SPRIGHTLY		D862	VIKING
D846	STEADFAST		D863	WARRIOR
D847	STRONGBOW		D864	ZAMBESI
D848	SULTAN		D865	ZEALOUS
D849	SUPERB			

CLASS 42 cont.

D866	01/72	vb	C	B.R. Swindon Works	(C10/72)	
D867	10/71	vb	C	B.R. Swindon Works	(C09/72)	
D868	10/71	vb	C	B.R. Swindon Works	(C04/72)	
D869	10/71	vb	C	B.R. Swindon Works	(C06/72)	
D870	08/71	vb	C	B.R. Swindon Works	(C05/72)	

Names:

D866	ZEBRA		D869	ZEST
D867	ZENITH		D870	ZULU
D868	ZEPHYR			

CLASS 52 B.R./MAYBACH/VOITH TYPE 4 2700 h.p. DH C-C

Built 1961-1964. WESTERN CLASS

D1000	02/74	xb	C	B.R. Swindon Works	(C07/74)
D1001	10/76	xb	C	B.R. Swindon Works	(C07/79)
D1002	01/74	xb	C	B.R. Swindon Works	(C06/74)
D1003	01/75	xb	C	B.R. Swindon Works	(C08/77)
D1004	08/73	xb	C	B.R. Swindon Works	(C09/74)
D1005	11/76	xb	C	B.R. Swindon Works	(C06/77)
D1006	04/75	xb	C	B.R. Swindon Works	(C03/77)
D1007	01/74	xb	C	B.R. Swindon Works	(C02/75)
D1008	10/74	xb	C	B.R. Swindon Works	(C10/75)
D1009	11/76	xb	C	B.R. Swindon Works	(C12/79)
D1010	02/77	xb	P	Foster Yeoman Ltd., Merehead	
D1011	10/75	xb	C	B.R. Swindon Works	(C01/79)
D1012	11/75	xb	C	B.R. Swindon Works	(C04/79)
D1013	02/77	xb	P	Severn Valley Railway	
D1014	09/74	xb	C	B.R. Swindon Works	(C02/75)
D1015	12/76	xb	P	B.R.E.L., Swindon	
D1016	12/75	xb	C	B.R. Swindon Works	(C08/77)
D1017	08/73	vb	C	B.R. Swindon Works	(C03/75)
D1018	06/73	vb	C	B.R. Swindon Works	(C03/74)
D1019	05/73	vb	C	B.R. Swindon Works	(C10/74)
D1020	06/73	vb	C	B.R. Swindon Works	(C04/74)
D1021	08/76	xb	C	B.R. Swindon Works	(C03/79)
D1022	01/77	xb	C	B.R. Swindon Works	(C12/78)
D1023	02/77	xb	P	Torbay & Dartmouth Railway	
D1024	11/73	xb	C	B.R. Swindon Works	(C08/74)
D1025	10/75	xb	C	B.R. Swindon Works	(C01/79)
D1026	10/75	xb	C	B.R. Swindon Works	(C08/76)
D1027	11/75	xb	C	B.R. Swindon Works	(C06/76)
D1028	10/76	xb	C	B.R. Swindon Works	(C06/79)
D1029	11/74	xb	C	B.R. Swindon Works	(C05/75)
D1030	04/76	xb	C	B.R. Swindon Works	(C09/76)
D1031	07/75	xb	C	B.R. Swindon Works	(C10/76)
D1032	06/73	xb	C	B.R. Swindon Works	(C12/74)
D1033	09/76	xb	C	B.R. Swindon Works	(C05/79)
D1034	10/75	xb	C	B.R. Swindon Works	(C02/79)
D1035	11/75	xb	C	B.R. Swindon Works	(C09/76)
D1036	11/76	xb	C	B.R. Swindon Works	(C02/77)
D1037	05/76	xb	C	B.R. Swindon Works	(C02/77)
D1038	10/73	xb	C	B.R. Swindon Works	(C11/74)
D1039	07/73	xb	C	B.R. Swindon Works	(C09/74)
D1040	02/76	xb	C	B.R. Swindon Works	(C08/76)
D1041	02/77	xb	P	Bury Transport Museum	
D1042	07/73	xb	C	B.R. Swindon Works	(C05/74)
D1043	04/76	xb	C	B.R. Swindon Works	(C02/77)
D1044	02/75	xb	C	B.R. Swindon Works	(C09/75)
D1045	12/74	xb	C	B.R. Swindon Works	(C08/75)
D1046	12/75	xb	C	B.R. Swindon Works	(C11/76)
D1047	02/76	xb	C	B.R. Swindon Works	(C09/76)
D1048	02/77	xb	P	Steamport Railway Museum	
D1049	04/76	xb	C	B.R. Swindon Works	(C02/77)
D1050	04/75	xb	C	B.R. Swindon Works	(C04/76)
D1051	09/76	xb	C	B.R. Swindon Works	(C08/77)
D1052	10/75	xb	C	B.R. Swindon Works	(C04/76)
D1053	11/76	xb	C	B.R. Swindon Works	(C06/77)

D1054	11/76	xb	C	B.R. Swindon Works	(C05/77)	
D1055	01/76	xb	C	B.R. Swindon Works	(C12/79)	
D1056	12/76	xb	C	B.R. Swindon Works	(C05/79)	
D1057	05/76	xb	C	B.R. Swindon Works	(C06/77)	
D1058	01/77	xb	C	B.R. Swindon Works	(C06/79)	
D1059	10/75	xb	C	B.R. Swindon Works	(C07/76)	
D1060	11/73	xb	C	B.R. Swindon Works	(C07/74)	
D1061	10/74	xb	C	B.R. Swindon Works	(C08/75)	
D1062	09/74	xb	C	Severn Valley Railway		
D1063	04/76	xb	C	B.R. Swindon Works	(C08/77)	
D1064	12/75	xb	C	B.R. Swindon Works	(C07/77)	
D1065	11/76	xb	C	B.R. Swindon Works	(C07/79)	
D1066	11/74	xb	C	B.R. Swindon Works	(C04/75)	
D1067	01/76	xb	C	B.R. Swindon Works	(C09/76)	
D1068	10/76	xb	C	B.R. Swindon Works	(C08/77)	
D1069	10/75	xb	C	B.R. Swindon Works	(C02/77)	
D1070	12/76	xb	C	B.R. Swindon Works	(C05/79)	
D1071	12/76	xb	C	B.R. Swindon Works	(C11/78)	
D1072	11/76	xb	C	B.R. Swindon Works	(C04/77)	
D1073	09/74	xb	C	B.R. Swindon Works	(C08/75)	

Names:

D1000	WESTERN ENTERPRISE	D1034	WESTERN DRAGOON
D1001	WESTERN PATHFINDER	D1035	WESTERN YEOMAN
D1002	WESTERN EXPLORER	D1036	WESTERN EMPEROR
D1003	WESTERN PIONEER	D1037	WESTERN EMPRESS
D1004	WESTERN CRUSADER	D1038	WESTERN SOVEREIGN
D1005	WESTERN VENTURER	D1039	WESTERN KING
D1006	WESTERN STALWART	D1040	WESTERN QUEEN
D1007	WESTERN TALISMAN	D1041	WESTERN PRINCE
D1008	WESTERN HARRIER	D1042	WESTERN PRINCESS
D1009	WESTERN INVADER	D1043	WESTERN DUKE
D1010	WESTERN CAMPAIGNER	D1044	WESTERN DUCHESS
D1011	WESTERN THUNDERER	D1045	WESTERN VISCOUNT
D1012	WESTERN FIREBAND	D1046	WESTERN MARQUIS
D1013	WESTERN RANGER	D1047	WESTERN LORD
D1014	WESTERN LEVIATHAN	D1048	WESTERN LADY
D1015	WESTERN CHAMPION	D1049	WESTERN MONARCH
D1016	WESTERN GLADIATOR	D1050	WESTERN RULER
D1017	WESTERN WARRIOR	D1051	WESTERN AMBASSADOR
D1018	WESTERN BUCCANEER	D1052	WESTERN VICEROY
D1019	WESTERN CHALLENGER	D1053	WESTERN PATRIARCH
D1020	WESTERN HERO	D1054	WESTERN GOVERNOR
D1021	WESTERN CAVALIER	D1055	WESTERN ADVOCATE
D1022	WESTERN SENTINEL	D1056	WESTERN SULTAN
D1023	WESTERN FUSILIER	D1057	WESTERN CHIEFTAIN
D1024	WESTERN HUNTSMAN	D1058	WESTERN NOBLEMAN
D1025	WESTERN GUARDSMAN	D1059	WESTERN EMPIRE
D1026	WESTERN CENTURION	D1060	WESTERN DOMINION
D1027	WESTERN LANCER	D1061	WESTERN ENVOY
D1028	WESTERN HUSSAR	D1062	WESTERN COURIER
D1029	WESTERN LEGIONNAIRE	D1063	WESTERN MONITOR
	(formerly WESTERN LEGIONAIRE)	D1064	WESTERN REGENT
D1030	WESTERN MUSKETEER	D1065	WESTERN CONSORT
D1031	WESTERN RIFLEMAN	D1066	WESTERN PREFECT
D1032	WESTERN MARKSMAN	D1067	WESTERN DRUID
D1033	WESTERN TROOPER	D1068	WESTERN RELIANCE

D1069	WESTERN VANGUARD		D1072	WESTERN GLORY
D1070	WESTERN GUANTLET		D1073	WESTERN BULWARK
D1071	WESTERN RENOWN			

CLASS 47 BRUSH & B.R./SULZER/BRUSH TYPE 4 2580 h.p. DE Co-Co
Built 1962-1968 (1702-5 formerly class 48)

D1100	47298	xi
D1101	47518	xd
D1102	47519	xd
D1103	47520	xd
D1104	47521	xd
D1105	47522	xe
D1106	47523	xd
D1107	47524	xd
D1108	47525	xe
D1109	47526	xd
D1110	47527	xd
D1111	47528	xd

Class Continued with D1500

CLASS 53   BRUSH/MAYBACH/BRUSH TYPE 4 2800 h.p. DE   Co-Co
Built 1961

| D1200 | | 06/75 | ab | C | J. Cashmore, Great Bridge | (C05/76) |

Name: 1200   FALCON

Class 47 continued

D1500	47401	xe
D1501	47402	xd
D1502	47403	xd
D1503	47404	xd
D1504	47405	xd
D1505	47406	xd
D1506	47407	xe
D1507	47408	xd
D1508	47409	xd
D1509	47410	xd
D1510	47411	xd
D1511	47412	xd
D1512	47413	xd
D1513	47414	xd
D1514	47415	xd
D1515	47416	xd
D1516	47417	xd
D1517	47418	xd
D1518	47419	xd
D1519	47420	xd
D1520	47421	xd
D1521	47001	xb
D1522	47002	xb
D1523	47003	xb
D1524	47004	xb
D1525	47422	xd
D1526	47005	xb
D1527	47423	xd

D1528	47006		xi			
D1529	47007		xb			
D1530	47008		xi			
D1531	47424		xe			
D1532	47009		xb			
D1533	47425		xd			
D1534	47426		xd			
D1535	47427		xe			
D1536	47428		xd			
D1537	47010		xb			
D1538	47011		xb			
D1539	47012		xb			
D1540	47013		xb			
D1541	47429		xd			
D1542	47430		xe			
D1543	47014		xb			
D1544	47015		xi			
D1545	47431		xd			
D1546	47016		xb			
D1547	47432		xe			
D1548	47433		xe			
D1549	47434		xe			
D1550	47435		xd			
D1551	47529		xe			
D1552	47436		xe			
D1553	47437		xe			
D1554	47438		xe			
D1555	47439		xe			
D1556	47440		xe			
D1557	47441		xe			
D1558	47442		xe			
D1559	47443		xe			
D1560	47444		xe			
D1561	47445		xe			
D1562		06/71	vb	C	B.R. Crewe Works	(C09/71)
D1563	47446		xe			
D1564	47447		xe			
D1565	47448		xe			
D1566	47449		xe			
D1567	47450		xe			
D1568	47451		xe			
D1569	47452		xe			
D1570	47017		xb			
D1571	47453		xe			
D1572	47018		xb			
D1573	47019		xi			
D1574	47454		xe			
D1575	47455		xe			
D1576	47456		xe			
D1577	47457		xd			
D1578	47458		xd			
D1579	47459		xe			
D1580	47460		xd			
D1581	47461		xd			
D1582	47462		xe			
D1583	47020	47556	xe			
D1584	47531		xe			

D1585	47542		xd	
D1586	47463		xe	
D1587	47464		xe	
D1588	47543		xe	
D1589	47465		xe	
D1590	47466		xe	
D1591	47024	47557	xe	
D1592	47544		xd	
D1593	47467		xe	
D1594	47468		xe	
D1595	47469		xe	
D1596	47470		xe	
D1597	47026	47597	xe	
D1598	47471		xe	
D1599	47027	47558	xe	
D1600	47472		xe	
D1601	47473		xe	
D1602	47474		xe	
D1603	47475		xe	
D1604	47476		xe	
D1605	47028	47559	xe	
D1606	47029		xb	
D1607	47477		xe	
D1608	47478		xe	
D1609	47030	47618	xe	
D1610	47031	47560	xe	
D1611	47032		xi	
D1612	47479		xe	
D1613	47033		xb	
D1614	47034	47561	xe	
D1615	47035	47594	xe	
D1616	47480		xe	
D1617	47036	47562	xe	
D1618	47037	47563	xe	
D1619	47038	47564	xe	
D1620	47039	47565	xe	
D1621	47040		xb	
D1622	47041		xb	
D1623	47042	47586	xe	
D1624	47043	47566	xe	
D1625	47044	47567	xe	
D1626	47045	47568	xe	
D1627	47481		xe	
D1628	47046	47601	xr	R Rebuilt as 47901
D1629	47047	47569	xe	
D1630	47048	47570	xe	
D1631	47049		xb	
D1632	47050		xb	
D1633	47051		xb	
D1634	47052		xr	
D1635	47053		xb	
D1636	47482		xe	
D1637	47483		xe	
D1638	47054		xi	
D1639	47055		xi	
D1640	47056		xi	
D1641	47532		xe	

D1642	47547		xe			
D1643	47059		xi			
D1644	47060		xi			
D1645	47061		xr			
D1646	47545		xe			
D1647	47063		xr			
D1648	47064		xr			
D1649	47535		xe			
D1650	47066		xr			
D1651	47533		xe			
D1652	47068		xi			
D1653	47069		xr			
D1654	47070	47620	xe			
D1655	47536		xe			
D1656	47072	47609	xe			
D1657	47537		xe			
D1658	47074		xi			
D1659	47075		xi			
D1660	47076		xi			
D1661	47077	47613	xe			
D1662	47484		xe			
D1663	47078		xi			
D1664	47079		xi			
D1665	47080	47612	xe			
D1666	47081	47606	xe			
D1667	47082		xr			
D1668	47083		xi			
D1669	47538		xe			
D1670	47085		xi			
D1671		04/66	xb	C	Bridgend	(C06/66)
D1672	47086		xi			
D1673	47087		xr			
D1674	47088		xr			
D1675	47089		xr			
D1676	47090		xi			
D1677	47091		xi			
D1678	47534		xe			
D1679	47093		xr			
D1680	47094		xr			
D1681	47095		xr			
D1682	47096		xb			
D1683	47485		xe			
D1684	47097		xr			
D1685	47098		xr			
D1686	47099		xi			
D1687	47100		xr			
D1688	47101		xb			
D1689	47486		xe			
D1690	47102		xb			
D1691	47103		xb			
D1692	47104		xb			
D1693	47105		xb			
D1694	47106		xb			
D1695	47107		xb			
D1696	47108		xb			
D1697	47109		xb			
D1698	47110		xr			

D1699	47111			xr			
D1700	47112			xr			
D1701	47113			xr			
D1702	47114			xi			
D1703	47115			xb			
D1704	47116			xb			
D1705	47117			xb			
D1706	47118			xb			
D1707	47487			xe			
D1708	47119			xi			
D1709	47120			xb			
D1710	47121			xb			
D1711	47122			xr			
D1712	47123			xb			
D1713	47488			xe			
D1714	47124			xb			
D1715	47125			xr			
D1716	47489			xe			
D1717	47126	47555		xe			
D1718	47539			xe			
D1719	47128			xr			
D1720	47129			xr			
D1721	47130			xb			
D1722	47131			xr			
D1723	47540			xe			
D1724	47549			xe			
D1725	47490			xe			
D1726	47134			xi			
D1727	47135			xb			
D1728	47136			xb			
D1729	47137			xi			
D1730	47138	47607		xe			
D1731	47550			xe			
D1732	47140			xb			
D1733	47141	47614		xe			
D1734			03/65	vb	C	B.R. Crewe Works	(C04/65)
D1735	47142			xr			
D1736	47143			xb			
D1737	47144			xi			
D1738	47145			xb			
D1739	47146			xb			
D1740	47147			xr			
D1741	47148			xb			
D1742	47149	47617		xe			
D1743	47150			xi			
D1744	47151			xi			
D1745	47152			xb			
D1746	47153	47551		xe			
D1747	47546			xe			
D1748	47155			xi			
D1749	47156			xb			
D1750	47157			xb			
D1751	47158			xb			
D1752	47159			xb			
D1753	47491			xe			
D1754	47160	47605		xe			
D1755	47541			xd			

D1756	47162		xi
D1757	47163	47610	xe
D1758	47164	47571	xe
D1759	47165	47590	xe
D1760	47492		xe
D1761	47166	47611	xe
D1762	47167	47580	xe
D1763	47168	47572	xe
D1764	47169	47581	xe
D1765	47170	47582	xe
D1766	47171	47592	xe
D1767	47172	47583	xe
D1768	47173	47573	xe
D1769	47174	47574	xe
D1770	47175	47575	xe
D1771	47176	47576	xe
D1772	47177	47599	xe
D1773	47178	47588	xe
D1774	47179	47577	xe
D1775	47180	47584	xe
D1776	47181	47578	xe
D1777	47182	47598	xe
D1778	47183	47579	xe
D1779	47184	47585	xe
D1780	47185	47602	xe
D1781	47186		xb
D1782	47301		xq
D1783	47302		xq
D1784	47303		xq
D1785	47304		xq
D1786	47305		xq
D1787	47306		xq
D1788	47307		xq
D1789	47308		xq
D1790	47309		xq
D1791	47310		xq
D1792	47311		xq
D1793	47312		xq
D1794	47313		xq
D1795	47314		xq
D1796	47315		xq
D1797	47316		xq
D1798	47317		xq
D1799	47318		xq
D1800	47319		xq
D1801	47320		xq
D1802	47321		xq
D1803	47322		xq
D1804	47323		xq
D1805	47324		xq
D1806	47325		xq
D1807	47326		xq
D1808	47327		xq
D1809	47328		xq
D1810	47329		xq
D1811	47330		xq
D1812	47331		xq

D1813	47332		xq			
D1814	47333		xq			
D1815	47334		xq			
D1816	47335		xq			
D1817	47336		xq			
D1818	47337		xq			
D1819	47338		xq			
D1820	47339		xq			
D1821	47340		xq			
D1822	47341		xq			
D1823	47342		xq			
D1824	47343		xq			
D1825	47344		xq			
D1826	47345		xq			
D1827	47346		xq			
D1828	47347		xq			
D1829	47348		xq			
D1830	47349		xq			
D1831	47350		xq			
D1832	47351		xq			
D1833	47352		xq			
D1834	47353		xq			
D1835	47354		xq			
D1836	47355		xq			
D1837	47187		xb			
D1838	47188		xr			
D1839	47189		xb			
D1840	47190		xr			
D1841	47191		xb			
D1842	47192		xr			
D1843	47193		xr			
D1844	47194		xb			
D1845	47195		xb			
D1846	47196		xb			
D1847	47197		xb			
D1848	47198		xr			
D1849	47199		xb			
D1850	47200		xr			
D1851	47201		xr			
D1852	47202		xb			
D1853	47203		xb			
D1854	47204		xr			
D1855	47205		xb			
D1856	47206		xb			
D1857	47207		xb			
D1858	47208		01/80	xb	C B.R. Dundee Works	(C04/80)
D1859	47209		xb			
D1860	47210		xb			
D1861	47211		xb			
D1862	47212		xr			
D1863	47213		xb			
D1864	47214		xb			
D1865	47215		xb			
D1866	47216	47299	xr			
D1867	47217		xb			
D1868	47218		xr			
D1869	47219		xb			

D1870	47220		xi				
D1871	47221		xr				
D1872	47222		xr				
D1873	47223		xb				
D1874	47224		xr				
D1875	47356		xq				
D1876	47357		xq				
D1877	47358		xq				
D1878	47359		xq				
D1879	47360		xq				
D1880	47361		xq				
D1881	47362		xq				
D1882	47363		xq				
D1883	47364		xq				
D1884	47365		xq				
D1885	47366		xq				
D1886	47367		xq				
D1887	47368		xq				
D1888	47369		xq				
D1889	47370		xq				
D1890	47371		xq				
D1891	47372		xq				
D1892	47373		xq				
D1893	47374		xq				
D1894	47375		xq				
D1895	47376		xq				
D1896	47377		xq				
D1897	47378		xq				
D1898	47379		xq				
D1899	47380		xq				
D1900	47381		xq				
D1901	47225		xr				
D1902	47226		xr				
D1903	47227		xi				
D1904	47228		xi				
D1905	47229		xr				
D1906	47230		xr				
D1907	47231		xr				
D1908		08/69	xr	C	B.R. Crewe Works	(C10/69)	
D1909	47232		xr				
D1910	47233		xr				
D1911	47234		xr				
D1912	47235		xr				
D1913	47236		xr				
D1914	47237		xr				
D1915	47238		xr				
D1916	47239		xr				
D1917	47240		xr				
D1918	47241		xr				
D1919	47242		xr				
D1920	47243		xr				
D1921	47244		xr				
D1922	47245		xr				
D1923	47246		xr				
D1924	47247		xr				
D1925	47248	47616	xe				
D1926	47249		xr				

D1927	47250	47600	xe
D1928	47251	47589	xe
D1929	47252	47615	xe
D1930	47530		xe
D1931	47254		xr
D1932	47493	47701	xe
D1933	47255	47596	xe
D1934	47256		xr
D1935	47257		xr
D1936	47494	47706	xe
D1937	47495	47704	xe
D1938	47258		xr
D1939	47496	47710	xe
D1940	47497		xe
D1941	47498	47711	xe
D1942	47499	47709	xe
D1943	47500		xe
D1944	47501		xe
D1945	47502		xe
D1946	47503		xe
D1947	47504	47702	xe
D1948	47505	47712	xe
D1949	47506	47707	xe
D1950	47552		xe
D1951	47507		xe
D1952	47508		xe
D1953	47509		xe
D1954	47510		xe
D1955	47511		xe
D1956	47260	47553	xe
D1957	47554	47705	xe
D1958	47512		xe
D1959	47513		xe
D1960	47514	47703	xf
D1961	47515		xf
D1962	47262	47608	xe
D1963	47263	47587	xe
D1964	47264	47619	xe
D1965	47265	47591	xe
D1966	47266		xr
D1967	47267	47603	xe
D1968	47516	47708	xe
D1969	47268	47595	xe
D1970	47269		xb
D1971	47270		xb
D1972	47271	47604	xe
D1973	47272	47593	xe
D1974	47273		xb
D1975	47517		xe
D1976	47274		xb
D1977	47275		xr
D1978	47276		xr
D1979	47277		xr
D1980	47278		xr
D1981	47279		xi
D1982	47280		xr
D1983	47281		xr

D1984	47282	xr
D1985	47283	xr
D1986	47284	xr
D1987	47285	xr
D1988	47286	xr
D1989	47287	xr
D1990	47288	xr
D1991	47289	xr
D1992	47290	xi
D1993	47291	xr
D1994	47292	xr
D1995	47293	xr
D1996	47294	xr
D1997	47295	xr
D1998	47296	xr
D1999	47297	xr

Names:

47076	CITY OF TRURO
47078	SIR DANIEL GOOCH
47079	G.J. CHURCHWARD
	(formerly - GEORGE JACKSON CHURCHWARD)
47082	ATLAS
47083	ORION
47085	MAMMOTH
D1671	THOR (Removed 27.4.66)
47086	COLOSSUS
47087	CYCLOPS
47088	SAMSON
47089	AMAZON
47090	VULCAN
47091	THOR
47158	Henry Ford
47222	Appleby-Frodingham
47361	Wilton Endeavour
47401	North Eastern
47402	Gateshead
47403	The Geordie
47404	Hadrian
47405	Northumbria
47406	Rail Riders
47408	Finsbury Park
47444	University of Nottingham
47461	Charles Rennie Mackintosh
47469	Glasgow Chamber of Commerce
47470	University of Edinburgh
47471	Norman Tunna G.C.
47480	Robin Hood
47484	ISAMBARD KINGDOM BRUNEL
47500	Great Western
47508	Great Britain
47509	Albion
47510	Fair Rosamund (Removed 7/84)
47511	Thames (Removed 6/84)
47513	Severn
47535	University of Leicester
47537	Sir Gwynedd-County of Gwynedd
	(Reversed opposite side)

47538	PYTHON
47539	Rochdale Pioneers
47541	The Queen Mother
47550	University of Dundee
47555	The Commonwealth Spirit
47558	Mayflower
47559	Sir Joshua Reynolds
47560	Tamar
47562	Sir William Burrell
47577	Benjamin Gimbert G.C.
47579	James Nightall G.C.
47580	County of Essex
47581	Great Eastern
47582	County of Norfolk
47583	County of Hertfordshire
47584	County of Suffolk
47585	County of Cambridgeshire
47590	Thomas Telford
47592	County of Avon
47593	Galloway Princess
47595	Confederation of British Industry
47596	Aldeburgh Festival
47606	ODIN
47611	Thames
47612	TITAN
47613	NORTH STAR
47617	University of Stirling
47701	Saint Andrew
47702	Saint Cuthbert
47703	Saint Mungo
47704	Dunedin
47705	Lothian
47706	Strathclyde
47707	Holyrood
47708	Waverley
47709	The Lord Provost
47710	Sir Walter Scott
47711	Greyfriars Bobby
47712	Lady Diana Spencer

D2000		05/69	v	C	Steelbreaking & Dismantling, Chesterfield	(C08/69)	
D2001		06/69	v	C	C.F. Booth, Rotherham	(C10/70)	
D2002		06/69	v	C	Ingot Metals, Kentish Town	(C09/69)	
D2003		05/69	v	C	Ingot Metals, Kentish Town	(C09/69)	
D2004	03004	05/76	v	C	G. Cohen, Kettering	(C09/76)	
D2005	03005	11/76	v	C	B.R. Doncaster Works	(C02/77)	
D2006		10/72	v	C	B.R. Swindon Works	(C06/73)	
D2007	03007	05/76	v	C	G. Cohen, Kettering	(C10/76)	
D2008	03008	12/78	v	C	B.R. Swindon Works	(C03/79)	
D2009	03009	07/76	v	C	G. Cohen, Kettering	(C12/77)	
D2010	03010	11/74	v	F	P. Wood, Queenborough	(E05/76)	
D2011		10/72	v	C	B.R. Swindon Works	(C08/73)	
D2012	03012	12/75	v	F	Mayer Newman, Snailwell	( )	
D2013	03013	07/76	v	C	B.R. Doncaster Works	(C03/77)	
D2014	03014	06/74	v	C	B.R. Doncaster Works	(C04/76)	
D2015		07/71	v	C	G. Cohen, Kettering	(C07/72)	
D2016	03016	12/78	v	C	B.R. Swindon Works	(C05/79)	
D2017	03017	02/82	v	C	B.R. Swindon Works	(C09/82)	
D2018	03018	11/75	v	F	600 Fragmentisers Ltd., Willesden		
D2019		07/71	v	E	Italy (via P. Wood, Queenborough)	(E /72)	
D2020	03020	12/75	v	F	Mayer Newman, Snailwell		
D2021	03021	11/82	v	C	B.R. Swindon Works	(C03/83)	
D2022	03022	11/82	v	P	Swindon & Cricklade Railway		
D2023		07/71	v	P	Kent & East Sussex Railway		
D2024		07/71	v	P	Kent & East Sussex Railway		
D2025	03025	09/77	v	C	B.R. Swindon Works	(C03/78)	
D2026	03026	02/83	v	C	C.F. Booth, Rotherham	(C)	
D2027	03027	01/76	v	F	P. Wood, Queenborough		
D2028		12/69	v	C	B.R. Doncaster Works	(C10/71)	
D2029	03029	09/79	v	C	B.R. Doncaster Works	(C11/79)	
D2030		08/69	v	C	C.F. Booth, Rotherham	(C10/70)	
D2031		05/69	v	C	Pollock & Brown, Northam, Southampton	(C09/79)	
D2032		07/71	v	E	Italy (via P. Wood, Queenborough)	(E /72)	
D2033		12/71	v	E	Italy (via P. Wood, Queenborough)	(E /72)	
D2034	03034	02/83	v	C	C.F. Booth, Rotherham	(C /83)	
D2035	03035	06/76	v	C	G. Cohen, Kettering	(C09/77)	
D2036		12/71	v	E	Italy (via P. Wood, Queenborough)	(C /72)	
D2037	03037	09/76	v	F	N.C.B.O.E., British Oak D.P., Crigglestone		
D2038		03/72	v	C	T.W. Ward, Beighton	(C05/73)	
D2039		02/72	v	C	T.W. Ward, Beighton	(C03/78)	
D2040		07/69	v	C	C.F. Booth, Rotherham	(C10/70)	
D2041		02/70	v	P	Colne Valley Railway, Essex		
D2042		08/69	v	C	Ingot Metals, Kentish Town	(C)	
D2043		09/71	v	F	P. Wood, Queenborough	(C09/73)	
D2044	03044	01/76	v	C	G. Cohen, Kettering	(C09/76)	
D2045	03045	02/79	v	C	B.R. Doncaster Works	(C10/79)	
D2046		10/71	v	F	Gulf Oil, Midford Haven		
D2047	02047	07/79	v	C	B.R. Doncaster Works	(C10/79)	
D2048		10/72	v	C	B.R. Swindon Works	(C05/73)	
D2049		08/71	v	F	N.C.B.O.E., West Hallam D.P., Mapperley		
D2050	03050	08/78	v	C	C.F. Booth, Rotherham	(C05/79)	
D2051		12/72	v	F	Ford Motor Co, Dagenham		
D2052		05/72	v	C	A. Draper, Hull	(C12/73)	
D2053		05/72	v	C	A. Draper, Hull	(C11/73)	

D2054		11/72	v	F	B.I.S., Middleton Towers, Kings Lynn		
D2055	03055	06/74	v	C	B.R. Doncaster Works	(C11/74)	
D2056	03056	06/80	v	C	B.R. Doncaster Works	(C04/81)	
D2057		10/71	v	F	N.C.B., Grimethorpe Colliery		
D2058	03058	06/75	v	C	B.R. Doncaster Works	(C02/77)	
D2059	03059		x				
D2060	03060	12/82	v	C	B.R. Doncaster Works	(C07/83)	
D2061	03061	10/80	v	C	B.R. Swindon Works	(C02/82)	
D2062	03062	12/80	v	P	Dean Forest Railway, Lydney		
D2063	03063		x				
D2064	03064	06/81	v	C	B.R. Doncaster Works	(C08/81)	
D2065		12/72	v	C	C.F. Booth, Rotherham	(C07/73)	
D2066	03066		x				
D2067	03067	08/81	v	C	B.R. Doncaster Works	(C04/82)	
D2068	03068	04/76	v	C	G. Cohen, Kettering	(C09/76)	
D2069	03069	12/83	v	F	V. Berry, Leicester		
D2070		11/71	v	F	P. Wood, Queenborough		
D2071		05/72	v	C	A. Draper, Hull	(C11/73)	
D2072	03072	03/81	v	P	Lakeside & Haverthwaite Railway		
D2073	03073		x				
D2074		05/72	v	C	A. Draper, Huil	(C11/73)	
D2075	03075	07/76	v	C	B.R. Doncaster Works	(C01/79)	
D2076	03076	04/76	v	C	G. Cohen, Kettering	(C09/76)	
D2077		10/72	v	C	B.R. Swindon Works	(C05/73)	
D2078	03078		x				
D2079	03079	04/84	v	D	97805		
D2080	03080	12/80	v	C	B.R. Swindon Works	(C03/81)	
D2081	03081	12/80	v	E	N.V. Sobermai, Belgium		
D2082		12/69	v	C	B.R. Doncaster Works	(C09/71)	
D2083		06/69	v	C	Pollock & Brown, Northam, Southampton	(C11/69)	
D2084	03084		x				
D2085		12/69	v	C	B.R. Doncaster Works	(C03/72)	
D2086	03086	11/83	x	C	B.R. Doncaster Works	(C03/84)	
D2087		06/71	v	C	Pounds Ltd., Fratton	(C03/73)	
D2088		06/72	v	C	C.F. Booth, Rotherham	(C03/73)	
D2089	03089		x				
D2090	03090	07/76	v	P	National Railway Museum, York		
D2091	03091	03/74	v	C	B.R. Doncaster Works	(C03/77)	
D2092	03092	08/77	v	C	B.R. Doncaster Works	(C01/78)	
D2093		10/71	v	F	N.C.B., Grimethorpe Colliery		
D2094	03094		x				
D2095	03095	12/75	v	C	G. Cohen, Kettering	(C08/76)	
D2096	03096	12/76	v	C	B.R. Doncaster Works	(C03/77)	
D2097	03097	06/76	v	C	B.R. Doncaster Works	(C03/79)	
D2098	03098	11/75	v	E	Italy (via P. Wood, Queenborough)	(E /76)	
D2099	03099	02/76	v	F	N.S.F., Monkton Coking Plant		
D2100		11/71	v	C	G. Cohen, Kettering	(C07/72)	
D2101		11/71	v	C	T.W. Ward, Beighton	(C06/72)	
D2102	03102	02/76	v	C	G. Cohen, Kettering	(C09/76)	
D2103	03103	02/79	v	C	B.R. Doncaster Works	(C06/79)	
D2104	03104	06/75	v	C	B.R. Doncaster Works	(C02/76)	
D2105	03105	02/76	v	C	G. Cohen, Kettering	(C09/76)	
D2106	03106	09/75	v	C	W. Heselwood, Attercliffe, Sheffield	(C05/76)	
D2107	03107	08/81	v	C	B.R. Doncaster Works	(C11/82)	
D2108	03108	11/76	v	C	B.R. Doncaster Works	(C03/77)	
D2109	03109	07/75	v	C	B.R. Doncaster Works	(C04/76)	
D2110	03110	02/76	v	C	G. Cohen, Kettering	(C09/76)	

D2111	03111	07/80	v	C	B.R. Swindon Works	(C02/81)
D2112	03112		x			
D2113	03113	08/75	v	F	Gulf Oil, Milford Haven	
D2114		05/68	v	F	Birds Comm. Motors, Long Marston	(C01/73)
D2115		05/68	v	C	G. Cohen, Kingsbury	(C11/68)
D2116		10/71	v	C	Marple & Gillott, Attercliffe, Sheffield	(C07/73)
D2117		10/71	v	P	Lakeside & Haverthwaite Railway	
D2118		06/72	v	F	Anglian Building Products, Lenwade	
D2119	03119		v			
D2120	03120		v			
D2121	03121	05/81	v			
D2122		11/72	v	F	Duport Steels, Briton Ferry	(C08/75)
D2123		12/68	v	F	Birds Comm. Motors, Bristol	(C11/78)
D2124		02/70	v	C	Slag Reduction Co., Barrow	(C09/70)
D2125		12/68	v	F	Birds Comm. Motors, Cardiff	(C06/78)
D2126		10/71	v	F	P. Wood, Queenborough	(C09/73)
D2127		05/68	v	C	G. Cohen, Kingsbury	(C10/68)
D2128	03128	07/76	v	F	Birds Comm. Motors, Long Marston	(E12/76)
D2129	02129	12/81	v	C	C.F. Booth, Rotherham	(C)
D2130		08/72	v	C	C.F. Booth, Rotherham	(C03/73)
D2131		06/68	v	C	G. Cohen, Kettering	(C11/68)
D2132		05/69	v	F	N.C.B., Pye Hill Colliery	
D2133		07/69	v	F	British Cellophane, Bridgwater	
D2134	03134	07/76	v	F	Birds Comm. Motors, Long Marston	(E12/76)
D2135	02135	01/76	v	C	P. Wood, Queenborough	(C)
D2136		01/72	v	C	Robinson & Hanon, Blaydon	(C12/12)
D2137	02137	07/76	v	C	B.R. Doncaster Works	(C12/77)
D2138		05/69	v	F	N.C.B., Pye Hill Colliery	
D2139		05/68	v	F	N.S.F., Nantgarw	
D2140		04/70	v	C	B.R. Swindon Works	(C02/72)
D2141	03141		v			
D2142	03142	10/83	v			
D2143		07/68	v	C	J. Cashmore, Newport	(C12/68)
D2144	03144		v			
D2145	03145		v			
D2146		09/68	v	F	Birds Comm. Motors, Long Marston	(C07/78)
D2147	03147	09/75	v	C	C.F. Booth, Doncaster	(C04/76)
D2148		11/72	v	F	N.C.B., Bowers Row, Astley	
D2149	03149	11/82	v	C	B.R. Doncaster Works	(C07/83)
D2150		11/72	v	F	British Salt Co. Ltd., Middlewich	
D2151	03151		v			
D2152	03152	10/83	v			
D2153	03153	11/75	v	E	Italy (via P. Wood, Queenborough)	(E /76)
D2154	03154	09/83	v	C	B.R. Doncaster Works	(C11/83)
D2155	03155	06/75	v	C	B.R. Doncaster Works	(C04/76)
D2156	03156	11/75	v	E	Italy (via P. Wood, Queenborough)	(E /76)
D2157	03157	12/75	v	E	Italy (via P. Wood, Queenborough)	(E02/77)
D2158	03158		x			
D2159	03159	10/77	v	C	B.R. Swindon Works	(C10/78)
D2160	03160	12/81	v	C	C.F. Booth, Rotherham	( )
D2161	03161	12/81	v	C	C.F. Booth, Rotherham	( )
D2162	03162		x			
D2163	03163	01/76	v	C	G. Cohen, Kettering	(C09/76)
D2164	03164	01/76	v	E	Italy (via P. Wood, Queenborough)	(E02/77)
D2165	03165	08/75	v	C	C.F. Booth, Doncaster	(C03/76)
D2166	03166	11/75	v	C	C.F. Booth, Rotherham	(C06/76)
D2167	03167	07/75	v	C	B.R. Doncaster Works	(C06/76)

D2168	03168	08/81	v	C	B.R. Doncaster	(C04/82)	
D2169	03169	11/75	v	C	A. Draper, Hull at Botanic Gardens	(C06/76)	
D2170	03170		x				
D2171	03171	10/77	v	C	G. Cohen, Kettering	(C04/78)	
D2172	03172	05/76	v	C	G. Cohen, Kettering	(C08/77)	
D2173		11/73	v	C	B.R. Doncaster	(C03/77)	
D2174	03174	11/75	v	C	C.F. Booth, Rotherham	(C05/76)	
D2175	03175	09/83	v	C	B.R. Doncaster	(C11/83)	
D2176		05/68	v	F	G. Cohen, Kettering	(C11/71)	
D2177		09/68	v	C	Birds Comm. Motors, Long Marston	(C06/70)	
D2178		09/69	v	F	N.S.F., Nantgarw Coking Plant		
D2179	03179		x				
D2180	03180	03/84	x	F	Mayer Newman, Snailwell		
D2181		05/68	v	F	Gwent Coal Distribution Centre, Newport		
D2182		05/68	v	F	N.C.B., Hugglescote		
D2183		09/68	v	C	Birds Comm. Motors, Long Marston	(C03/70)	
D2184		12/68	v	F	N.C.B., Southern Depot, Southend		
D2185		12/68	v	F	Abercarn Tinplate Works	(C01/81)	
D2186		09/69	v	F	A.R. Adams, Newport	(C01/81)	
D2187		05/68	v	F	Birds Comm. Motors, Long Marston	(C06/78)	
D2188		05/68	v	F	Birds Comm. Motors, Long Marston	(C02/78)	
D2189	03189		v				
D2190		12/68	v	C	Birds Comm. Motors, Long Marston	(C06/70)	
D2191		05/68	v	C	G. Cohen, Kingsbury	(C11/68)	
D2192		01/69	v	O	Torbay & Dartmouth Railway, Paignton		
D2193		01/69	v	F	A.R. Adams, Newport	(C01/81)	
D2194		09/68	v	F	Birds Comm. Motors, Long Marston	(C07/78)	
D2195		09/68	v	F	Duport Steels, Llanelli	(C09/81)	
D2196	03196	06/83	x	F	Boddy Industries, Carnforth		
D2197	03197		x				
D2198		11/70	v	C	B.R. Doncaster	(C02/72)	
D2199		06/72	v	F	N.C.B., Royston Drift Mine		

CLASS 04 DREWRY/GARDNER/WILSON 204 h.p. DM 0-6-0
Built 1952-1962 (DS1173 1948)

11100	D2200	04/68	n	C	Barnsley & District Coking Co.	(C07/78)	
11101	D2201	04/68	n	F	Barnsley & District Coking Co.	(C07/78)	
11102	D2202	02/68	v	C	G. Cohen, Kettering	(C06/68)	
11103	D2203	12/67	v	P	Yorkshire Dales Railway		
11104		07/50	v	D	52 West Hartlepool Signal Depot	(D07/50)	
11105	D2204	10/69	v	F	Duport Steels, Briton Ferry	(C09/79)	
11106	D2205	07/69	v	F	Kent & East Sussex Railway		
11107	D2206	07/69	v	C	Hughes Bolckow, Blyth	(C12/69)	
11108	D2207	12/67	v	P	North Yorkshire Moors Railway		
11109	D2208	07/68	v	F	N.C.B., Silverwood Colliery	(C06/76)	
11110	D2209	07/68	v	F	N.C.B. Kiveton Park Colliery		
11111	D2210	05/70	v	C	R.A. King, Norwich	(C09/70)	
11112	D2211	07/70	v	F	Rees Industries Ltd, Llanelli	(C11/80)	
11113	D2212	11/70	v	C	C.F. Booth, Rotherham at Norwich	(C07/72)	
11114	D2213	08/68	v	F	N.C.B., Manvers Main Coal Prep. Plant	(C02/80)	
11115	D2214	07/68	v	C	C.F. Booth, Rotherham	(C09/69)	
11121	D2215	02/69	v	C	Birds Comm. Motors, Long Marston	(C06/70)	

11122	D2216	05/71	v	E	Italy (via P. Wood, Queenborough)	(E /72)	
11123	D2217	05/72	v	F	N.C.B., Treeton Colliery	(C10/73)	
11124	D2218	08/68	v	C	Steelbreaking & Dismantling Co, Chesterfield	(C01/70)	
11125	D2219	04/68	v	F	N.C.B., Barrow Colliery	(C05/77)	
11126	D2220	02/68	v	C	G. Cohen, Kettering	(C06/68)	
11127	D2221	07/68	v	C	C.F. Booth, Rotherham	(C09/69)	
11128	D2222	11/68	v	C	C.F. Booth, Rotherham	(C07/69)	
11129	D2223	05/71	v	C	G. Cohen, Kettering	(C11/71)	
11130	D2224	04/68	v	C	A. Draper, Hull	(C10/69)	
11131	D2225	03/69	v	F	N.C.B., Wath Colliery		
11132	D2226	04/68	v	C	A. Draper, Hull	(C10/69)	
11133	D2227	04/68	v	C	A. Draper, Hull	(C10/69)	
11134	D2228	07/68	v	F	Bowaters, Sittingbourne	(C02/79)	
11135	D2229	12/69	v	F	N.C.B., Manton Colliery		
11149	D2230	03/68	v	C	Steelbreaking & Dismantling Co, Chesterfield	(C02/69)	
11150	D2231	06/69	v	C	Steelbreaking & Dismantling Co, Chesterfield	(C05/70)	
11151	D2232	03/68	v	E	Italy (via P. Wood, Queenborough)	(E /)	
11152	D2233	09/68	v	C	Steelbreaking & Dismantling Co, Chesterfield	(C07/70)	
11153	D2234	04/68	v	C	A. Draper, Hull	(C05/69)	
11154	D2235	04/68	v	C	A. Finlay, Worsbrough	(C07/68)	
11155	D2236	02/68	v	C	G. Cohen, Kettering	(C05/68)	
11156	D2237	10/69	v	C	Hughes Bolckow, Blyth	(C04/70)	
11157	D2238	07/68	V	F	N.C.B., Manvers Main Coal Prep. Plant	(C03/82)	
11158	D2239	09/71	v	F	N.C.B., Dodworth Colliery, Barnsley		
11159	D2240	04/68	v	C	R.A. King, Norwich	(C10/70)	
11160	D2241	05/71	v	F	G. Cohen, Kettering	(C11/76)	
11212	D2242	10/69	v	F	P. Wood, Queenborough	(C09/71)	
11213	D2243	07/69	v	F	Tees & Hartlepool Port Authority	(C03/73)	
11214	D2244	06/70	v	F	A.R. Adams, Newport	(C01/81)	
11215	D2245	12/68	v	P	Market Bosworth Light Railway		
11216	D2246	07/68	v	F	Coal Mechanisation Ltd., Tolworth		
11217	D2247	11/69	v	F	Duport Steels, Briton Ferry	(C09/79)	
11218	D2248	06/70	v	F	N.C.B., Maltby Colliery		
11219	D2249	12/70	v	C	P. Wood, Queenborough	(C04/73)	
11220	D2250	06/68	v	C	Pounds Ltd., Fratton	(C06/69)	
11221	D2251	12/68	v	C	Pollock & Brown, Northam, Southampton	(C11/69)	
11222	D2252	10/68	v	C	Pollock & Brown, Northam, Southampton	(C08/69)	
11223	D2253	03/69	v	C	G. Cohen, Kettering	(C02/70)	
11224	D2254	06/67	v	C	B.R. Selhurst Depot	(C07/67)	
11225	D2255	03/68	v	C	Pollock & Brown, Northam, Southampton	(C08/68)	
11226	D2256	09/68	v	C	Pollock & Brown, Northam, Southampton	(C08/69)	
11227	D2257	01/68	v	C	Pollock & Brown, Northam, Southampton	(C07/68)	
11228	D2258	09/70	v	F	N.C.B.O.E., Shilo Disposal Pt., Bennerley		
11229	D2259	12/68	v	F	Bowaters, Sittingbourne	(C01/78)	
	D2260	10/70	v	F	P.D. Fuels, Coed Bach D.P., Kidwelly		
	D2261	03/70	v	F	C.F. Booth, Rotherham	(C08/70)	
	D2262	09/68	v	F	Ford Motor Co., Dagenham	(C07/78)	
	D2263	11/67	v	C	Pollock & Brown, Northam, Southampton	(C12/68)	
	D2264	10/69	v	C	C.F. Booth, Rotherham	(C07/71)	
	D2265	03/70	v	C	C.F. Booth, Rotherham	(C09/70)	
	D2266	11/67	v	C	C.F. Booth, Rotherham	(C04/68)	
	D2267	12/69	v	F	Ford Motor Co., Dagenham		
	D2268	06/68	v	C	T.W. Ward, Beighton	(C11/68)	
	D2269	08/68	v	C	Pounds Ltd., Fratton	(C06/69)	
	D2270	02/68	v	F	Duport Steels, Briton Ferry	(C09/79)	
	D2271	10/69	v	P	West Somerset Railway, Minehead		
	D2272	10/70	v	F	British Fuels Ltd., Blackburn		

D2273	10/67	v	C	C.F. Booth, Rotherham	(C11/68)
D2274	05/69	v	F	N.C.B., Maltby Colliery	(C09/80)
D2275	10/67	v	C	B.R. Swindon	(C02/68)
D2276	08/69	v	F	A.R. Adams, Newport	(C05/77)
D2277	05/69	v	C	H. Brahams, Bury-St-Edmunds	(C12/69)
D2278	04/70	v	C	Pounds Ltd, Fratton at Stratford Depot	(C01/71)
D2279	05/71	v	P	Stour Valley Railway	
D2280	03/71	v	F	Ford Motor Co., Dagenham	
D2281	10/68	v	F	Duport Steels, Briton Ferry	(C08/71)
D2282	12/70	v	C	P. Wood, Queenborough	(C09/72)
D2283	11/69	v	C	Hartwood, Barnsley at Stratford Depot	(C05/70)
D2284	04/71	v	F	N.C.B., Woolley Colliery, Darton	
D2285	08/69	v	C	H. Braham, Bury-St-Edmunds	(C03/70)
D2286	06/68	v	C	Pounds Ltd., Fratton	(C06/69)
D2287	06/68	v	C	Pounds Ltd., Fratton	(C08/69)
D2288	12/67	v	C	Pollock & Brown, Northam, Southampton	(C08/68)
D2289	09/71	v	E	Italy (via P. Wood, Queenborough)	(E10/72)
D2290	11/67	v	C	Pollock & Brown, Northam, Southampton	(C08/68)
D2291	12/67	v	C	Pollock & Brown, Northam, Southampton	(C07/68)
D2292	12/67	v	C	Pollock & Brown, Northam, Southampton	(C08/68)
D2293	04/71	v	F	P. Wood, Queenborough	(C)
D2294	02/71	v	F	P. Wood, Queenborough	(C)
D2295	04/71	v	E	Italy (via P. Wood, Queenborough)	(C10/72)
D2296	11/69	v	C	H. Braham, Bury-St-Edmunds	(C03/71)
D2297	07/70	v	C	H. Braham, Bury-St-Edmunds	(C03/71)
D2298	12/68	v	P	Quainton Railway Centre, Aylesbury	
D2299	01/70	v	F	N.C.B., Calverton Colliery	(C04/84)
D2300	05/69	v	F	N.C.B., Manton Colliery	
D2301	09/68	v	C	Steelbreaking & Dismantling, Chesterfield	(C01/70)
D2302	06/69	v	F	Papworth Ltd., Ely	
D2303	11/67	v	C	B.R. Doncaster	(C01/69)
D2304	02/68	v	F	Duport Steels, Llanelli	(C05/77)
D2305	02/68	v	F	Duport Steels, Llanelli	(C09/81)
D2306	02/68	v	F	Duport Steels, Llanelli	(C09/81)
D2307	02/68	v	F	Duport Steels, Llanelli	(C10/79)
D2308	02/68	v	F	Duport Steels, Llanelli	(C05/80)
D2309	07/68	v	C	C.F. Booth, Rotherham	(C05/69)
D2310	01/69	v	F	Coal Mechanisation Ltd., Tolworth	
D2311	02/68	v	C	Slag Reduction Co., Ickles	(C08/68)
D2312	02/68	v	C	Slag Reduction Co., Ickles	(C08/68)
D2313	02/68	v	C	Slag Reduction Co., Ickles	(C08/68)
D2314	02/68	v	C	Slag Reduction Co., Ickles	(C08/68)
D2315	02/68	v	C	Hughes Bolckow, Blyth	(C08/68)
D2316	02/68	v	C	C.F. Booth, Rotherham	(C11/68)
D2317	08/69	v	F	N.C.B., Cortonwood Colliery	
D2318	02/68	v	C	Hughes Bolckow, Blyth	(C05/68)
D2319	02/68	v	C	A. Young, Dinsdale	(C07/69)
D2320	02/68	v	C	C.F. Booth, Rotherham	(C02/69)
D2321	07/68	v	C	G. Cohen, Middlesborough	(C12/68)
D2322	08/68	v	F	N.C.B., Kiveton Park Colliery	
D2323	07/68	v	C	C.F. Booth, Rotherham	(C05/69)
D2324	07/68	v	F	G.W. Talbot Ltd., Aylesbury C.C.D.	
D2325	07/68	v	F	N.C.B., Norwich C.C.D.	
D2326	08/68	v	F	N.C.B., Manvers Main Coal Prep. Plant	(C04/75)
D2327	08/68	v	F	N.C.B., Dinnington Main Colliery	(C02/84)
D2238	09/68	v	F	N.C.B., Kiveton Park Colliery	

	D2329		07/68	v	F	Derwent Valley Railway, York	(C04/70)	
	D2330		07/69	v	C	M. Turnbull, Thornaby	(C08/70)	
	D2331		07/68	v	C	T.W. Ward, Beighton	(C11/68)	
	D2332		06/69	v	F	N.C.B., Shireoaks Colliery		
	D2333		09/69	v	F	Ford Motor Co., Dagenham		
	D2334		07/68	v	F	N.C.B., Thurcroft Colliery		
	D2335		07/68	v	F	N.C.B., Maltby Colliery	(C02/80)	
	D2336		07/68	v	F	N.C.B., Manvers Main Coal Prep. Plant	(C02/78)	
	D2337		07/68	v	F	N.C.B., Manvers Main Colliery		
	D2338		07/68	v	C	T.W. Ward, Beighton	(C11/68)	
	D2339		10/67	v	C	Hughes Bolckow, Blyth	(C05/68)	
	D2340		10/68	v	F	Duport Steels, Briton Ferry	(C09/79)	
*DS1173	D2341		12/68	n	C	Pollock & Brown, Northam, Southampton	(C08/69)	

CLASS 03 continued

Dep 91	D2370	03370	12/82	v	C	B.R. Doncaster	(C07/83)	
Dep 92	D2371	03371		x				
	D2372		11/70	v	C	G. Cohen, Kettering	(C12/71)	
	D2373		05/68	v	F	N.C.B., Manvers Main Colliery	(C03/82)	
	D2374		05/68	v	C	G. Cohen, Kettering	(C12/68)	
	D2375		05/68	v	C	G. Cohen, Kettering	(C11/68)	
	D2376		05/68	v	C	G. Cohen, Kettering	(C11/68)	
	D2377		05/68	v	C	B.R. Swindon	(C09/69)	
	D2378		06/71	v	C	B.R. Swindon	(C10/72)	
	D2379		05/68	v	C	B.R. Swindon	(C09/69)	
	D2380		05/68	v	C	G. Cohen, Kettering	(C12/68)	
	D2381		06/72	v	P	Steamtown, Carnforth		
	D2382	03382	10/83	v				
	D2383		04/71	v	C	T.W. Ward, Beighton	(C02/72)	
	D2384		05/68	v	C	G. Cohen, Kettering	(C11/68)	
	D2385		02/70	v	C	C.F. Booth, Rotherham	(C08/70)	
	D2386	03386	03/76	v	C	G. Cohen, Kettering	(C12/76)	
	D2387		12/72	v	C	C.F. Booth, Rotherham	(C04/73)	
	D2388		07/72	v	C	C.F. Booth, Rotherham	(C02/73)	
	D2389	03389	02/83	v	C	C.F. Booth, Rotherham	( )	
	D2390		05/68	v	C	G. Cohen, Kettering	(C11/68)	
	D2391		11/70	v	C	G. Cohen, Kettering	(C12/71)	
	D2392		06/71	v	C	C.F. Booth, Rotherham	(C02/72)	
	D2393		12/69	v	C	C.F. Booth, Rotherham	(C05/71)	
	D2394		11/68	v	C	C.F. Booth, Rotherham	(C08/69)	
	D2395		05/68	v	C	G. Cohen, Kettering	(C12/68)	
	D2396		05/68	v	C	G. Cohen, Kettering	(C11/68)	
	D2397	03397		x				
	D2398		10/71	x	C	Pounds Ltd., Fratton	(C09/72)	
	D2399	03399		x				

CLASS 05   ANDREW BARCLAY/GARDNER/WILSON 204 h.p. DM   0-6-0
Built 1955. Note: These are different to the main batch classified 05 (D2550-D2618)

11177	D2400	10/67	n	C	Slag Reduction Co., Ickles	(C04/68)	
11178	D2401	12/68	n	C	C.F. Booth, Rotherham	(C01/70)	
11179	D2402	09/67	n	C	C.F. Booth, Rotherham	(C04/68)	
11180	D2403	01/69	n	C	C.F. Booth, Rotheham	(C01/70)	
11181	D2404	01/69	n	C	C.F. Booth, Rotherham	(C01/70)	
11182	D2405	12/68	n	C	W. Heselwood, Attercliffe, Sheffield	(C05/69)	
11183	D2406	05/67	n	C	T.W. Ward, Beighton	(C04/68)	
11184	D2407	01/69	n	C	C.F. Booth, Rotherham	(C08/70)	

| 11185 | D2408 | 05/67 | n | C | T.W. Ward, Beighton | (C04/68) | |
| 11186 | D2409 | 12/68 | n | C | C.F. Booth, Rotherham | (C03/70) | |

CLASS 06   ANDREW BARCLAY/GARDNER/WILSON 204 h.p. DM   0-4-0
Built 1958-1960

D2410		01/69	v	C	G.H. Campbell, Airdrie	(C06/69)	
D2411		06/68	v	C	G.H. Campbell, Airdrie	(C01/69)	
D2412		06/68	v	C	G.H. Campbell, Airdrie	(C01/69)	
D2413	06001	09/76	v	C	G.H. Campbell, Airdrie	(C02/78)	
D2414	06002	09/81	v	C	B.R. Swindon Works	(C05/82)	
D2415		06/68	v	C	G.H. Campbell, Airdrie	(C03/69)	
D2416		11/72	v	C	B.R. Glasgow Works	(C11/73)	
D2417		06/68	v	C	G.H. Campbell, Airdrie	(C03/69)	
D2418		12/68	v	C	G.H. Campbell, Airdrie	(C10/69)	
D2419		01/69	v	C	G.H. Campbell, Airdrie	(C01/69)	
D2420	06003	03/81	v	D	97804 Reading Signal Works		
D2421	06004	03/79	v	C	B.R. Glasgow Works	(C03/80)	
D2422	06005	10/80	v	C	B.R. Dundee Works	(C07/83)	
D2423	06006	06/80	v	C	B.R. Dundee Works	(C07/83)	
D2424		11/72	v	C	B.R. Glasgow Works	(C01/74)	
D2425		06/68	v	C	G.H. Campbell, Airdrie	(C12/68)	
D2426	06007	09/77	v	C	B.R. Glasgow Works	(C03/78)	
D2427		09/69	v	C	J.McWilliam, Shettleston	(C10/71)	
D2428		06/68	v	C	G.H. Campbell, Airdrie	(C02/69)	
D2429		04/69	v	C	J.McWilliam, Shettleston	(C10/71)	
D2430		06/68	v	C	G.H. Campbell, Airdrie	(C01/69)	
D2431		11/71	v	C	B.R. Glasgow Works	(C03/72)	
D2432		12/68	v	F	P. Wood, Queenborough	(E03/77)	
D2433		06/72	v	C	B.R. Glasgow Works	(C05/73)	
D2434		07/69	v	C	J.McWilliam, Shettleston	(C10/71)	
D2435		11/71	v	C	G.H. Campbell, Airdrie	(C09/74)	
D2436		11/71	v	C	B.R. Glasgow Works	(C11/73)	
D2437	06008	10/80	v	C	G.H. Campbell, Airdrie at Polmadie	(C08/83)	
D2438		11/72	v	C	G.H. Campbell, Airdrie	(C12/74)	
D2439		11/71	v	C	B.R. Glasgow Works	(C03/72)	
D2440	06009	11/75	v	C	G.H. Campbell, Airdrie	(C)	
D2441		03/67	v	C	Slag Reduction Co., Ickles	(C12/67)	
D2442		11/72	v	C	G.H. Campbell, Airdrie	(C12/74)	
D2443		06/72	v	C	B.R. Glasgow Works	(C05/73)	
D2444	06010	11/75	v	C	B.R. Glasgow Works	(C04/79)	

UNCLASSIFIED   HUDSWELL-CLARKE/GARDNER/POWERFLOW 204 h.p. DM   0-6-0
Built 1955-1961

11116	D2500	05/67	n	C	C.F. Booth, Rotherham	(C04/68)	
11117	D2501	02/67	n	C	Slag Reduction Co., Ickles	(C08/67)	
11118	D2502	10/67	n	C	C.F. Booth, Rotherham	(C03/68)	
11119	D2503	08/67	n	C	C.F. Booth, Rotherham	(C04/68)	
11120	D2504	03/67	n	C	C.F. Booth, Rotherham	(C04/68)	
11144	D2505	08/67	n	C	C.F. Booth, Rotherham	(C04/68)	
11145	D2506	11/67	n	C	Steelbreaking & Dismantling, Chesterfield	(C06/70)	
11146	D2507	03/67	n	C	Slag Reduction Co., Ickles	(C08/67)	
11147	D2508	05/67	n	C	C.F. Booth, Rotherham	(C04/68)	
11148	D2509	08/67	n	C	C.F. Booth, Rotherham	(C04/68)	
	D2510	08/67	v	C	C.F. Booth, Rotherham	(C04/68)	
	D2511	12/67	v	P	Keighley & Worth Valley Railway		

	D2512		05/67	v	C	C.F. Booth, Rotherham	(C03/68)	
	D2513		08/67	v	F	N.C.B., Cadeby Colliery	(C10/75)	
	D2515		08/67	v	C	W. Hatton Ltd., at Bolton Depot	(C05/68)	
	D2516		08/67	v	C	W. Hatton Ltd., at Bolton Depot	(C05/68)	
	D2517		02/67	v	C	Slag Reduction Co., Ickles	(C08/67)	
	D2518		02/67	v	F	N.C.B., Hatfield Main Colliery	(C06/73)	
	D2519		07/67	v	P	Keighley & Worth Valley Railway	(C04/82)	

CLASS 05 HUNSLET/GARDNER/WILSON 204 h.p. DM 0-6-0
Built 1955-1961

11136	D2550		10/66	v	C	B.R. Doncaster	(C12/66)	
11137	D2551		01/68	v	C	C.F. Booth, Rotherham	(C06/68)	
11138	D2552		06/67	v	C	C.F. Booth, Rotherham	(C04/68)	
11139	D2553		01/68	v	C	C.F. Booth, Rotherham	(C06/68)	
11140	D2554	05001	01/81	v	P	Isle of Wight Steam Railway		
11141	D2555		01/68	v	C	C.F. Booth, Rotherham	(C06/68)	
11142	D2556		07/67	v	C	G.H. Campbell, Airdrie	(C03/68)	
11143	D2557		04/67	v	C	C.F. Booth, Rotherham	(C04/68)	
11161	D2558		07/67	v	C	C.F. Booth, Rotherham	(C03/68)	
11162	D2559		07/67	v	C	G.H. Campbell, Airdrie	(C03/68)	
11163	D2560		11/67	v	C	Slag Reduction Co., Ickles	(C07/68)	
11164	D2561		08/67	v	F	Duport Steels, Llanelli	(C10/72)	
11165	D2562		01/68	v	C	C.F. Booth, Rotherham	(C06/68)	
11166	D2563		08/67	v	C	C.F. Booth, Rotherham	(C04/68)	
11167	D2564		08/67	v	C	C.F. Booth, Rotherham	(C03/68)	
11168	D2565		03/67	v	C	C.F. Booth, Rotherham	(C03/68)	
11169	D2566		01/68	v	C	C.F. Booth, Rotherham	(C06/68)	
11170	D2567		11/67	v	C	Slag Reduction Co., Ickles	(C09/68)	
11171	D2568		08/67	v	F	Duport Steels, Briton Ferry	(C05/69)	
11172	D2569		08/67	v	F	Duport Steels, Briton Ferry	(C05/69)	
11173	D2570		07/67	v	F	Duport Steels, Briton Ferry	(C06/71)	
11174	D2571		01/68	v	C	B.R. Glasgow	(C10/68)	
11175	D2572		02/67	v	C	Slag Reduction Co., Ickles	(C08/67)	
11176	D2573		01/68	v	C	J.McWilliam, Shettleston	(C09/69)	
	D2574		06/68	v	C	G.H. Campbell, Airdrie	(C02/69)	
	D2575		06/68	v	C	G.H. Campbell, Airdrie	(C02/69)	
	D2576		06/68	v	C	Machinery & Scrap Ltd., Motherwell	(C08/68)	
	D2577		06/67	v	C	Machinery & Scrap Ltd., Motherwell	(C12/67)	
	D2578		06/77	v	P	Bulmer Railway Centre, Hereford		
	D2579		06/68	v	C	G.H. Campbell, Airdrie	(C01/69)	
	D2580		06/68	v	C	G.H. Campbell, Airdrie	(C01/69)	
	D2581		06/68	v	C	G.H. Campbell, Airdrie	(C01/69)	
	D2582		06/68	v	C	G.H. Campbell, Airdrie	(C01/69)	
	D2583		06/68	v	C	G.H. Campbell, Airdrie	(C01/69)	
	D2584		06/67	v	C	Hunsley Engine Co., Leeds	(C08/68)	
	D2585		06/68	v	C	G.H. Campbell, Airdrie	(C01/69)	
	D2586		04/67	v	C	Slag Reduction Co., Ickles	(C10/67)	
	D2587		12/67	v	P	Bury Transport Museum		
	D2588		04/67	v	C	Slag Reduction Co., Ickles	(C11/67)	
	D2589		12/67	v	C	G.H. Campbell, Airdrie	(C12/69)	
	D2590		06/68	v	C	G.H. Campbell, Airdrie	(C01/69)	
	D2591		04/67	v	C	Slag Reduction Co., Ickles	(C10/67)	
	D2592		03/68	v	C	G.H. Campbell, Airdrie	(C02/69)	
	D2593		12/67	v	P	Bury Transport Museum		
	D2594		04/67	v	C	Slag Reduction Co., Ickles	(C12/67)	

	D2595	06/68	v	C	Hunslet Engine Co., Leeds	(C10/68)	
	D2596	06/68	v	C	G.H. Campbell, Airdrie	(C01/69)	
	D2597	12/67	v	C	G.H. Campbell, Airdrie	(C01/69)	
	D2598	12/67	v	F	N.C.B., Lambton Engine Works	(C05/75)	
	D2599	12/67	v	F	N.C.B., Askern Colliery	(C05/81)	
	D2600	12/67	v	F	Duport Steels, Briton Ferry	(C06/71)	
	D2601	12/67	v	F	Duport Steels, Llanelli	(C09/79)	
	D2602	07/67	v	C	Slag Reduction Co., Ickles	(C12/67)	
	D2603	08/67	v	C	C.F. Booth, Rotherham	(C04/68)	
	D2604	12/67	v	C	G. Cohen, Morriston, Swansea	(C03/68)	
	D2605	12/67	v	C	G. Cohen, Morriston, Swansea	(C03/68)	
	D2606	02/67	v	C	Slag Reduction Co., Ickles	(C12/67)	
	D2607	12/67	v	F	N.C.B., Steetley Colliery	(C07/84)	
	D2608	12/67	v	C	G.H. Campbell, Airdrie	(C01/69)	
	D2609	12/67	v	C	C.F. Booth, Rotherham	(C05/68)	
	D2610	12/67	v	C	C.F. Booth, Rotherham	(C08/68)	
	D2611	12/67	v	F	N.C.B., Yorkshire Main Colliery	(C12/76)	
	D2612	02/61	v	D	Dep 88	(C12/67)	
	D2613	12/67	v	F	N.C.B., Bentley Colliery	(C06/77)	
	D2614	04/67	v	C	A. Draper Hull	(C11/67)	
	D2615	01/64	v	D	Dep 89	(C08/68)	
	D2616	12/67	v	F	N.C.B., Hatfield Main Colliery	(C10/73)	
	D2617	12/67	v	C	Hunslet Engine Co., Leeds	(C04/76)	
	D2618	06/68	v	C	G.H. Campbell, Airdrie	(C02/69)	

UNCLASSIFIED   N.B.L./PAXMAN/VOITH 200 h.p. DH   0-4-0
Built 1953-1956

11700	D2700	11/63	n	C	B.R. Darlington	(C11/64)	
11701	D2701	03/67	n	C	A. Draper, Hull	(C11/67)	
11702	D2702	03/67	n	C	A. Draper, Hull	(C11/67)	
11703	D2703	02/68	n	C	Shipbreaking Industries, Faslane	(C05/68)	
11704	D2704	06/67	v	C	A. Young, Carmyle	(C10/67)	
11705	D2705	08/67	n	C	J.N. Connel, Calder	(C11/67)	
11706	D2706	03/67	v	C	Slag Reduction Co., Ickles	(C08/67)	
11707	D2707	03/67	v	C	Slag Reduction Co., Ickles	(C08/67)	

UNCLASSIFIELD   N.B.L./M.A.N./VOITH 225 h.p. DH   0-4-0
Built 1957-1961

11708	D2708	02/67	v	C	Slag Reduction Co., Ickles	(C12/67)	
11709	D2709	02/67	v	C	Slag Reduction Co., Ickles	(C12/67)	
11710	D2710	03/67	v	C	Slag Reduction Co., Ickles	(C08/67)	
11711	D2711	02/67	v	C	Slag Reduction Co., Ickles	(C11/67)	
11712	D2712	03/67	v	C	Slag Reduction Co., Ickles	(C11/67)	
11713	D2713	03/67	v	C	Slag Reduction Co., Ickles	(C09/67)	
11714	D2714	03/67	v	C	Slag Reduction Co., Ickles	(C09/67)	
11715	D2715	03/67	v	C	Slag Reduction Co., Ickles	(C09/67)	
11716	D2716	03/67	v	C	Slag Reduction Co., Ickles	(C08/67)	
11717	D2717	07/67	v	C	Argosy Salvage Co., Shettleston	(C12/67)	
11718	D2718	07/67	v	C	Argosy Salvage Co., Shettleston	(C12/67)	
11719	D2719	02/67	v	C	Slag Reduction Co., Ickles	(C11/67)	
	D2720	07/67	v	F	J.N. Connel Ltd., Coatbridge	(C07/71)	
	D2721	07/67	v	C	Argosy Salvage Co., Shettleston	(C12/67)	
	D2722	02/67	v	C	Slag Reduction Co., Ickles	(C11/67)	
	D2723	07/67	v	C	J.N. Connel Ltd., Calder	(C11/67)	
	D2724	03/67	v	C	Slag Reduction Co., Ickles	(C08/67)	

D2725	06/67	v	C	Motherwell Machine & Scrap Co.	(C09/67)
D2726	02/67	v	F	P. Wood, Queenborough	(C10/71)
D2727	03/67	v	C	Slag Reduction Co., Ickles	(C08/67)
D2728	07/67	v	C	Argosy Salvage Co., Shettleston	(C12/67)
D2729	03/67	v	C	Slag Reduction Co., Ickles	(C08/67)
D2730	10/67	v	C	Argosy Salvage Co., Shettleston	(C06/68)
D2731	10/67	v	C	Argosy Salvage Co., Shettleston	(C06/68)
D2732	02/67	v	C	Slag Reduction Co., Ickles	(C10/67)
D2733	02/67	v	C	Slag Reduction Co., Ickles	(C11/67)
D2734	09/67	v	C	Argosy Salvage Co., Shettleston	(C12/67)
D2735	03/67	v	C	Slag Reduction Co., Ickles	(C08/67)
D2736	03/67	v	F	Birds Comm. Motors, Tremorfa Works	(C07/69)
D2737	03/67	v	C	Slag Reduction Co., Ickles	(C07/67)
D2738	06/67	v	F	N.C.B., Killoch Colliery	(C08/79)
D2739	03/67	v	F	Birds Comm. Motors, Long Marston	(C09/69)
D2740	03/67	v	C	Slag Reduction Co., Ickles	(C08/67)
D2741	02/67	v	C	Slag Reduction Co., Ickles	(C12/67)
D2742	02/67	v	C	Slag Reduction Co., Ickles	(C12/67)
D2743	02/67	v	C	Slag Reduction Co., Ickles	(C11/67)
D2744	07/67	v	C	Argosy Salvage Co., Shettleston	(C11/67)
D2745	04/67	v	C	Slag Reduction Co., Ickles	(C08/67)
D2746	03/67	v	C	Slag Reduction Co., Ickles	(C08/67)
D2747	07/67	v	C	Argosy Salvage Co., Shettleston	(C12/67)
D2748	06/67	v	C	Argosy Salvage Co., Shettleston	(C12/67)
D2749	07/67	v	C	Argosy Salvage Co., Shettleston	(C12/67)
D2750	07/67	v	C	J.N. Connel Ltd., Calder	(C11/67)
D2751	07/67	v	C	J.N. Connel Ltd., Calder	(C07/67)
D2752	03/67	v	C	Slag Reduction Co., Ickles	(C12/67)
D2753	06/67	v	C	Motherwell Machinery & Scrap Co.	(C11/67)
D2754	07/67	v	C	J.N. Connel Ltd., Coatbridge	(C06/69)
D2755	07/67	v	C	Argosy Salvage Co., Shettleston	(C12/67)
D2756	02/68	v	C	G.H. Campbell, Airdrie	(C11/68)
D2757	07/67	v	F	Birds Comm. Motors, Tremorfa Works	(C10/70)
D2758	02/68	v	C	G.H. Campbell, Airdrie	(C11/68)
D2759	10/67	v	C	Argosy Salvage Co., Shettleston	(C05/68)
D2760	02/68	v	C	G.H. Campbell, Airdrie	(C11/68)
D2761	10/67	v	C	Argosy Salvage Co., Shettleston	(C05/68)
D2762	03/67	v	C	Slag Reduction Co., Ickles	(C08/67)
D2763	06/67	v	F	B.S.C., Swansea	(C04/77)
D2764	02/68	v	C	Barnes & Bell, Coatbridge	(C05/68)
D2765	03/67	v	C	Slag Reduction Co., Ickles	(C09/67)
D2766	03/67	v	C	Slag Reduction Co., Ickles	(C08/67)
D2767	06/67	v	F	Bury Transport Museum	
D2768	02/68	v	C	Shipbreaking Industries Ltd, Faslane	(C05/68)
D2769	02/68	v	C	G.H. Campbell, Airdrie	(C11/68)
D2770	02/68	v	C	G.H. Campbell, Airdrie	(C11/68)
D2771	03/67	v	C	Slag Reduction Co., Ickles	(C08/67)
D2772	03/67	v	C	Slag Reduction Co., Ickles	(C08/67)
D2773	02/68	v	C	Barnes & Bell, Coatbridge	(C05/68)
D2774	06/67	v	F	N.C.B., Celynen South Colliery, Abercarn	
D2775	02/68	v	C	G.H. Campbell, Airdrie	(C10/68)
D2776	10/67	v	C	Argosy Salvage Co., Shettleston	(C05/68)
D2777	03/67	v	F	Birds Comm. Motors, Pontymister	(C05/68)
D2778	03/67	v	C	Slag Reduction Co., Ickles	(C09/67)
D2779	02/68	v	C	G.H. Campbell, Airdrie	(C11/68)
D2780	02/68	v	C	Barnes & Bell, Coatbridge	(C05/68)

CLASS 02   Y.E.C./ROLLS ROYCE/Y.E.C. 170 h.p. DH   0-4-0
Built 1960-1961

D2850		07/70	v	C	W. Heselwood, Attercliffe, Sheffield	(C06/71)	
D2851	02001	06/75	v	C	A. Young, Dudley Hill at Allerton	(C03/76)	
D2852		10/73	v	C	Avon Transmission Services at Allerton	(C03/76)	
D2853	02003	06/75	v	F	L.C.P. Fuels, Shut End, Brierley Hill		
D2854		02/70	v	F	C.F. Booth, Rotherham		
D2855		10/70	v	C	W. Heselwood, Attercliffe, Sheffield	(C06/71)	
D2856	02004	06/75	v	F	Redland Roadstone, Barrow-on-Soar, Mountsorrel	(C10/78)	
D2857		04/71	v	F	Birds Comm. Metals, Long Marston		
D2858		02/70	v	F	Lowton Metals, Haydock		
D2859		03/70	v	C	Birds Comm. Metals, Long Marston	(C04/71)	
D2860		12/70	v	P	National Railway Museum, York		
D2861		12/69	v	C	C.F. Booth, Rotherham	(C05/71)	
D2862		12/69	v	F	N.C.B., Norton Colliery	(C04/79)	
D2863		12/69	v	C	T.W. Ward, Beighton	(C08/71)	
D2864		02/70	v	C	W. Heselwood, Attercliffe, Sheffield	(C04/71)	
D2865		03/70	v	F	A.P.C.M., Kilvington		
D2866		02/70	v	F	A. Young, Dalmuir		
D2867		09/70	v	F	Redland Roadstone, Barrow-on-Soar		
D2868		12/69	v	F	L.C.P. Fuels, Shut End, Brierley Hill		
D2869		12/69	v	C	T.W. Ward, Beighton	(C08/71)	

UNCLASSIFIED   N.B.L./M.A.N./VOITH 330 h.p.   0-4-0
Built 1958-1960

D2900	02/67	v	C	Slag Reduction Co., Ickles	(C10/67)	
D2901	02/67	v	C	Slag Reduction Co., Ickles	(C10/67)	
D2902	02/67	v	C	Slag Reduction Co., Ickles	(C10/67)	
D2903	02/67	v	C	Slag Reduction Co., Ickles	(C11/67)	
D2904	02/67	v	C	Slag Reduction Co., Ickles	(C11/67)	
D2905	02/67	v	C	Slag Reduction Co., Ickles	(C11/67)	
D2906	02/67	v	C	Slag Reduction Co., Ickles	(C11/67)	
D2907	02/67	v	C	Slag Reduction Co., Ickles	(C11/67)	
D2908	02/67	v	C	Slag Reduction Co., Ickles	(C12/67)	
D2909	02/67	v	C	Slag Reduction Co., Ickles	(C10/67)	
D2910	02/67	v	C	Slag Reduction Co., Ickles	(C11/67)	
D2911	02/67	v	C	Slag Reduction Co., Ickles	(C11/67)	
D2912	02/67	v	C	Slag Reduction Co., Ickles	(C11/67)	
D2913	02/67	v	C	Slag Reduction Co., Ickles	(C11/67)	

UNCLASSIFIED   HUNSLET/GARDNER/HUNSLET 153 h.p. DM   0-4-0
Built 1954-1955

11500	D2950	12/67	n	P	Stored at Thyssen Ltd., Llanelli	(C /82)	
11501	D2951	12/67	n	C	C.F. Booth, Rotherham	(C08/68)	
11502	D2952	12/66	n	C	Slag Reduction Co., Ickles	(C08/67)	

CLASS 01   ANDREW BARCLAY/GARDNER/WILSON 153 h.p. DM   0-4-0
Built 1956 (81 in 1959)

11503	D2953		06/66	n	F	Thames Matex, West Thurrock		
11504	D2954	01001	09/79	n	C	O.R. Davies at Holyhead Breakwater	(C02/82)	
11505	D2955	01002	03/81	n	C	O.R. Davies at Holyhead Breakwater	(C02/82)	
11506	D2956		05/66	n	F	Mayer Newman, Snailwell	(C)	
Dep 81	D2956		11/67	v	F	Duport Steels, Briton Ferry	(C08/69)	

UNCLASSIFIED RUSTON & HORNSEY 165 h.p. DM 0-4-0
Built 1956

| 11507 | D2957 | | 03/67 | n | C | Slag Reduction Co., Ickles | (C08/67) | |
| 11508 | D2958 | | 01/68 | n | F | C.F. Booth, Rotherham | | |

CLASS 07 RUSTON & HORNSBY/A.E.I. 275 h.p. DE 0-6-0
Built 1962

	D2985	07001	07/77	x	F	Peakstone Ltd., Peak Dale		
	D2986	07002	07/77	v	F	P.D. Fuels, Cwm Mawr D.P.		
	D2987	07003	10/76	x	F	British Industrial Sand, Oakamoor		
	D2988		05/73	v	C	M.C. Laydon at Battersea Yard	(C11/73)	
	D2989	07005	07/77	x	F	I.C.I., Wilton Works, Middlesborough		
	D2990	07006	07/77	v	F	P.D. Fuels, Coed Bach D.P.		
	D2991		05/73	v	D	Generator at Eastleigh Works		
	D2992		05/73	v	C	B.R. Eastleigh	(C12/73)	
	D2993	07009	10/76	x	E	Italy (via P. Wood, Queenborough)	(E03/77)	
	D2994	07010	10/76	v	P	West Somerset Railway, Minehead		
	D2995	07011	07/77	x	F	I.C.I., Wilton Works, Middlesborough		
	D2996	07012	07/77	v	F	P.D. Fuels, Coed Bach D.P.		
	D2997	07013	07/77	x	F	Dow Chemicals Ltd., King Lynn		
	D2998		05/73	v	C	B.R. Eastleigh	(C07/76)	

UNCLASSIFIED BRUSH/PETTER/BRUSH 200 h.p. DE 0-4-0
Built 1960

| | D2999 | | 10/67 | n | C | C.F. Booth, Rotherham | (C04/68) | |

CLASS 08/09 B.R./ENGLISH ELECTRIC/ENGLISH ELECTRIC 400 h.p. DE 0-6-0
Built 1952-1962

13000	D3000		11/72	v	F	N.C.B., Mardy Colliery		
13001	D3001		11/72	v	C	B.R. Doncaster Works	(C11/75)	
13002	D3002		07/72	v	P	Plym Valley Railway		
13003	D3003		07/72	v	F	Somerset C.C. Wanstrow Playground		
13004	D3004	08001	06/78	v	C	B.R. Swindon Works	(C03/79)	
13005	D3005	08002	09/77	v	C	B.R. Swindon Works	(C01/78)	
13006	D3006		11/72	v	D	ADB966507 Snowplough	(C08/79)	
13007	D3007	08003	12/77	v	C	B.R. Glasgow Works	(C03/79)	
13008	D3008	08004	08/83	v				
13009	D3009	08005	10/78	v	C	B.R. Doncaster Works	(C02/79)	
13010	D3010	08006	02/80	v	C	B.R. Swindon Works	(C04/80)	
13011	D3011		10/72	v	F	British Leyland Ltd., Longbridge		
13012	D3012		01/73	v	C	B.R. Swindon Works	(C10/73)	
13013	D3013		10/72	v	C	J. Cashmore, Newport	(C11/73)	
13014	D3014		10/72	v	F	N.C.B., Merthyr Vale Colliery		
13015	D3015	08008	11/83	v				
13016	D3016	08009	11/75	v	C	B.R. Swindon Works	(C06/76)	
13017	D3017	08010	12/77	v	C	B.R. Eastleigh Works		
13018	D3018	08011		v				
13019	D3019		06/73	v	F	P.D. Fuels, Gwaun-Cae-Gurwen D.P.		
13020	D3020		12/73	v	E	LAMCO, Liberia	(E01/73)	
13021	D3021	08014	05/80	v	C	C.F. Booth, Rotherham	(C11/81)	
13022	D3022	08015	09/80	v	P	Severn Valley Railway		
13023	D3023	08016	05/80	v	F	.N.C.B.C.E. British Oak D.P. Crigglestone		

13024	D3024		08/73	v	C	B.R. Doncaster Works	(C10/75)
13025	D3025	08018	07/83	v			
13026	D3026		11/72	v	C	B.R. Swindon Works	(C04/73)
13027	D3027	08019	09/83	v			
13028	D3028		08/73	v	C	B.R. Doncaster Works	(C11/75)
13029	D3029	08021		v			
13030	D3030	08022		v			
13031	D3031	08023	09/83	v			
13032	D3032	08024	12/82	v	C	B.R. Doncaster Works	(C08/83)
13033	D3033	08025	12/77	v	C	B.R. Swindon Works	(C03/78)
13034	D3034		11/72	v	C	B.R. Derby Works	(C11/73)
13035	D3035		12/72	v	D	ADB966508 Snowplough	(C05/79)
13036	D3036	08026	07/82	v			
13037	D3037		12/72	v	D	ADB966510 Snowplough	(C03/79)
13038	D3038		12/72	v	F	N.C.B., Bates Colliery, Blyth	(C05/80)
13039	D3039	08027	11/80	v	C	B.R. Swindon Works	(C04/82)
13040	D3040	08028	04/81	v	C	B.R. Swindon Works	(C04/82)
13041	D3041	08029	03/78	v	C	B.R. Swindon Works	(C05/78)
13042	D3042	08030	07/82	v			
13043	D3043	08031	07/82	v			
13044	D3044	08032	08/74	v	F	Foster Yeoman Ltd., Merehead	
13045	D3045		11/72	v	C	B.R. Glasgow Works	(C04/76)
13046	D3046	08033		v			
13047	D3047		07/73	v	E	LAMCO, Liberia	(E /75)
13048	D3048	08035	09/79	v	C	B.R. Swindon Works	(C01/80)
13049	D3049	08036	09/81	v	C	B.R. Swindon Works	(C03/83)
13050	D3050	08037	02/80	v	C	B.R. Swindon Works	(C10/80)
13051	D3051		06/73	v	C	B.R. Derby Works	(C08/73)
13052	D3052		12/73	v	C	J. Cashmore, Newport	(C09/74)
13053	D3053		06/73	v	C	B.R. Doncaster Works	(C10/75)
13054	D3054	08041	08/78	v	C	B.R. Swindon Works	(C03/81)
13055	D3055	08042	03/79	v	C	B.R. Doncaster Works	(C05/79)
13056	D3056	08043	12/77	v	C	B.R. Swindon Works	(C04/78)
13057	D3057	08044	01/78	v	C	B.R. Doncaster Works	(C01/79)
13058	D3058	08045	07/82	v			
13059	D3059	08046	05/80	v	F	Associated British Maltsters, Airdrie	
13060	D3060	08047	10/79	v	C	B.R. Swindon Works	(C07/80)
13061	D3061	08048	12/77	v	C	B.R. Doncaster Works	(C04/78)
13062	D3062	08049	05/81	v	C	B.R. Swindon Works	(C07/83)
13063	D3063	08050	10/81	v	C	B.R. Swindon Works	(C01/83)
13064	D3064	08051	07/82	v			
13065	D3065	08052	01/81	v	C	C.F. Booth, Rotherham at March Depot	(C01/82)
13066	D3066	08053	03/81	v	C	B.R. Swindon Works	(C06/81)
13067	D3067	08054	02/80	v	F	Tilcon Construction Ltd., Grassington	
13068	D3068	08055	11/80	v	C	B.R. Swindon Works	(C)
13069	D3069		01/73	v	D	ADB966509 Snowplough	(C04/80)
13070	D3070	08056		v			
13071	D3071	08057	07/76	v	C	B.R. Doncaster Works	(C03/77)
13072	D3072	08058	04/82	v	C	B.R. Doncaster Works	(C05/83)
13073	D3073	08059	09/80	v			
13074	D3074	08060	06/84	v			
13075	D3075	08061	05/84	v			
13076	D3076	08062		v			
13077	D3077	08063	07/84	v			
13078	D3078		11/72	v	D	ADB966506 Snowplough	(C02/79)
13079	D3079	08064		v			
13080	D3080	08065	09/77	v	C	B.R. Doncaster Works	(C11/78)

13081	D3081	08066	09/77	v	C	B.R Doncaster Works	(C11/78)	
13082	D3082	08067	07/83	v	D	TS1 at Tyseley Depot (out of use)		
13083	D3083	08068	07/83	v				
13084	D3084	08069	02/83	v	C	B.R. Doncaster Works	(C03/84)	
13085	D3085	08070	12/77	v	D	Clyderail Electrification	(C04/80)	
13086	D3086	08071	02/78	v	C	B.R. Doncaster Works	(C07/78)	
13087	D3087		06/73	v	F	C.E.G.B. Walsall Power Station	(C06/82)	
13088	D3088		12/73	v	F	N.C.B., Bates Colliery, Blyth		
13089	D3089	08074	12/73	v	C	B.R. Derby Works	(C06/77)	
13090	D3090	08075	12/81	v	C	B.R. Swindon Works	(C04/82)	
13091	D3091	08076	09/80	v	C	B.R. Swindon Works	(C04/82)	
13092	D3092		10/72	n	E	LAMCO, Liberia	(E04/74)	
13093	D3093		05/72	n	C	G. Cohen, Kettering	(C01/74)	
13094	D3094		10/72	n	E	LAMCO, Liberia	(C04/74)	
13095	D3095		05/72	n	C	B.R. Swindon Works	(C12/73)	
13096	D3096		05/72	n	C	B.R. Selhurst Depot	(C09/72)	
13097	D3097		05/72	n	C	B.R. Swindon Works	(C12/73)	
13098	D3098		10/72	n	E	LAMCO, Liberia	(E04/74)	
13099	D3099		10/72	n	F	P. Wood, Queenborough	(C07/77)	
13100	D3100		10/72	n	E	LAMCO, Liberia	(E04/74)	
13101	D3101		05/72	n	P	Great Central Railway		
13102	D3102	08077	11/77	v	F	Wiggins Teape & Co.Ltd., Fort William		
13103	D3103	08078	08/83	v				
13104	D3104	08079	12/83	v				
13105	D3105	08080	11/80	v	C	B.R. Swindon Works	(C05/81)	
13106	D3106	08081	04/80	v	C	B.R. Swindon Works	(C07/80)	
13107	D3107	08082	11/80	v	C	B.R. Swindon Works	(C03/82)	
13108	D3108	08083	07/84	v				
13109	D3109	08084	11/80	v	C	B.R. Swindon Works	(C12/81)	
13110	D3110	08085		v				
13111	D3111	08086	08/80	v	C	B.R. Swindon Works	(C01/81)	
13112	D3112	08087	10/79	v	C	B.R. Swindon Works	(C05/80)	
13113	D3113	08088	09/83	v				
13114	D3114	08089	09/80	v	C	B.R. Swindon Works	(C12/80)	
13115	D3115	08090	11/77	v	C	B.R. Swindon Works	(C01/79)	
13116	D3116	08091	11/82	v	C	B.R. Doncaster Works	(C01/84)	

Class continued with 13127

UNCLASSIFIED   B.R./CROSSLEY/C.P. 350 h.p. DE   0-6-0
Built 1955

13117	D3117		07/67	v	C	J. Cashmore, Great Bridge	(C10/67)	
13118	D3118		07/67	v	C	J. Cashmore, Great Bridge	(C07/68)	
13119	D3119		07/67	v	C	J. Cashmore, Great Bridge	(C07/68)	
13120	D3120		04/67	v	C	G. Cohen, Kettering	(C06/68)	
13121	D3121		04/67	v	C	B.R. Derby Works	(C05/68)	
13122	D3122		11/66	v	C	Steelbreaking & Dismantling, Chesterfield	(C08/67)	
13123	D3123		11/66	v	C	J. Cashmore, Great Bridge	(C09/67)	
13124	D3124		11/66	v	C	J. Cashmore, Great Bridge	(C09/67)	
13125	D3125		07/67	v	C	G. Cohen, Kettering	(C05/68)	
13126	D3126		11/66	v	C	J. Cashmore, Great Bridge	(C07/67)	

Class 08 continued

13127	D3127	08092	11/78	v	C	B.R Doncaster Works	(C01/79)	
13128	D3128	08093	07/81	v	C	B.R. Swindon Works	(C04/82)	
13129	D3129	08094	06/83	v				
13130	D3130	08095	02/83	v				

13131	D3131	08096	09/84	v			
13132	D3132	08097	03/81	v	C	B.R. Swindon Works	(C06/81)
13133	D3133	08098	11/80	v	C	B.R. Swindon Works	(C01/81)
13134	D3134	08099	09/82	v	C	B.R. Doncaster Works	(C10/83)
13135	D3135	08100	12/82	v			
13136	D3136	08101	07/83	v			

Class continued with 13167

CLASS 10   B.R./BLACKSTONE/G.E.C. 350 h.p. DE   0-6-0
Built 1955-1962

13137	D3137	07/70	v	C	C.F. Booth, Doncaster	(C01/71)
13138	D3138	04/72	v	C	C.F. Booth, Rotherham	(C09/73)
13139	D3139	06/68	v	C	C.F. Booth, Rotherham	(C05/69)
13140	D3140	06/68	v	C	C.F. Booth, Rotherham	(C03/69)
13141	D3141	07/71	v	C	C.F. Booth, Rotherham	(C06/72)
13142	D3142	06/68	v	C	C.F. Booth, Rotherham	(C03/69)
13143	D3143	08/69	v	C	G. Cohen, Kettering	(C04/70)
13144	D3144	07/69	v	C	Hughes Bolckow, Blyth	(C10/69)
13145	D3145	04/72	v	C	C.F. Booth, Rotherham	(C02/73)
13146	D3146	02/68	v	C	Hughes Bolckow, Blyth	(C05/68)
13147	D3147	05/68	v	C	C.F. Booth, Rotherham	(C04/69)
13148	D3148	03/68	v	C	C.F. Booth, Rotherham	(C05/69)
13149	D3149	07/70	v	C	C.F. Booth, Rotherham	(C11/70)
13150	D3150	06/68	v	C	C.F. Booth, Rotherham	(C04/69)
13151	D3151	11/67	v	C	Hughes Bolckow, Blyth	(C04/68)

Class continued with D3439

UNCLASSIFIED   B.R./BLACKSTONE/B.T.H. 350 h.p. DE   0-6-0
Built 1955

13152	D3152	09/67	v	C	Slag Reduction Co., Ickles	(C03/68)
13153	D3153	07/67	v	C	C.F. Booth, Rotherham	(C02/68)
13154	D3154	07/67	v	C	C.F. Booth, Rotherham	(C04/68)
13155	D3155	09/67	v	C	C.F. Booth, Rotherham	(C03/68)
13156	D3156	07/67	v	C	C.F. Booth, Rotherham	(C03/68)
13157	D3157	09/67	v	C	Slag Reduction Co., Ickles	(C10/68)
13158	D3158	02/67	v	C	Slag Reduction Co., Ickles	(C08/67)
13159	D3159	09/67	v	C	C.F. Booth, Rotherham	(C04/68)
13160	D3160	11/67	v	C	Slag Reduction Co., Ickles	(C04/68)
13161	D3161	09/67	v	C	C.F. Booth, Rotherham	(C04/68)
13162	D3162	11/67	v	C	Slag Reduction Co., Ickles	(C10/68)
13163	D3163	09/67	v	C	C.F. Booth, Rotherham	(C04/68)
13164	D3164	12/67	v	C	Slag Reduction Co., Ickles	(C10/68)
13165	D3165	07/67	v	C	C.F. Booth, Rotherham	(C03/68)
13166	D3166	07/67	v	C	C.F. Booth, Rotherham	(C04/68)

CLASS 08 continued

13167	D3167	08102		v			
13168	D3168	08103	09/83	v			
13169	D3169	08104	07/82	v	C	B.R. Doncaster Works	(C03/84)
13170	D3170	08105	07/83	v	C	B.R. Doncaster Works	(C08/84)
13171	D3171	08106	01/82	v	C	B.R. Swindon Works	(C01/83)
13172	D3172		05/72	v	C	B.R. Derby Works	(C08/72)
13173	D3173	08107	12/82	v	C	B.R. Doncaster Works	(C03/84)
13174	D3174	08108	07/84	v	F	Dormer Wood, Newmarket	
13175	D3175	08109	04/81	v	C	B.R. Swindon Works	(C10/81)

13176	D3176	08110	10/79	v	C	B.R. Swindon Works	(C04/80)	
13177	D3177	08111	02/77	v	D	ADB966512-ADB968012 Snowplough	(C /)	
13178	D3178	08112	07/82	v	C	B.R. Swindon Works	(C04/84)	
13179	D3179	08113	03/84	v	F	P.D. Fuels, Annanford		
13180	D3180	08114	11/83	v	C	B.R. Swindon Works	(C08/84)	
13181	D3181	08115	07/84	v				
13182	D3182	08116	08/82	v	C	B.R. Doncaster Works	(C08/83)	
13183	D3183		12/72	v	F	N.C.B., Merthyr Vale Colliery		
13184	D3184	08117	02/77	v	D	ADB966513-ADB968013 Snowplough	(C03/79)	
13185	D3185	08118	03/80	v	C	B.R. Swindon Works	(C07/80)	
13186	D3186	08119	02/77	v	D	ADB966511-ADB968011 Snowplough	(C02/80)	
13187	D3187	08120	10/81	v	C	B.R. Swindon Works	(C08/82)	
13188	D3188	08121	06/84	v				
13189	D3189	08122	06/77	v	C	B.R. Doncaster Works	(C11/77)	
13190	D3190	08123	03/84	v				
13191	D3191	08124	03/81	v	C	B.R. Swindon Works	(C02/83)	
13192	D3192	08125	12/81	v	C	B.R. Swindon Works	(C02/84)	
13193	D3193		09/67	v	C	B.R. Derby Works	(C09/67)	
13194	D3194	08126	11/80	v	C	B.R. Swindon Works	(C12/81)	
13195	D3195	08127	08/80	v	C	B.R. Swindon Works	(C12/80)	
13196	D3196	08128	08/80	v	C	B.R. Swindon Works	(C02/84)	
13197	D3197	08129	07/83	v	C	B.R. Doncaster Works	(C04/84)	
13198	D3198	08130	12/82	v				
13199	D3199	08131	03/81	v	C	B.R. Swindon Works	(C08/81)	
13200	D3200	08132		v				
13201	D3201	08133	09/80	v	F	Sheerness Iron & Steel Co.		
13202	D3202	08134	08/81	v				
13203	D3203	08135	02/77	v	C	B.R. Swindon Works	(C03/77)	
13204	D3204	08136	08/83	v				
13205	D3205	08137	11/82	v				
13206	D3206	08138	01/78	v	C	B.R. Swindon Works	(C05/78)	
13207	D3207	08139	09/80	v	C	B.R. Swindon Works	(C04/82)	
13208	D3208	08140	06/77	v	C	B.R. Swindon Works	(C09/77)	
13209	D3209	08141		v				
13210	D3210	08142	11/83	v	F	N.C.B., Hickleton Main Colliery		
13211	D3211	08143	03/76	v	C	B.R. Swindon Works	(C02/77)	
13212	D3212	08144	12/77	v	C	B.R. Glasgow Works	(C10/79)	
13213	D3213	08145	12/77	v	C	B.R. Glasgow Works	(C08/78)	
13214	D3214	08146	10/80	v	C	B.R. Swindon Works	(C05/81)	
13215	D3215	08147	07/83	v				
13216	D3216	08148	03/84	v				
13217	D3217	08149	04/81	v	C	B.R. Swindon Works	(C02/84)	
13218	D3218	08150		v				
13219	D3219	08151	01/79	v	C	B.R. Eastleigh Works	(C06/79)	
13220	D3220	08152	07/80	v	C	B.R. Swindon Works	(C11/80)	
13221	D3221	08153	12/82	v				
13222	D3222	08154	10/79	v	C	B.R. Swindon Works	(C03/80)	
13223	D3223	08155	12/78	v	C	B.R. Swindon Works	(C03/80)	
13224	D3224	08156	12/78	v	C	B.R. Swindon Works	(C02/80)	
13225	D3225	08157	04/77	v	F	Independent Sea Terminals, Ridham Dock		
13226	D3226	08158	02/79	v	C	B.R. Swindon Works	(C10/79)	
13227	D3227	08159		v				
13228	D3228	08160		v				
13229	D3229	08161		v				
13230	D3230	08162	07/80	v	C	B.R. Swindon Works	(C01/81)	
13231	D3231	08163	12/82	v	C	B.R. Doncaster Works	(C02/84)	
13232	D3232	08164		v				

13233	D3233	08165	07/80	v	C	B.R. Swindon Works	(C10/80)
13234	D3234	08166	07/82	v	C	B.R. Doncaster Works	(C09/83)
13235	D3235	08167	09/77	v	C	B.R. Glasgow Works	(C07/79)
13236	D3236	08168		v			
13237	D3237	08169	03/81	v	C	B.R. Swindon Works	(C10/81)
13238	D3238	08170		v			
13239	D3239	08171	04/83	v	C	B.R. Doncaster Works	(C09/83)
13240	D3240	08172		v			
13241	D3241	08173	12/78	v	D	PO1 Polmadie Depot	
13242	D3242	08174	08/81	v	C	B.R. Swindon Works	(C03/82)
13243	D3243	08175	12/78	v			
13244	D3244	08176		v			
13245	D3245	08177		v			
13246	D3246	08178	05/82	v	C	B.R. Swindon Works	(C03/84)
13247	D3247	08179	06/75	v	C	B.R. Swindon Works	(C08/76)
13248	D3248	08180	05/81	v	C	B.R. Swindon Works	(C08/81)
13249	D3249	08181	07/82	v			
13250	D3250	08182	03/81	v	C	B.R. Swindon Works	(C03/82)
13251	D3251	08183	03/84	v			
13252	D3252	08184	06/81	v	C	B.R. Swindon Works	(C04/82)
13253	D3253	08185	02/82	v	C	B.R. Swindon Works	(C10/82)
13254	D3254	08186		v			
13255	D3255		12/72	v	F	N.C.B., Mardy Colliery	
13256	D3256	08187	07/83	v			
13257	D3257	08188	04/83	v			
13258	D3258	08189	12/81	v	C	B.R. Swindon Works	(C03/84)
13259	D3259	08190	10/80	v	C	B.R. Swindon Works	(C12/80)
13260	D3260	08191		v			
13261	D3261		12/72	v	F	N.C.B.,Tower Colliery,Hirwaun	
13262	D3262	08192	07/82	v			
13263	D3263	08193	06/83	v			
13264	D3264	08194	11/80	v	C	B.R. Swindon Works	(C10/83)
13265	D3265	08195	09/83	v			
13266	D3266	08196	10/83	v			
13267	D3267	08197	04/82	v	C	B.R. Doncaster Works	(C02/84)
13268	D3268	08198	12/80	v	C	B.R. Swindon Works	(C11/81)
13269	D3269	08199	01/83	v	C	B.R. Doncaster Works	(C07/84)
13270	D3270	08200		v			
13271	D3271	08201	12/82	v	C	B.R. Doncaster Works	(C05/84)
13272	D3272	08202		v			
13273	D3273	08203	07/84	v			
13274	D3274	08204	08/83	v	C	B.R. Swindon Works	(C09/84)
13275	D3275	08205	11/83	v	C	B.R. Doncaster Works	(C08/84)
13276	D3276	08206		v			
13277	D3277	08207	09/80	v	C	B.R. Swindon Works	(C05/83)
13278	D3278	08208		v			
13279	D3279	08209	02/83	v	C	B.R. Doncaster Works	(C08/83)
13280	D3280	08210		v			
13281	D3281	08211		v			
13282	D3282	08212	09/81	v	C	B.R. Swindon Works	(C02/82)
13283	D3283	08213	11/80	v	C	B.R. Swindon Works	(C08/81)
13284	D3284	08214	02/84	v			
13285	D3285	08215	09/82	v	C	B.R. Doncaster Works	(C06/83)
13286	D3286	08216	11/80	v	F	Sheerness Iron & Steel Co.Ltd.	
13287	D3287	08217	04/82	v	C	B.R. Doncaster Works	(C05/83)
13288	D3288	08218	07/80	v	C	B.R. Swindon Works	(C08/81)
13289	D3289	08219	03/83	v	C	B.R. Swindon Works	(C08/83)

13290	D3290	08220		v			
13291	D3291	08221	03/81	v	C	B.R. Swindon Works	(C11/81)
13292	D3292	08222		v			
13293	D3293	08223	06/79	v	C	B.R. Swindon Works	(C11/80)
13294	D3294	08224		v			
13295	D3295	08225		v			
13296	D3296	08226		v			
13297	D3297	08227	10/83	v			
13298	D3298	08228		v			
13299	D3299	08229	12/77	v	C	B.R. Swindon Works	(C12/78)
13300	D3300	08230	09/80	v	C	B.R. Swindon Works	(C06/83)
13301	D3301	08231	06/81	v	C	B.R. Swindon Works	(C10/81)
13302	D3302	08232	09/82	v	C	B.R. Doncaster Works	(C07/83)
13303	D3303	08233	05/81	v	C	G. Morris, Romford at Stratford Depot	(C03/82)
13304	D3304	08234	09/82	v	C	B.R. Swindon Works	(C01/83)
13305	D3305	08235	07/83	v	C	B.R. Doncaster Works	(C09/84)
13306	D3306	08236	09/75	v	C	B.R. Swindon Works	(C09/76)
13307	D3307	08237		v			
13308	D3308	08238	03/84	v			
13309	D3309	08239	07/84	v			
13310	D3310	08240	07/82	v			
13311	D3311	08241	10/81	v	C	B.R. Swindon Works	(C05/82)
13312	D3312	08242		v			
13313	D3313	08243		a			
13314	D3314	08244		v			
13315	D3315	08245	05/84	v			
13316	D3316	08246	08/82	v			
13317	D3317	08247	03/81	v	C	B.R. Swindon Works also carried PO1	(C11/81)
13318	D3318	08248	09/84	v			
13319	D3319	08249		v			
13320	D3320	08250		v			
13321	D3321	08251	09/80	v	C	B.R. Swindon Works	(C01/81)
13322	D3322	08252	08/81	v	C	B.R. Swindon Works	(C04/82)
13323	D3323	08253		v			
13324	D3324	08254		v			
13325	D3325	08255		v			
13326	D3326	08256	02/84	v			
13327	D3327	08257		v			
13328	D3328	08258		v			
13329	D3329	08259		v			
13330	D3330	08260	08/83	v	C	B.R. Doncaster Works	(C10/83)
13331	D3331	08261	12/83	v			
13332	D3332	08262	01/84	v			
13333	D3333	08263	03/84	v	C	B.R. Doncaster Works	(C08/84)
13334	D3334	08264	07/84	v			
13335	D3335	08265	12/81	v			
13336	D3336	08266		v			
13337	D3337	08267	12/77	v	D	RDB968020 then 97201 RTC	
13338	D3338	08268		v			
13339	D3339	08269	07/84	v			
13340	D3340	08270	12/82	v	C	B.R. Doncaster Works	(C01/84)
13341	D3341	08271	09/81	v	C	B.R. Swindon Works	(C04/83)
13342	D3342	08272		v			
13343	D3343	08273	12/82	v	C	B.R. Doncaster Works	(C03/84)
13344	D3344	08274		v			
13345	D3345	08275	02/83	v	C	B.R. Doncaster Works	(C07/84)
13346	D3346	08276	06/77	v	C	B.R. Doncaster Works	(C11/77)

13347	D3347	08277	11/81	v	C	B.R. Doncaster Works	(C07/83)
13348	D3348	08278	06/77	v	C	B.R. Glasgow Works	(C12/77)
13349	D3349	08279	04/81	v	C	B.R. Swindon Works	(C05/83)
13350	D3350	08280	10/80	v	C	B.R. Swindon Works	(C03/83)
13351	D3351	08281	12/80	v			
13352	D3352	08282	11/80	v	C	B.R. Swindon Works	(C08/81)
13353	D3353	08283		v			
13354	D3354	08284		v			
13355	D3355	08285		v			
13356	D3356	08286	04/82	v			
13357	D3357	08287	12/82	v	C	B.R. Doncaster Works	(C09/83)
	D3358	08288	01/83	v	P	Mid Hants Railway	
	D3359	08289		v			
	D3360	08290	04/82	v	C	B.R. Swindon Works	(C03/84)
	D3361	08291	12/82	v	C	B.R. Doncaster Works	(C12/83)
13362	D3362	08292	05/84	v	F	Carntyne Transport Co., Glasgow	
13363	D3363	08293		v			
13364	D3364	08294	11/80	v	C	B.R. Swindon Works	(C12/81)
13365	D3365	08295		v			
13366	D3366	08296		v			
	D3367	08297		v			
	D3368	08298	03/81	v	C	B.R. Swindon Works	(C07/81)
	D3369	08299	07/81	v	C	B.R. Swindon Works	(C10/82)
	D3370	08300	07/83	v	C	B.R. Doncaster Works	(C04/84)
	D3371	08301	12/81	v			
	D3372	08302	06/81	v	C	B.R. Swindon Works	(C03/82)
	D3373	08303	12/81	v			
	D3374	08304		v			
	D3375	08305		v			
	D3376	08306	12/77	v	C	B.R. Swindon Works	(C11/78)
	D3377	08307	12/77	v	C	B.R. Swindon Works	(C06/78)
	D3378	08308		v			
	D3379	08309		v			
	D3380	08310	09/77	v	C	B.R. Doncaster Works	(C10/78)
	D3381	08311	12/82	v	C	B.R. Doncaster Works	(C02/84)
	D3382	08312	05/83	v			
	D3383	08313	05/82	v	C	B.R. Doncaster Works	(C05/83)
	D3384	08314	02/81	v	C	B.R. Glasgow Works	(C10/81)
	D3385	08315	02/79	v	C	B.R. Doncaster Works	(C01/80)
	D3386	08316	03/76	v	C	B.R. Swindon Works	(C02/77)
	D3387	08317	10/82	v	C	B.R. Doncaster Works	(C10/83)
	D3388	08318	10/76	v	C	B.R. Eastleigh Works	(C10/77)
	D3389	08319	04/83	v			
	D3390	08320	12/82	v	F	Chepstow Industries	
	D3391	08321	06/84	v			
	D3392	08322	09/83	v			
	D3393	08323	06/81	v	C	B.R. Swindon Works	(C02/82)
	D3394	08324		v			
	D3395	08325	07/84	v			
	D3396	08326	10/83	v			
	D3397	08327	02/83	v			
	D3398	08328	12/81	v			
	D3399	08329	06/84	v			
	D3400	08330		v			
	D3401	08331		v			
	D3402	08332		v			
	D3403	08333	12/82	v			

D3404	08334		v			
D3405	08335		v			
D3406	08336	04/81	v	C	B.R. Swindon Works	(C03/82)
D3407	08337		v			
D3408	08338		v			
D3409	08339		v			
D3410	08340	08/81	v	C	B.R. Swindon Works	(C03/82)
D3411	08341	10/83	v			
D3412	08342	07/82	v	C	B.R. Swindon Works	(C11/83)
D3413	08343	10/83	v			
D3414	08344	05/84	v			
D3415	08345	10/83	v			
D3416	08346		v			
D3417	08347	10/83	v			
D3418	08348	07/82	v			
D3419	08349	07/83	v			
D3420	08350	01/84	v	P	North Staffordshire Railway	
D3421	08351	01/84	v			
D3422	08352	07/83	v			
D3423	08353	07/81	v	C	B.R. Swindon Works	(C03/82)
D3424	08354		v			
D3425	08355	04/83	v	C	B.R. Doncaster Works	(C03/84)
D3426	08356	11/82	v	C	B.R. Swindon Works	(C12/83)
D3427	08357	09/77	v	C	B.R. Swindon Works	(C04/79)
D3428	08358	10/77	v	C	B.R. Doncaster Works	(C11/77)
D3429	08359	10/77	v	P	North Staffordshire Railway	
D3430	08360	01/83	v			
D3431	08361		v			
D3432	08362	03/82	v	C	B.R. Swindon Works	(C04/83)
D3433	08363	08/82	v	C	B.R. Swindon Works	(C04/83)
D3434	08364	01/83	v	C	B.R. Swindon Works	(C10/83)
D3435	08365	09/80	v	C	B.R. Swindon Works	(C04/81)
D3436	08366	12/80	v	C	B.R. Swindon Works	(C03/82)
D3437	08367		v			
D3438	08368	12/80	v			

Class continued with D3454

CLASS 10 continued

D3439	09/68	v	C	Steelbreaking & Dismantling, Chesterfield	(C01/69)
D3440	12/68	v	C	G. Cohen, Kettering	(C05/69)
D3441	09/68	v	C	G. Cohen, Kettering	(C03/69)
D3442	06/68	v	C	C.F. Booth, Rotherham	(C01/69)
D3443	12/68	v	C	C.F. Booth, Rotherham	(C06/69)
D3444	12/68	v	C	G. Cohen, Kettering	(C11/69)
D3445	11/68	v	C	Cox & Danks, North Acton	(C02/69)
D3446	07/68	v	C	Steelbreaking & Dismantling, Chesterfield	(C09/69)
D3447	03/68	v	C	C.F. Booth, Rotherham	(C01/69)
D3448	06/68	v	C	Steelbreaking & Dismantling, Chesterfield	(C06/69)
D3449	12/67	v	C	C.F. Booth, Rotherham	(C08/68)
D3450	06/68	v	C	C.F. Booth, Rotherham	(C01/69)
D3451	06/68	v	C	C.F. Booth, Rotherham	(C06/69)
D3452	06/68	v	F	English China Clay Ports Ltd., Fowey	
D3453	06/68	v	C	C.F. Booth, Rotherham	(C06/69)

Class continued with D3473

CLASS 08 continued

D3454	08369		v			
D3455	08370	03/84	v			
D3456	08371	10/83	v			
D3457	08372		v			
D3458	08373		v			
D3459	08374	12/82	v	C	B.R. Doncaster Works	(C09/84)
D3460	08375		v			
D3461	08376	07/83	v	C	B.R. Doncaster Works	(C04/84)
D3462	08377	06/83	v			
D3463	08378	06/81	v	C	B.R. Swindon Works	(C04/82)
D3464	08379	12/80	v	C	B.R. Swindon Works	(C03/81)
D3465	08380	08/82	v	C	B.R. Swindon Works	(C05/83)
D3466	08381	12/82	v	C	B.R. Doncaster Works	(C05/84)
D3467	08382		v			
D3468	08383		v			
D3469	08384		v			
D3470	08385		v			
D3471	08386		v			
D3472	08387	05/82	v			

Class continued with D3503

CLASS 10 continued

D3473		07/68	v	C	C.F. Booth, Rotherham	(C01/69)
D3474		06/68	v	C	C.F. Booth, Rotherham	(C01/69)
D3475		07/68	v	C	C.F. Booth, Rotherham	(C01/69)
D3476		06/68	v	F	English China Clay Ports Ltd., Fowey	
D3477		06/68	v	C	G. Cohen, Kettering	(C03/69)
D3478		06/68	v	C	C.F. Booth, Rotherham	(C07/69)
D3479		04/69	v	C	G. Cohen, Kettering	(C07/69)
D3480		08/68	v	C	Steelbreaking & Dismantling, Chesterfield	(C01/69)
D3481		12/68	v	C	C.F. Booth, Rotherham	(C05/68)
D3482		06/68	v	C	C.F. Booth, Rotherham	(C01/69)
D3483		03/69	v	C	G. Cohen, Kettering	(C10/69)
D3484		08/68	v	C	Steelbreaking & Dismantling, Chesterfield	(C01/69)
D3485		12/68	v	C	G. Cohen, Kettering	(C07/69)
D3486		11/70	v	C	C.F. Booth, Rotherham	(C08/71)
D3487		06/68	v	C	C.F. Booth, Rotherham	(C06/69)
D3488		12/68	v	C	G. Cohen, Kettering	(C11/69)
D3489		04/68	v	F	Felixstowe Dock & Railway Co.	
D3490		06/68	v	C	C.F. Booth, Rotherham	(C01/69)
D3491		12/68	v	C	G. Cohen, Kettering	(C11/69)
D3492		06/69	v	C	G. Cohen, Kettering	(C10/69)
D3493		06/68	v	C	C.F. Booth, Rotherham	(C01/69)
D3494		05/68	v	C	G. Cohen, Kettering	(C03/69)
D3495		06/68	v	C	C.F. Booth, Rotherham	(C01/69)
D3496		10/67	v	C	B.R. Doncaster Works	(C09/68)
D3497		04/68	v	F	English China Clay Ports Ltd., Fowey	( )
D3498		06/68	v	C	C.F. Booth, Rotherham	(C01/69)
D3499		01/68	v	C	C.F. Booth, Rotherham	(C09/68)
D3500		01/68	v	C	J. Cashmore, Great Bridge	(07/68)
D3501		06/68	v	C	C.F. Booth, Rotherham	(C01/69)
D3502		02/68	v	C	J. Cashmore, Great Bridge	(C07/68)

Class continued with D3612

D3503	08388		a				
D3504	08389		a				
D3505	08390		a				
D3506	08391		v				
D3507	08392		v				
D3508	08393		a				
D3509	08394		v				
D3510	08395		v				
D3511	08396		v				
D3512	08397		a				
D3513	08398		v				
D3514	08399		a				
D3515	08400		v				
D3516	08401		a				
D3517	08402		a				
D3518	08403		v				
D3519	08404	07/78	v	C	B.R. Doncaster Works	(C01/79)	
D3520	08405		a				
D3521	08406		v				
D3522	08407		a				
D3523	08408		v				
D3524	08409		v				
D3525	08410		a				
D3526	08411		a				
D3527	08412		v				
D3528	08413		a				
D3529	08414		a				
D3530	08415		v				
D3531	08416		a				
D3532	08417		a				
D3533	08418		a				
D3534	08419		a				
D3535	08420		v				
D3536	08421		a				
D3537	08422		v				
D3538	08423		a				
D3539	08424		v				
D3540	08425		v				
D3541	08426	07/76	v	C	B.R. Doncaster Works	(C04/77)	
D3542	08427		v				
D3543	08428		a				
D3544	08429	09/83	v	C	B.R. Doncaster Works	(C10/83)	
D3545	08430		v				
D3546	08431		v				
D3547	08432	10/83	v	C	B.R. Doncaster Works	(C01/84)	
D3548	08433		v				
D3549	08434		v				
D3550	08435	11/80	v	C	B.R. Swindon Works	(C05/83)	
D3551	08436		v				
D3552	08437		v				
D3553	08438		v				
D3554	08439		v				
D3555	08440		a				
D3556	08441		a				
D3557	08442		a				

D3558	08443		v			
D3559	08444		v			
D3560	08445		a			
D3561	08446		v			
D3562	08447		a			
D3563	08448		a			
D3564	08449		a			
D3565	08450		v			
D3566	08451		v			
D3567	08452		v			
D3568	08453	10/80	v	C	B.R. Swindon Works	(C08/82)
D3569	08454		v			
D3570	08455		v			
D3571	08456		v			
D3572	08457		v			
D3573	08458		v			
D3574	08459		v			
D3575	08460		a			
D3576	08461		v			
D3577	08462		a			
D3578	08463		a			
D3579	08464		v			
D3580	08465		v			
D3581	08466		a			
D3582	08467	11/81	v	C	B.R. Swindon Works	(C10/82)
D3583	08468		v			
D3584	08469		v			
D3585	08470		v			
D3586	08471		v			
D3587	08472		a			
D3588	08473		v			
D3589	08474		v			
D3590	08475		v			
D3591	08476		v			
D3592	08477		v			
D3593	08478		v			
D3594	08479		v			
D3595	08480		a			
D3596	08481		v			
D3597	08482		a			
D3598	08483		a			
D3599	08484		a			
D3600	08485		a			
D3601	08486		v			
D3602	08487		v			
D3603	08488		v			
D3604	08489		a			
D3605	08490		v			
D3606	08491		v			
D3607	08492		a			
D3608	08493		a			
D3609	08494		v			
D3610	08495		v			
D3611	08496		a			

Class continued with D3652

CLASS 10 continued

D3612	03/69	v	C	G. Cohen, Kettering	(C07/69)
D3613	02/69	v	F	N.C.B., Moor Green Colliery	
D3614	02/69	v	C	Steelbreaking & Dismantling, Chesterfield	(C08/69)
D3615	12/68	v	C	G. Cohen, Kettering	(C07/69)
D3616	07/69	v	C	Steelbreaking & Dismantling, Chesterfield	(C10/69)
D3617	07/69	v	C	Steelbreaking & Dismantling, Chesterfield	(C11/69)
D3618	04/69	v	F	N.C.B., Moor Green Colliery	
D3619	02/69	v	F	N.C.B., Moor Green Colliery	
D3620	02/67	v	C	Slag Reduction Co., Ickles	(C08/67)
D3621	07/69	v	C	C.F. Booth, Rotherham	(C01/70)
D3622	02/69	v	C	C.F. Booth, Rotherham	(C07/69)
D3623	02/69	v	C	C.F. Booth, Rotherham	(C09/69)
D3624	11/68	v	C	C.F. Booth, Rotherham	(C07/69)
D3625	07/68	v	C	C.F. Booth, Rotherham	(C01/69)
D3626	07/68	v	C	C.F. Booth, Rotherham	(C01/69)
D3627	07/68	v	C	C.F. Booth, Rotherham	(C01/69)
D3628	12/67	v	C	C.F. Booth, Rotherham	(C09/68)
D3629	05/69	v	C	G. Cohen, Kettering	(C11/69)
D3630	12/68	v	C	Cox & Danks, North Acton	(C06/69)
D3631	05/67	v	C	G. Cohen, Canning Town at Stratford Depot	(C10/67)
D3632	07/68	v	C	C.F. Booth, Rotherham	(C01/69)
D3633	12/68	v	C	G. Cohen, Kettering	(C06/69)
D3634	11/71	v	C	C.F. Booth, Rotherham	(C06/72)
D3635	12/68	v	C	G. Cohen, Kettering	(C06/59)
D3636	04/68	v	C	J.E. McMurray, Greenford at Stratford Depot	(C05/69)
D3637	11/68	v	C	G. Cohen, Kettering	(C08/69)
D3638	11/70	v	F	N.C.B., Ashington Central Workshops	(C09/75)
D3639	07/69	v	E	Conakry, Guinea (via C.F. Booth)	(E03/70)
D3640	12/68	v	C	G. Cohen, Kettering	(C05/69)
D3641	11/71	v	C	C.F. Booth, Rotherham	(C02/73)
D3642	06/69	v	F	B.S.C., Appleby Frodingham	(C10/78)
D3643	10/68	v	C	G. Cohen, Kettering	(C07/69)
D3644	06/70	v	C	C.F. Booth, Rotherham	(C05/71)
D3645	03/69	v	C	C.F. Booth, Rotherham	(C08/69)
D3646	05/71	v	C	C.F. Booth, Rotherham	(C12/71)
D3647	03/70	v	C	C.F. Booth, Rotherham	(C09/70)
D3648	01/71	v	F	N.C.B., Bates Colliery, Blyth	(C02/77)
D3649	07/69	v	E	Conakry, Guinea (via C.F. Booth)	(E03/70)
D3650	11/71	v	C	C.F. Booth, Rotherham	(C06/72)
D3651	12/71	v	C	C.F. Booth, Rotherham	(C06/72)

Class continued with D4049

CLASS 08/09 continued

D3652	08497		v			
D3653	08498		a			
D3654	08499		a			
D3655	08500		v			
D3656	08501		v			
D3657	08502		a			
D3658	08503		a			
D3659	08504		a			
D3660	08505	02/81	v	C	B.R. Swindon Works	(C03/83)
D3661	08506		a			
D3662	08507		a			
D3663	08508		v			
D3664	08509		a			

D3665	09001		x				
D3666	09002		x				
D3667	09003		x				
D3668	09004		x				
D3669	09005		x				
D3670	09006		x				
D3671	09007		x				
D3672	08510		a				
D3673	08511		a				
D3674	08512		a				
D3675	08513	03/78	v	C	B.R. Doncaster Works	(C10/78)	
D3676	08514		a				
D3677	08515		a				
D3678	08516		a				
D3679	08517		a				
D3680	08518		a				
D3681	08519		a				
D3682	08520		v				
D3683	08521		a				
D3684	08522		v				
D3685	08523		v				
D3686	08524		v				
D3687	08525		x				
D3688	08526		x				
D3689	08527		x				
D3690	08528		x				
D3691	08529		x				
D3692	08530		x				
D3693	08531		x				
D3694	08532		x				
D3695	08533		x				
D3696	08534		x				
D3697		07/65	v	R	Converted to class 13 D4502 slave		
D3698		05/65	v	R	Converted to class 13 D4500 slave		
D3699	08535		x				
D3700	08536		x				
D3701	08537		x				
D3702	08538		x				
D3703	08539		x				
D3704	08540		x				
D3705	08541		x				
D3706	08542		x				
D3707	08543		x				
D3708	08544		x				
D3709	08545	11/83	v	C	B.R. Swindon Works	(C)	
D3710	08546		v				
D3711	08547	12/81	v	C	B.R. Swindon Works	(C05/82)	
D3712	08548	12/82	v	C	B.R. Doncaster Works	(C12/83)	
D3713	08549		v				
D3714	08550	03/83	v				
D3715	08551	10/82	v	C	B.R. Doncaster Works	(C11/83)	
D3716	08552	08/82	v	C	B.R. Doncaster Works	(C01/83)	
D3717	08553	05/81	v	C	B.R. Swindon Works	(C04/83)	
D3718	08554	08/82	v	C	B.R. Doncaster Works	(C03/83)	
D3719	09008		x				
D3720	09009		x				
D3721	09010		x				

D3722	08555	08/82	v	C	B.R. Doncaster Works	(C11/83)	
D3723	08556		v				
D3724	08557	12/82	v	C	B.R. Doncaster Works	(C12/83)	
D3725	08558		v				
D3726	08559	12/81	v	C	B.R. Swindon Works	(C10/83)	
D3727	08560	05/81	v	C	B.R. Swindon Works	(C03/82)	
D3728	08561		v				
D3729	08562		v				
D3730	08563		v				
D3731	08564		v				
D3732	08565		v				
D3733	08566	10/75	v	C	B.R. Glasgow Works	(C11/77)	
D3734	08567		v				
D3735	08568		v				
D3736	08569		v				
D3737	08570		x				
D3738	08571		v				
D3739	08572	02/81	v	C	B.R. Swindon Works	(C10/83)	
D3740	08573		x				
D3741	08574	03/81	v				
D3742	08575		v				
D3743	08576		v				
D3744	08577		x				
D3745	08578		x				
D3746	08579		v				
D3747	08580		v				
D3748	08581		v				
D3749	08582		a				
D3750	08583		x				
D3751	08584		x				
D3752	08585		x				
D3753	08586		a				
D3754	08587		x				
D3755	08588		v				
D3756	08589		v				
D3757	08590		v				
D3758	08591		x				
D3759	08592		v				
D3760	08593		x				
D3761	08594		v				
D3762	08595		v				
D3763	08596	03/77	a	F	Bowater, Sittingbourne		
D3764	08597		x				
D3765	08598		v				
D3766	08599		v				
D3767	08600	01/79	a	D	97800 Slade Green Depot		
D3768	08601		v				
D3769	08602		v				
D3770	08603		x				
D3771	08604		x				
D3772	08605		v				
D3773	08606		v				
D3774	08607		v				
D3775	08608		v				
D3776	08609		x				
D3777	08610		v				
D3778	08611		x				

D3779	08612		x		
D3780	08613		v		
D3781	08614		v		
D3782	08615		x		
D3783	08616		v		
D3784	08617		x		
D3785	08618		v		
D3786	08619		x		
D3787	08620		x		
D3788	08621		a		
D3789	08622		x		
D3790	08623		v		
D3791	08624		v		
D3792	08625		x		
D3793	08626		v		
D3794	08627		a		
D3795	08628		x		
D3796	08629		x		
D3797	08630		x		
D3798	08631		v		
D3799	08632		x		
D3800	08633		v		
D3801	08634		v		
D3802	08635		x		
D3803	08636	07/80	v	C B.R. Swindon Works	(C06/83)
D3804	08637		v		
D3805	08638		x		
D3806	08639		v		
D3807	08640		x		
D3808	08641		x		
D3809	08642		x		
D3810	08643		x		
D3811	08644		x		
D3812	08645		x		
D3813	08646		x		
D3814	08647		x		
D3815	08648		x		
D3816	08649		x		
D3817	08650		x		
D3818	08651		x		
D3819	08652		x		
D3820	08653		x		
D3821	08654		x		
D3822	08655		x		
D3823	08656		a		
D3824	08657		a		
D3825	08658		v		
D3826	08659		a		
D3827	08660		v		
D3828	08661		a		
D3829	08662		v		
D3830	08663		a		
D3831	08664		v		
D3832	08665		v		
D3833	08666		x		
D3834	08667		v		
D3835	08668		v		

D3836	08669		a				
D3837	08670		a				
D3838	08671		v				
D3839	08672		a				
D3840	08673		v				
D3841	08674	07/81	v	C	B.R. Swindon Works	(C07/83)	
D3842	08675		v				
D3843	08676		v				
D3844	08677		v				
D3845	08678		a				
D3846	08679	06/76	a	F	N.C.B., North Gawber Colliery		
D3847	08680		x				
D3848	08681		v				
D3849	08682		v				
D3850	08683		x				
D3851	08684		v				
D3852	08685		v				
D3853	08686		a				
D3854	08687		a				
D3855	08688		a				
D3856	08689		a				
D3857	08690		v				
D3858	08691		v				
D3859	08692		v				
D3860	08693		x				
D3861	08694		x				
D3862	08695		x				
D3863	08696		a				
D3864	08697		v				
D3865	08698		a				
D3366	08699		v				
D3867	08700		a				
D3868	08701		v				
D3869	08702		v				
D3870	08703		a				
D3871	08704		x				
D3872	08705		a				
D3873	08706		x				
D3874	08707		a				
D3875	08708		a				
D3876	08709		x				
D3877	08710		x				
D3878	08711		v				
D3879	08712		x				
D3880	08713		a				
D3881	08714		v				
D3882	08715		v				
D3883	08716		v				
D3884	08717		x				
D3885		02/72	v	C	B.R. Glasgow Works	(C03/72)	
D3886	08718		x				
D3887	08719		x				
D3888	08720		a				
D3889	08721		v				
D3890	08722		v				
D3891	08723		v				
D3892	08724		v				

D3893	08725	x
D3894	08726	a
D3895	08727	v
D3896	08728	a
D3897	08729	a
D3898	08730	v
D3899	08731	x
D3900	08732	x
D3901	08733	x
D3902	08734	v
D3903	08735	x
D3904	08736	a
D3905	08737	x
D3906	08738	x
D3907	08739	x
D3908	08740	x
D3909	08741	x
D3910	08742	x
D3911	08743	x
D3912	08744	x
D3913	08745	x
D3914	08746	x
D3915	08747	x
D3916	08748	x
D3917	08749	x
D3918	08750	x
D3919	08751	x
D3920	08752	x
D3921	08753	x
D3922	08754	x
D3923	08755	x
D3924	08756	x
D3925	08757	x
D3926	08758	x
D3927	08759	x
D3928	08760	x
D3929	08761	x
D3930	08762	x
D3931	08763	x
D3932	08764	x
D3933	08765	x
D3934	08766	x
D3935	08767	x
D3936	08768	x
D3937	08769	v
D3938	08770	a
D3939	08771	x
D3940	08772	x
D3941	08773	x
D3942	08774	a
D3943	08775	x
D3944	08776	a
D3945	08777	x
D3946	08778	x
D3947	08779	v
D3948	08780	x
D3949	08781	x

D3950	08782		a		
D3951	08783		v		
D3952	08784		v		
D3953	08785		a		
D3954	08786		a		
D3955	08787		x		
D3956	08788		x		
D3957	08789		a		
D3958	08790		v		
D3959	08791		a		
D3960	08792		x		
D3961	08793		a		
D3962	08794		v		
D3963	08795		x		
D3964	08796		a		
D3965	08797		x		
D3966	08798		v		
D3967	08799		v		
D3968	08800		x		
D3969	08801		x		
D3970	08802		v		
D3971	08803		v		
D3972	08804		x		
D3973	08805		x		
D3974	08806		a		
D3975	08807		v		
D3976	08808		x		
D3977	08809		x		
D3978	08810		a		
D3979	08811		a		
D3980	08812	02/78	v	C B.R. Swindon Works	(C03/78)
D3981	08813		a		
D3982	08814		a		
D3983	08815		x		
D3984	08816		a		
D3985	08817		x		
D3986	08818		x		
D3987	08819		x		
D3988	08820		a		
D3989	08821		v		
D3990	08822		x		
D3991	08823		a		
D3992	08824		a		
D3993	08825		a		
D3994	08826		a		
D3995	08827		a		
D3996	08828		a		
D3997	08829		a		
D3998	08830		x		
D3999	08831		x		
D4000	08832		x		
D4001	08833		x		
D4002	08834		x		
D4003	08835		x		
D4004	08836		x		
D4005	08837		x		
D4006	08838		x		

D4007	08839		x			
D4008	08840		x			
D4009	08841		x			
D4010	08842		x			
D4011	08843		x			
D4012	08844		x			
D4013	08845		x			
D4014	08846		x			
D4015	08847		x			
D4016	08848		x			
D4017	08849		x			
D4018	08850		x			
D4019	08851		x			
D4020	08852		x			
D4021	08853		x			
D4022	08854		x			
D4023	08855		x			
D4024	08856		x			
D4025	08857		x			
D4026	08858		x			
D4027	08859		x			
D4028	08860	03/81	v	C	B.R. Swindon Works	(C06/81)
D4029	08861	10/81	v	C	B.R. Swindon Works	(C03/82)
D4030	08862	09/80	v	C	B.R. Swindon Works	(C09/81)
D4031	08863	09/80	v	C	B.R. Swindon Works	(C10/81)
D4032	08864	08/81	v	C	B.R. Swindon Works	(C03/82)
D4033	08865		x			
D4034	08866		x			
D4035	08867		x			
D4036	08868		x			
D4037	08869		x			
D4038	08870		x			
D4039	08871		x			
D4040	08872		x			
D4041	08873		x			
D4042	08874		x			
D4043	08875		x			
D4044	08876		x			
D4045	08877		x			
D4046	08878		x			
D4047	08879		x			
D4048	08880		x			

Class continued with D4095

CLASS 10 continued

D4049	01/72	v	C	G. Cohen, Kettering	(C08/72)
D4050	12/71	v	C	C. F. Booth, Rotherham	(C08/73)
D4051	07/71	v	C	C. F. Booth, Rotherham	(C07/72)
D4052	10/70	v	C	C. F. Booth, Rotherham	(C02/71)
D4053	12/71	v	C	C. F. Booth, Rotherham	(C08/73)
D4054	06/72	v	C	G. Cohen, Kettering	(C05/73)
D4055	12/71	v	C	C. F. Booth, Rotherham	(C05/73)
D4056	06/72	v	F	N.C.B., Shilbottle Colliery	
D4057	01/72	v	C	C. F. Booth, Rotherham	(C04/73)
D4058	01/72	v	C	G. Cohen, Kettering	(C08/72)

D4059	12/71	v	C	G. Cohen, Kettering	(C08/72)	
D4060	12/71	v	C	C. F. Booth, Rotherham	(C06/72)	
D4061	01/72	v	C	C. F. Booth, Rotherham	(C11/72)	
D4062	01/72	v	C	C. F. Booth, Rotherham	(C11/72)	
D4063	06/72	v	C	G. Cohen, Kettering	(C05/73)	
D4064	07/68	v	C	C. F. Booth, Rotherham	(C01/69)	
D4065	11/71	v	C	C. F. Booth, Rotherham	(C06/72)	
D4066	06/72	v	C	G. Cohen, Kettering	(C02/73)	
D4067	12/70	v	P	Main Line Steam Trust, Loughborough		
D4068	06/72	v	F	N.C.B., Whittle Colliery		
D4069	04/72	v	F	N.C.B., Whittle Colliery		
D4070	04/72	v	F	N.C.B., Whittle Colliery		
D4071	06/68	v	C	G. Cohen, Kettering	(C03/69)	
D4072	04/72	v	F	N.C.B., Lambton Engine Works		
D4073	06/72	v	C	G. Cohen, Kettering	(C04/73)	
D4074	04/72	v	F	N.C.B., Lambton Engine Works	(C08/78)	
D4075	06/72	v	C	G. Cohen, Kettering	(C04/73)	
D4076	06/68	v	C	C. F. Booth, Rotherham	(C05/69)	
D4077	11/70	v	C	G. Cohen, Kettering	(C08/71)	
D4078	06/72	v	C	G. Cohen, Kettering	(C05/73)	
D4079	06/72	v	C	G. Cohen, Kettering	(C05/73)	
D4080	02/68	v	C	C. F. Booth, Rotherham	(C11/68)	
D4081	06/68	v	C	C. F. Booth, Rotherham	(C04/69)	
D4082	06/68	v	C	C. F. Booth, Rotherham	(C04/69)	
D4083	06/68	v	C	C. F. Booth, Rotherham	(C05/69)	
D4084	06/68	v	C	C. F. Booth, Rotherham	(C05/69)	
D4085	06/68	v	C	C. F. Booth, Rotherham	(C01/69)	
D4086	07/68	v	C	G. Cohen, Kettering	(C01/69)	
D4087	09/68	v	C	G. Cohen, Kettering	(C03/69)	
D4088	08/68	v	C	C. F. Booth, Rotherham	(C01/69)	
D4089	08/68	v	C	C. F. Booth, Rotherham	(C01/69)	
D4090	08/68	v	C	G. Cohen, Kettering	(C04/69)	
D4091	08/68	v	C	Slag Reduction Co., Ickles	(C02/69)	
D4092	09/68	v	F	P.D. Fuels, Gwaun-cae-Gurwen D.P.		
D4093	08/68	v	C	G. Cohen, Kettering	(C04/69)	
D4094	08/68	v	C	G. Cohen, Kettering	(C04/69)	

CLASS 08/09 continued

D4095	08881	x	
D4096	08882	x	
D4097	08883	x	
D4098	08884	x	
D4099	09011	x	
D4100	09012	x	
D4101	09013	x	
D4102	09014	x	
D4103	09015	x	
D4104	09016	x	
D4105	09017	x	
D4106	09018	x	
D4107	09019	x	
D4108	09020	x	
D4109	09021	x	
D4110	09022	x	
D4111	09023	x	
D4112	09024	x	

D4113	09025	x
D4114	09026	x
D4115	08885	x
D4116	08886	x
D4117	08887	x
D4118	08888	x
D4119	08889	x
D4120	08890	x
D4121	08891	x
D4122	08892	x
D4123	08893	x
D4124	08894	x
D4125	08895	x
D4126	08896	x
D4127	08897	x
D4128	08898	x
D4129	08899	x
D4130	08900	x
D4131	08901	x
D4132	08902	x
D4133	08903	x
D4134	08904	x
D4135	08905	x
D4136	08906	x
D4137	08907	x
D4138	08908	x
D4139	08909	x
D4140	08910	x
D4141	08911	x
D4142	08912	x
D4143	08913	x
D4144	08914	x
D4145	08915	x
D4146	08916	x
D4147	08917	x
D4148	08918	x
D4149	08919	x
D4150	08920	x
D4151	08921	x
D4152	08922	x
D4153	08923	x
D4154	08924	x
D4155	08925	x
D4156	08926	x
D4157	08927	x
D4158	08928	x
D4159	08929	x
D4160	08930	x
D4161	08931	x
D4162	08932	x
D4163	08933	x
D4164	08934	x
D4165	08935	x
D4166	08936	x
D4167	08937	x
D4168	08938	x
D4169	08939	x

D4170	08940		x			
D4171	08941		x			
D4172	08942		x			
D4173	08943		x			
D4174	08944		x			
D4175	08945		x			
D4176	08946		x			
D4177	08947		x			
D4178	08948		x			
D4179	08949		x			
D4180	08950		x			
D4181	08951		x			
D4182	08952		x			
D4183	08953		x			
D4184	08954		x			
D4185	08955		x			
D4186	08956		x			
D4187		07/67	v	R	Converted to class 13 D4502 master	
D4188		05/65	v	R	Converted to class 13 D4500 master	
D4189		06/65	v	R	Converted to class 13 D4501 slave	
D4190		06/65	v	R	Converted to class 13 D4501 master	
D4191	08957		x			
D4192	08958		x			

CLASS 13   B.R./E.E./E.E. 800 h.p. DE   0-6-0 + 0-6-0
Re-built 1965 from Class 08

D4500	13001		v			
D4501	13002	06/81	v	C	B.R. Swindon Works	(C10/82)
D4502	13003		v			

CLASS 24 B.R./SULZER/B.T.H. * or A.E.I. TYPE 2 1160 h.p. DE Bo-Bo
*Built 1958-1961 (*D5000-D5019)*

D5000	24005	01/76	vi	C	B.R. Swindon Works	(C04/77)
D5001	24001	10/75	vi	C	B.R. Doncaster Works	(C11/77)
D5002	24002	10/75	vi	C	B.R. Glasgow Works	(C07/78)
D5003	24003	08/75	vi	C	B.R. Doncaster Works	(C07/76)
D5004	24004	10/75	vb	C	B.R. Glasgow Works	(C05/77)
D5005		01/69	vb	C	B.R. Derby Loco Works	(C12/69)
D5006	24006	08/75	vb	C	B.R. Glasgow Works	(C12/80)
D5007	24007	10/75	vi	C	B.R. Doncaster Works	(C01/78)
D5008	24008	08/75	vb	C	B.R. Doncaster Works	(C05/76)
D5009	24009	07/76	vb	C	B.R. Doncaster Works	(C11/77)
D5010	24010	10/75	vi	C	B.R. Doncaster Works	(C01/77)
D5011	24011	10/75	vb	C	B.R. Glasgow Works	(C04/77)
D5012	24012	08/75	vi	C	B.R. Doncaster Works	(C02/76)
D5013	24013	10/75	vb	C	B.R. Doncaster Works	(C02/78)
D5014	24014	10/75	vb	C	B.R. Doncaster Works	(C03/78)
D5015	24015	08/75	vi	C	B.R. Doncaster Works	(C01/77)
D5016	24016	08/75	vb	C	B.R. Doncaster Works	(C01/77)
D5017	24017	10/75	vb	C	B.R. Doncaster Works	(C01/77)
D5018	24018	08/75	vb	C	B.R. Doncaster Works	(C06/76)
D5019	24019	10/75	vb	C	B.R. Doncaster Works	(C06/78)
D5020	24020	08/75	vb	C	B.R. Swindon Works	(C04/77)
D5021	24021	08/75	vb	C	B.R. Swindon Works	(C03/77)
D5022	24022	01/76	vb	C	B.R. Doncaster Works	(C09/78)

D5023	24023	09/78	vi	C	B.R. Doncaster Works	(C12/78)	
D5024	24024	08/75	vb	C	B.R. Swindon Works	(C04/77)	
D5025	24025	01/76	vi	C	B.R. Swindon Works	(C07/77)	
D5026	24026	08/75	vb	C	B.R. Swindon Works	(C01/77)	
D5027	24027	07/76	vr	C	B.R. Swindon Works	(C05/77)	
D5028		06/72	vb	C	B.R. Crewe Works	(C09/72)	
D5029	24029	08/75	vb	C	B.R. Swindon Works	(C03/77)	
D5030	24030	07/76	vb	C	B.R. Swindon Works	(C05/77)	
D5031	24031	10/75	vb	C	B.R. Swindon Works	(C12/76)	
D5032	24032	07/76	vb	P	North Yorkshire Moors Railway		
D5033	24033	10/75	vb	C	B.R. Swindon Works	(C03/77)	
D5034	24034	01/76	vi	C	B.R. Swindon Works	(C05/77)	
D5035	24035	10/78	vi	C	B.R. Doncaster Works	(C12/78)	
D5036	24036	11/77	vb	C	B.R. Doncaster Works	(C05/78)	
D5037	24037	07/76	vb	C	B.R. Swindon Works	(C06/77)	
D5038	24038	07/76	vb	C	B.R. Swindon Works	(C06/77)	
D5039	24039	07/76	vb	C	B.R. Swindon Works	(C07/78)	
D5040	24040	01/76	vb	C	B.R. Swindon Works	(C02/77)	
D5041	24041	07/76	vb	C	B.R. Swindon Works	(C06/78)	
D5042	24042	08/75	vb	C	B.R. Swindon Works	(C02/76)	
D5043		08/69	vb	C	J. Cashmore, Great Bridge	(C06/70)	
D5044	24044	01/76	vb	C	B.R. Swindon Works	(C01/77)	
D5045	24045	08/75	vb	C	B.R. Swindon Works	(C12/76)	
D5046	24046	07/76	vb	C	B.R. Swindon Works	(C07/77)	
D5047	24047	11/78	vi	C	B.R. Doncaster Works	(C03/79)	
D5048	24048	08/75	vb	C	B.R. Swindon Works	(C03/76)	
D5049	24049	01/76	vb	C	B.R. Swindon Works	(C11/76)	
D5050	24050	10/75	vb	C	B.R. Swindon Works	(C12/76)	
D5051		12/67	vb	C	B.R. Inverurie Works	(C08/68)	
D5052	24052	12/76	vb	C	B.R. Swindon Works	(C05/78)	
D5053	24053	01/76	vb	C	B.R. Swindon Works	(C05/76)	
D5054	24054	07/76	vb	P	Bury Transport Museum		
D5055	24055	10/75	vb	C	B.R. Swindon Works	(C12/76)	
D5056	24056	10/75	vb	C	B.R. Swindon Works	(C11/76)	
D5057	24057	01/78	vi	C	B.R. Doncaster Works	(C08/78)	
D5058	24058	10/75	vb	C	B.R. Swindon Works	(C10/76)	
D5059	24059	10/75	vb	C	B.R. Swindon Works	(C03/77)	
D5060	24060	10/75	vb	C	B.R. Swindon Works	(C01/77)	
D5061	24061	08/75	vb	D	97201 Research Dept Derby		
D5062	24062	10/75	vb	C	B.R. Swindon Works	(C10/76)	
D5063	24063	04/79	vi	C	B.R. Doncaster Works	(C08/79)	
D5064	24064	01/76	vb	C	B.R. Swindon Works	(C12/76)	
D5065	24065	12/76	vi	C	B.R. Swindon Works	(C06/77)	
D5066	24066	02/76	vb	C	B.R. Doncaster Works	(C09/78)	
D5067		10/72	vb	C	B.R. Glasgow Works	(C10/73)	
D5068		10/72	vb	C	B.R. Glasgow Works	(C04/73)	
D5069	24069	12/76	vi	C	B.R. Doncaster Works	(C09/77)	
D5070	24070	02/76	vb	C	B.R. Doncaster Works	(C06/76)	
D5071	24071	08/75	vb	C	B.R. Doncaster Works	(C01/77)	
D5072	24072	10/75	vb	C	B.R. Doncaster Works	(C12/77)	
D5073	24073	11/77	vb	C	B.R. Doncaster Works	(C10/78)	
D5074	24074	10/75	vb	C	J. Cashmore, Great Bridge	(C06/76)	
D5075	24075	01/76	vb	C	B.R. Swindon Works	(C07/76)	
D5076	24076	10/75	vb	C	B.R. Swindon Works	(C01/77)	
D5077	24077	07/76	vb	C	B.R. Swindon Works	(C08/78)	
D5078	24078	04/76	vb	C	B.R. Swindon Works	(C06/78)	
D5079	24079	07/76	vb	C	B.R. Swindon Works	(C09/78)	

D5080	24080	09/76	vb	C	B.R. Doncaster Works	(C06/78)
D5081	24081	10/80	vi	P	Steamport Railway Museum, Southport	
D5082	24082	03/79	vb	C	B.R. Doncaster Works	(C05/79)
D5083	24083	03/76	vb	C	B.R. Swindon Works	(C05/77)
D5084	24084	07/76	vi	C	B.R. Swindon Works	(C12/78)
D5085	24085	07/76	vb	C	B.R. Swindon Works	(C10/78)
D5086	24086	01/76	vb	C	B.R. Doncaster Works	(C01/77)
D5087	24087	02/78	vb	C	B.R. Doncaster Works	(C09/78)
D5088		07/70	vb	C	G. Cohen, Kettering	(C01/72)
D5089	24089	01/76	vb	C	B.R. Swindon Works	(C07/77)
D5090	24090	02/76	vb	C	B.R. Doncaster Works	(C01/78)
D5091	24091	11/77	vb	C	B.R. Doncaster Works	(C05/78)
D5092	24092	10/75	vb	C	B.R. Swindon Works	(C12/76)
D5093		08/69	vb	C	J. Cashmore, Great Bridge	(C06/70)
D5094	24094	09/76	vb	C	B.R. Doncaster Works	(C09/77)
D5095	24095	08/75	vb	C	B.R. Doncaster Works	(C06/76)
D5096	24096	08/75	vb	C	B.R. Doncaster Works	(C08/76)
D5097	24097	02/76	vb	C	B.R. Doncaster Works	(C02/77)
D5098	24098	08/75	vb	C	B.R. Doncaster Works	(C05/76)
D5099	24099	02/76	vb	C	B.R. Doncaster Works	(C07/77)
D5100	24100	02/76	vb	C	B.R. Doncaster Works	(C05/76)
D5101	24101	02/76	vb	C	B.R. Doncaster Works	(C03/76)
D5102	24102	02/76	vq	C	B.R. Doncaster Works	(C03/78)
D5103	24103	12/76	vq	C	B.R. Doncaster Works	(C07/77)
D5104	24104	12/76	vq	C	B.R. Doncaster Works	(C09/77)
D5105	24105	10/75	vq	C	B.R. Doncaster Works	(C02/78)
D5106	24106	12/76	vq	C	B.R. Doncaster Works	(C10/77)
D5107	24107	12/76	vq	C	B.R. Swindon Works	(C06/77)
D5108	24108	07/76	vq	C	B.R. Doncaster Works	(C01/78)
D5109	24109	02/76	vq	C	B.R. Doncaster Works	(C03/78)
D5110	24110	12/76	vq	C	B.R. Doncaster Works	(C04/77)
D5111	24111	02/76	vq	C	B.R. Doncaster Works	(C02/78)
D5112	24112	12/76	vi	C	B.R. Doncaster Works	(C10/77)
D5113	24113	12/76	vi	C	B.R. Doncaster Works	(C09/77)
D5114		10/72	vb	C	B.R. Glasgow Works	(C10/73)
D5115	24115	12/76	vi	C	B.R. Swindon Works	(C06/77)
D5116	24116	09/76	vb	C	B.R. Doncaster Works	(C07/77)
D5117	24117	02/76	vb	C	B.R. Doncaster Works	(C01/77)
D5118	24118	12/76	vi	C	B.R. Doncaster Works	(C05/77)
D5119	24119	07/76	vb	C	B.R. Doncaster Works	(C05/77)
D5120	24120	12/76	vi	C	B.R. Doncaster Works	(C07/77)
D5121	24121	12/76	vi	C	B.R. Doncaster Works	(C05/78)
D5122		09/68	vb	C	B.R. Glasgow Works	(C03/71)
D5123	24123	07/76	vb	C	B.R. Doncaster Works	(C08/77)
D5124	24124	12/76	vi	C	B.R. Swindon Works	(C05/77)
D5125	24125	03/76	vb	C	B.R. Doncaster Works	(C08/77)
D5126	24126	02/76	vb	C	B.R. Doncaster Works	(C08/77)
D5127	24127	02/76	vb	C	B.R. Doncaster Works	(C04/77)
D5128	24128	07/76	vb	C	B.R. Doncaster Works	(C10/77)
D5129	24129	12/76	vi	C	B.R. Doncaster Works	(C04/77)
D5130	24130	12/76	vi	C	B.R. Doncaster Works	(C09/77)
D5131		09/71	vb	C	B.R. Glasgow Works	(C02/72)
D5132	24132	02/76	vb	C	B.R. Doncaster Works	(C03/76)
D5133	24133	03/78	vb	C	B.R. Doncaster Works	(C10/78)
D5134	24134	12/76	vi	C	B.R. Swindon Works	(C09/78)
D5135	24135	01/76	vb	C	B.R. Swindon Works	(C07/77)
D5136	24136	10/75	vb	C	B.R. Swindon Works	(C01/77)

D5137	24137	07/76	vb	C	B.R. Doncaster Works	(C08/78)	
D5138		08/69	vb	C	J. Cashmore, Great Bridge	(C06/70)	
D5139		08/69	vb	C	J. Cashmore, Great Bridge	(C06/70)	
D5140	24140	01/76	vb	C	B.R. Swindon Works	(C09/76)	
D5141	24141	07/76	vb	C	B.R. Swindon Works	(C06/78)	
D5142	24142	07/76	vb	D	ADB968009 Power Plant	(C09/84)	
D5143	24143	01/76	vb	C	B.R. Swindon Works	(C05/76)	
D5144	24144	01/76	vb	C	B.R. Swindon Works	(C09/76)	
D5145	24145	01/76	vb	C	B.R. Swindon Works	(C05/76)	
D5146	24146	01/76	vb	C	B.R. Swindon Works	(C10/76)	
D5147	24147	07/76	vb	C	B.R. Doncaster Works	(C11/77)	
D5148	24148	10/75	vb	C	B.R. Doncaster Works	(C12/77)	
D5149	24149	10/72	vb	C	B.R. Glasgow Works	(C04/73)	
D5150	24150	12/76	vi	C	B.R. Doncaster Works	(C07/77)	

CLASS 25   B.R./SULZER/A.E.I. TYPE 2 1250 h.p. DE   Bo-Bo
Built 1961-1967

D5151	25001	09/80	vq	C	B.R. Swindon Works	(C11/80)	
D5152	25002	12/80	vq	C	B.R. Swindon Works	(C04/81)	
D5153	25003	08/76	vq	C	B.R. Glasgow Works	(C10/78)	
D5154	25004	09/76	vq	C	B.R. Glasgow Works	(C09/77)	
D5155	25005	12/80	vq	C	B.R. Swindon Works	(C08/81)	
D5156	25006	12/80	vq	C	B.R. Swindon Works	(C07/83)	
D5157	25007	12/80	vq	C	B.R. Swindon Works	(C09/82)	
D5158	25008	06/80	vq	C	B.R. Glasgow Works	(C08/80)	
D5159	25009	07/80	vq	C	B.R. Glasgow Works	(C10/80)	
D5160	25010	02/81	vq	C	B.R. Swindon Works	(C05/81)	
D5161	25011	12/80	vq	C	B.R. Swindon Works	(C03/81)	
D5162	25012	02/77	vq	C	B.R. Glasgow Works	(C09/77)	
D5163	25013	09/80	vq	C	B.R. Swindon Works	(C01/81)	
D5164	25014	07/77	vq	C	B.R. Glasgow Works	(C09/77)	
D5165	25015	12/75	vq	C	B.R. Doncaster Works	(C02/77)	
D5166	25016	01/76	vq	C	B.R. Swindon Works	(C12/76)	
D5167	25017	01/76	vq	C	B.R. Swindon Works	(C07/76)	
D5168	25018	11/76	vq	C	B.R. Glasgow Works	(C11/78)	
D5169	25019	09/80	vq	C	B.R. Swindon Works	(C01/81)	
D5170	25020	01/76	vq	C	B.R. Swindon Works	(C08/76)	
D5171	25021	09/80	vq	C	B.R. Swindon Works	(C12/80)	
D5172	25022	01/76	vq	C	B.R. Glasgow Works	(C12/76)	
D5173	25023	09/80	vq	C	B.R. Swindon Works	(C04/83)	
D5174	25024	01/76	vq	C	B.R. Glasgow Works	(C12/76)	
D5175	25025	04/77	vq	C	B.R. Glasgow Works	(C03/78)	
D5176	25026	11/80	vb	C	B.R. Swindon Works	(C03/81)	
D5177	25027	05/83	vb				
D5178	25028	12/80	xb				
D5179	25029	08/77	vr	C	B.R. Glasgow Works	(C03/78)	
D5180	25030	08/76	vr	C	B.R. Derby Works	(C05/80)	
D5181	25031	12/77	vr	C	B.R. Glasgow Works	(C06/78)	
D5182	25032		xr				
D5183	25033	04/83	xb				
D5184	25034		xb				
D5185	25035		xb				
D5186	25036	12/82	xb				
D5187	25037		xi				
D5188	25038	05/81	vb	C	B.R. Derby Works	(C09/82)	
D5189	25039	05/81	vb	C	B.R. Swindon Works	(C12/81)	

D5190	25040	11/80	vb	C	B.R. Swindon Works	(C02/82)	
D5191	25041	05/81	vb	C	B.R. Swindon Works	(C06/83)	
D5192	25042		vd				
D5193	25043	02/81	vb	C	B.R. Derby Works	(C08/81)	
D5194	25044		xb				
D5195	25045	10/75	vb	C	B.R. Derby Works	(C03/79)	
D5196	25046	02/81	vb				
D5197	25047	09/80	vb	C	B.R. Swindon Works	(C01/81)	
D5198	25048		xb				
D5199	25049	01/84	xi				
D5200	25050	04/83	xb				
D5201	25051		xb				
D5202	25052	10/80	vb	C	B.R. Swindon Works	(C11/80)	
D5203	25053	12/80	xb	C	B.R. Swindon Works	(C11/81)	
D5204	25054		xi				
D5205	25055	11/80	vb	C	B.R. Swindon Works	(C12/81)	
D5206	25056	08/82	vb				
D5207	25057		xb				
D5208	25058		xb				
D5209	25059		xi				
D5210	25060		xb				
D5211	25061	11/80	vb	C	B.R. Swindon Works	(C03/83)	
D5212	25062	12/82	vb				
D5213	25063	11/80	vb	C	B.R. Swindon Works	(C03/83)	
D5214	25064		xi				
D5215	25065	02/81	vb	C	B.R. Swindon Works	(C02/82)	
D5216	25066	06/81	vb	C	B.R. Derby Works	(C02/83)	
D5217	25067	12/82	vb				
D5218	25068	07/80	vb	C	B.R. Glasgow Works	(C03/82)	
D5219	25069	12/83	vb				
D5220	25070	11/80	vb	C	B.R. Swindon Works	(C06/83)	
D5221	25071	06/81	vb	C	B.R. Swindon Works	(C02/83)	
D5222	25072		xi				
D5223	25073	09/81	vb	C	B.R. Swindon Works	(C08/82)	
D5224	25074	09/80	vb	C	B.R. Swindon Works	(C05/82)	
D5225	25075	03/83	vb				
D5226	25076		xi				
D5227	25077	05/78	xb	C	B.R. Glasgow Works	( )	
D5228	25078		xi				
D5229	25079	08/83	xi	C	B.R. Swindon Works	(C01/84)	
D5230	25080		vb				
D5231	25081	02/82	vb	C	B.R. Swindon Works	(C07/82)	
D5232	25082	05/81	xb	C	B.R. Swindon Works	(C01/83)	
D5233	25083	07/84	vb				
D5234	25084	12/83	vb				
D5235	25085	03/82	vb	C	B.R. Derby Works	(C05/83)	
D5236	25086	10/83	vb				
D5237	25087	09/80	vb	C	B.R. Swindon Works	(C04/81)	
D5238	25088	08/81	xq				
D5239	25089		xq				
D5240	25090	05/83	vq				
D5241	25091	10/78	vq	C	B.R. Glasgow Works	(C10/79)	
D5242	25092	05/80	vq	C	B.R. Derby Works	(C08/82)	
D5243	25093	11/82	vq				
D5244	25094	02/81	vq	C	B.R. Derby Works	(C05/82)	
D5245	25095		xq				
D5246	25096	12/77	vq	C	B.R. Glasgow Works	(C06/78)	

D5247	25097	11/83	xq				
D5248	25098	10/78	vq	C	B.R. Glasgow Works	(C06/79)	
D5249	25099	12/80	xq	C	B.R. Swindon Works	(C02/81)	
D5250	25100	02/81	vq	C	B.R. Swindon Works	(C02/83)	
D5251	25101	01/83	vq				
D5252	25102	05/80	vq	C	B.R. Swindon Works	(C10/80)	
D5253	25103	09/80	vq	C	B.R. Swindon Works	(C04/83)	
D5254	25104	09/82	vq				
D5255	25105	04/82	vq				
D5256	25106	10/83	xq	C	B.R. Swindon Works	(C02/84)	
D5257	25107	05/81	vq	C	B.R. Swindon Works	(C09/81)	
D5258	25108	07/80	vq	C	B.R. Glasgow Works	(C03/81)	
D5259	25109		xq				
D5260	25110	11/80	vq	C	B.R. Swindon Works	(C03/82)	
D5261	25111	03/80	vq	C	B.R. Swindon Works	(C10/80)	
D5262	25112	11/80	vq	C	B.R. Swindon Works	(C03/82)	
D5263	25113	06/83	xq	C	B.R. Swindon Works	(C10/83)	
D5264	25114	02/81	vq	C	B.R. Swindon Works	(C07/81)	
D5265	25115	10/83	vq				
D5266	25116	11/80	vq	C	B.R. Swindon Works	(C07/82)	
D5267	25117	01/84	xq	C	B.R. Swindon Works	(C06/84)	
D5268	25118	01/81	vq	C	B.R. Swindon Works	(C08/83)	
D5269	25119		vq				
D5270	25120	11/83	xq	C	B.R. Swindon Works	(C06/84)	
D5271	25121	11/80	vq	C	B.R. Swindon Works	(C08/82)	
D5272	25122	11/80	vq	C	B.R. Swindon Works	(C06/83)	
D5273	25123	05/83	vq				
D5274	25124	10/83	vq				
D5275	25125	12/81	vq	C	B.R. Swindon Works	(C04/83)	
D5276	25126	11/82	vq				
D5277	25127	11/80	vq	C	B.R. Swindon Works	(C07/83)	
D5278		05/71	vq	C	G. Cohen, Tinsley at Peak Forest	(C10/71)	
D5279	25129	02/82	vq				
D5280	25130	12/82	vq				
D5281	25131	01/83	vq				
D5282	25132	12/82	vq				
D5283	25133	08/83	vq				
D5284	25134	12/82	vq				
D5285	25135	01/83	vq				
D5286	25136	03/83	vq				
D5287	25137	11/80	vq	C	B.R. Swindon Works	(C06/83)	
D5288	25138	12/83	vq				
D5289	25139	11/82	vq				
D5290	25140	12/83	vq				
D5291	25141	09/82	vq				
D5292	25142	10/81	vq	C	B.R. Swindon Works	(C12/82)	
D5293	25143	11/82	vq				
D5294	25144	04/83	vq				
D5295	25145		xq				
D5296	25146	08/83	vq				
D5297	25147	03/80	vq	C	B.R. Swindon Works	(C09/80)	
D5298	25148	09/81	vq	C	B.R. Swindon Works	(C05/82)	
D5299	25149	01/82	vq	C	B.R. Swindon Works	(C06/83)	

Class continued with D7500

CLASS 26 B.R.C. & W./SULZER/C.P. TYPE 2 1160 h.p. DE Bo-Bo
Built 1958-1959

D5300	26007		xr			
D5301	26001		xr			
D5302	26002		xr			
D5303	26003		xr			
D5304	26004		xr			
D5305	26005		xr			
D5306	26006		xr			
D5307	26020	02/77	vb	C	B.R. Glasgow Works	(C03/78)
D5308	26008		vb			
D5309	26009	01/77	vb	C	B.R. Glasgow Works	(C03/78)
D5310	26010		vr			
D5311	26011		vr			
D5312	26012	01/82	vb	C	B.R. Glasgow Works	(C08/82)
D5313	26013		vi			
D5314	26014		vr			
D5315	26015		xr			
D5316	26016	10/75	vb	C	B.R. Glasgow Works	(C11/76)
D5317	26017	08/77	vb	C	B.R. Glasgow Works	(C02/78)
D5318	26018	01/82	vb	C	B.R. Glasgow Works	(C05/82)
D5319	26019		vb			
D5320	26028		xr			
D5321	26021		vb			
D5322	26022	02/81	vb	C	B.R. Glasgow Works	(C08/81)
D5323	26023		xr			
D5324	26024		vb			
D5325	26025		vr			
D5326	26026		vb			
D5327	26027		xr			
D5328		05/72	vb	C	B.R. Glasgow Works	(C12/72)
D5329	26029		xr			
D5330	26030		vb			
D5331	26031		vb			
D5332	26032		vb			
D5333	26033		vb			
D5334	26034		vb			
D5335	26035		vb			
D5336	26036		vb			
D5337	26037		vb			
D5338	26038		vb			
D5339	26039		xr			
D5340	26040		vb			
D5341	26041		vb			
D5342	26042		vb			
D5343	26043		vb			
D5344	26044	01/84	vb			
D5345	26045	07/83	vb			
D5346	26046		xr			

CLASS 27 B.R.C. & W./SULZER/G.E.C. TYPE 2 1250 h.p. DE Bo-Bo
Built 1961-1962

D5347	27001		xb
D5348	27002		vb

D5349	27003			xb			
D5350	27004			vb			
D5351	27005			xb			
D5352	27006		01/76	vb	C	B.R. Glasgow Works	(C01/77)
D5353	27007			vb			
D5354	27008			xb			
D5355	27009		07/80	vb	C	B.R. Glasgow Works	(C02/82)
D5356	27010			vb			
D5357	27011		03/81	vb	C	B.R. Derby Works	(C09/82)
D5358	27012			vb			
D5359	27013		07/76	vb	C	B.R. Glasgow Works	(C07/77)
D5360	27014			vb			
D5361	27015		01/77	vb	C	B.R. Glasgow Works	(C04/77)
D5362	27016		04/84	vb			
D5363	27017			vb			
D5364	27018			vb			
D5365	27019		05/84	vb			
D5366	27020			vb			
D5367	27021			vb			
D5368	27022			vb			
D5369	27023			vb			
D5370	27024			xq			
D5371	27025			xq			
D5372	27026			xq			
D5373	27027		06/83	vq			
D5374	27101	27045		xt			
D5375	27028		08/83	vq			
D5376	27029			vo			
D5377	27030			vo			
D5378	27031		05/78	vo	C	B.R. Glasgow Works	(C09/78)
D5379	27032			vb			
D5380	27102	27046		xb			
D5381	27033			vb			
D5382	27034		07/83	xb			
D5383			01/66	vb	C	J. Cashmore, Great Bridge	(C07/67)
D5384	27035		09/76	vb	C	B.R. Glasgow Works	(C03/77)
D5385	27036			vb			
D5386	27103	27212		xr		Now 27066	
D5387	27104	27048		xb			
D5388	27105	27049		xb			
D5389	27037			vb			
D5390	27038			xb			
D5391	27119	27201	01/79	xr	C	B.R. Glasgow Works	(C09/79)
D5392	27120	27202	08/80	xr	C	B.R. Glasgow Works	(C02/82)
D5393	27121	27203	05/83	xb		Now 27057	
D5394	27106	27050		xb			
D5395	27107	27051		xb			
D5396	27108			xb			
D5397	27109	27053		xb			
D5398	27039		10/75	vb	C	B.R. Glasgow Works	(C04/77)
D5399	27110	27054		xb			
D5400	27111	27055		xb			
D5401	27112	27056		xb			
D5402	27040			vb			
D5403	27122	27204		xr			
D5404	27113	27207		xr			
D5405	27041			xb			

D5406	27042		xb			
D5407	27114	27208	xr			
D5408	27115	27209	xr		Now 27063	
D5409	27210	27064	xr			
D5410	27123	27205	xr		Now 27059	
D5411	27117	27211	xr			
D5412	27124	27206	xr			
D5413	27118	27103	xb			
D5414	27043		04/80	vb	D	Re-railing Training Loco	
D5415	27044		07/80	vb	C	B.R. Glasgow Works	(C05/82)

CLASS 31 BRUSH/ENGLISH ELECTRIC/BRUSH TYPE 2 1470 h.p. DE A1A-A1A
Built 1957-1962. Formerly Brush/Mirrlees/Brush Class 30 (1250 hp)

D5500	31018	07/76	vb	P	National Railway Museum, York	
D5501	31001	07/76	vb	C	B.R. Doncaster Works	(C01/77)
D5502	31002	01/80	vi	D	ADB968014 Power Plant at ZC	(C03/84)
D5503	31003	02/80	vi	C	B.R. Doncaster Works	(C04/80)
D5504	31004	10/80	vi	C	B.R. Swindon Works	(C08/81)
D5505	31005	02/80	vi	C	B.R. Doncaster Works	(C03/80)
D5506	31006	01/80	vi	C	B.R. Doncaster Works	(C12/80)
D5507	31007	11/76	vb	C	B.R. Doncaster Works	(C08/78)
D5508	31008	10/80	vi	D	ADB968016 Power Plant	
D5509	31009	07/76	vb	C	B.R. Doncaster Works	(C11/77)
D5510	31010	07/76	vb	C	B.R. Doncaster Works	(C01/77)
D5511	31011	07/76	vb	C	B.R. Doncaster Works	(C01/77)
D5512	31012	11/76	vb	C	B.R. Doncaster Works	(C11/78)
D5513	31013	03/79	vi	D	ADB968013 Power Plant	
D5514	31014	11/76	vb	D	ADB968015 Power Plant	(C06/83)
D5515	31015	05/80	vi	C	B.R. Doncaster Works	(C11/80)
D5516	31016	07/76	vb	C	B.R. Doncaster Works	(C07/78)
D5517	31017	05/80	vb			(C02/83)
D5518	31101		xr			
D5519	31019	10/80	vb	C	B.R. Swindon Works	(C08/81)
D5520	31102		vb			
D5521	31103	10/80	vb	C	B.R. Swindon Works	(C02/83)
D5522	31418		xe			
D5523	31105		xi			
D5524	31106		xb			
D5525	31107		xi			
D5526	31108		vb			
D5527	31109		xr			
D5528	31110		xi			
D5529	31111	06/83	vb			
D5530	31112		xi			
D5531	31113		xi			
D5532	31114		vb			
D5533	31115		vb			
D5534	31116		xr			
D5535	31117		xb			
D5536	31118		xr			
D5537	31119		xi			
D5538	31120		vr			
D5539	31121		xr			
D5540	31122		xi			
D5541	31123		xr			
D5542	31124		xr			

D5543	31125			vb			
D5544	31126			vb			
D5545	31127			xb			
D5546	31128			xi			
D5547	31129			vi			
D5548	31130			xr			
D5549	31131			xi			
D5550	31132			vr			
D5551	31133	31450		xe			
D5552	31134			vr			
D5553	31135			xb			
D5554	31136		08/80	vb	C	B.R. Swindon Works	(C11/80)
D5555	31137	31444		xe			
D5556	31138			xr			
D5557	31139	31438		ve			
D5558	31140	31421		xe			
D5559	31141			xr			
D5560	31142			xb			
D5561	31143			xr			
D5562	31144			xr			
D5563	31145			xr			
D5564	31146			vr			
D5565	31147			xr			
D5566	31148	31448		xe			
D5567	31149			xr			
D5568	31150		10/75	xb	C	B.R. Doncaster Works	(C02/76)
D5569	31151	31436		xe			
D5570	31152			xi			
D5571	31153	31432		xe			
D5572	31154			xi			
D5573	31155			xr			
D5574	31156			xi			
D5575	31157	31424		xe			
D5576	31158			xb			
D5577	31159			xi			
D5578	31160			vb			
D5579	31161			vb			
D5580	31162			xi			
D5581	31163			xi			
D5582	31164			vi			
D5583	31165			xr			
D5584	31166			xr			
D5585	31167			vr			
D5586	31168			xb			
D5587	31169			vi			
D5588	31170			xi			
D5589	31401			xe			
D5590	31171			xr			
D5591	31172	31420		xe			
D5592	31402			xd			
D5593	31173			xb			
D5594	31174			xb			
D5595	31175			xb			
D5596	31403			xe			
D5597	31176			xb			
D5598	31177	31443		xe			
D5599	31178			xr			

D5600	31179	31435		xe				
D5601	31180			xi				
D5602	31181			xi				
D5603	31182	31437		xe				
D5604	31183			vb				
D5605	31404			xd				
D5606	31405			xd				
D5607	31184			xb				
D5608	31185			xi				
D5609	31186			xb				
D5610	31187			xb				
D5611	31188			xb				
D5612	31189			xi				
D5613	31190			xb				
D5614	31191			xi				
D5615	31192		10/82	xb	C	B.R. Doncaster Works	(01/83)	
D5616	31406			xd				
D5617	31193	31426		xe				
D5618	31194	31427		xe				
D5619	31195			xb				
D5620	31196			xi				
D5621	31197	31423		xe				
D5622	31198			xi				
D5623	31199			xi				
D5624	31200			vi				
D5625	31201			xr				
D5626	31202			xi				
D5627	31203			xr				
D5628	31204	31440		xe				
D5629	31205			xb				
D5630	31206			xb				
D5631	31207			vb				
D5632	31208			xb				
D5633	31209			xi				
D5634	31210			xi				
D5635	31211	31428		xe				
D5636	31212			xr				
D5637	31213			xi				
D5638	31214		05/83	vb	C	B.R. Doncaster Works	(C10/83)	
D5639	31215			vi				
D5640	31407			xd				
D5641	31216			xi				
D5642	31217			xi				
D5643	31218			xb				
D5644	31219			xi				
D5645	31220	31441		xe				
D5646	31408			xd				
D5647	31221			xr				
D5648	31222			xb				
D5649	31223			xi				
D5650	31224			xi				
D5651	31225			xb				
D5652	31226			xb				
D5653	31227			xr				
D5654	31228			vi				
D5655	31229			vb				
D5656	31409			xd				

D5657	31230		xb				
D5658	31231		xi				
D5659	31232		xi				
D5660	31233		xr				
D5661	31234		vi				
D5662	31235		xb				
D5663	31236	31433	xe				
D5664	31237		vi				
D5665	31238		xr				
D5666	31239	31439	xe				
D5667	31240		vr				
D5668	31241	03/82	xb	C	B.R. Swindon Works	(C05/82)	
D5669	31410		xd				
D5670	31242		xb				
D5671	31243		xi				
D5672	31244	09/82	vb	C	B.R. Doncaster Works	(C09/83)	
D5673	31245		xr				
D5674	31246		vb				
D5675	31247		xi				
D5676	31248		vi				
D5677	31249		xi				
D5678	31250		xi				
D5679	31251	31442	xe				
D5680	31252		xi				
D5681	31253	31431	xe				
D5682	31254	12/79	vb	C	B.R. Old Oak Common Depot	(C12/79)	
D5683	31255		xb				
D5684	31256		xi				
D5685	31257		xi				
D5686	31258	31434	xe				
D5687	31259		xb				
D5688	31260		xr				
D5689	31261		vb				
D5690	31262	05/83	vb	C	B.R. Doncaster Works	(C07/83)	
D5691	31411		xd				
D5692	31412		xe				
D5693	31263		xb				
D5694	31264		xb				
D5695	31265	31430	xe				
D5696	31266		vr				
D5697	31419		xe				
D5698	31268		xb				
D5699	31269	31429	xe				

Class continued with D5800

CLASS 28 MET. VIC./CROSSLEY/MET. VIC TYPE 2 1200 h.p. DE Co-Bo
Built 1958-1959

D5700	12/67	vb	C	J. McWilliams, Shettleston	(C11/68)	
D5701	09/68	vb	C	J. Cashmore, Great Bridge	(C10/69)	
D5702	09/68	vb	C	J. Cashmore, Great Bridge	(C11/69)	
D5703	12/67	vb	C	J. McWilliams, Shettleston	(C07/68)	
D5704	12/67	vb	C	J. McWilliams, Shettleston	(C11/68)	
D5705	09/68	vb	P	B.R. Swindon Works		
D5706	09/68	vb	C	J. Cashmore, Great Bridge	(C11/69)	
D5707	09/68	vb	C	J. Cashmore, Great Bridge	(C10/69)	

D5708			09/68	vb	C	J. Cashmore, Great Bridge	(C11/69)
D5709			12/67	vb	C	J. McWilliams, Shettleston	(C12/68)
D5710			12/67	vb	C	J. McWilliams, Shettleston	(C12/68)
D5711			09/68	vb	C	J. Cashmore, Great Bridge	(C11/69)
D5712			09/68	vb	C	J. Cashmore, Great Bridge	(C12/69)
D5713			12/67	vb	C	J. McWilliams, Shettleston	(C11/68)
D5714			09/68	vb	C	J. Cashmore, Great Bridge	(C10/69)
D5715			05/68	vb	C	J. McWilliams, Shettleston	(C10/68)
D5716			09/68	vb	C	J. Cashmore, Great Bridge	(C12/69)
D5717			09/68	vb	C	J. Cashmore, Great Bridge	(C11/69)
D5718			05/68	vb	C	J. McWilliams, Shettleston	(C10/68)
D5719			09/68	vb	C	J. Cashmore, Great Bridge	(C10/69)

CLASS 31 continued

D5800	31270		vb
D5801	31271		vr
D5802	31272		xi
D5803	31273		xi
D5804	31274	31425	xe
D5805	31275		vr
D5806	31276		xr
D5807	31277		vr
D5808	31278		xr
D5809	31279		vb
D5810	31280		xr
D5811	31281		xr
D5812	31413		xe
D5813	31282		xr
D5814	31413		xd
D5815	31283		xr
D5816	31284		xr
D5817	31285		xr
D5818	31286		xb
D5819	31287		xr
D5820	31288		xr
D5821	31289		xr
D5822	31290		vr
D5823	31291		vb
D5824	31415		xd
D5825	31292		xr
D5826	31293		xi
D5827	31294		xi
D5828	31295	31447	xe
D5829	31296		xr
D5830	31297		vr
D5831	31298		vr
D5832	31299		vr
D5833	31300	31445	xe
D5834	31301		xr
D5835	31302		xr
D5836	31303		vr
D5837	31304		xi
D5838	31305		xi
D5839	31306		vr
D5840	31307	31449	xe
D5841	31308		vr
D5842	31416		xe

D5843	31309			xi			
D5844	31310	31422		xe			
D5845	31311			xr			
D5846	31312			vb			
D5847	31313		09/82	vb	C	B.R. Doncaster Works	(C05/83)
D5848	31314		09/82	xr	C	B.R. Doncaster Works	(C02/83)
D5849	31315			vr			
D5850	31316	31446		xe			
D5851	31317			vi			
D5852	31318	31451		xe			
D5853	31319			vi			
D5854	31320			xr			
D5855	31321			vi			
D5856	31317			xd			
D5857	31322			xr			
D5858	31323			xi			
D5859	31324			vr			
D5860	31325			vi			
D5861	31326			xi			
D5862	31327			xb			

CLASS 23   E.E./NAPIER/E.E.   TYPE 2 1100 h.p. DE   Bo-Bo
Built 1959. "Baby Deltics"

D5900	12/68	vb	C	G. Cohen, Kettering	(C08/69)	
D5901	12/69	vb	D	B.R. Reasearch Dept. Derby	(C01/77)	
D5902	11/69	vb	C	G. Cohen, Kettering	(C10/70)	
D5903	12/68	vb	C	G. Cohen, Kettering	(C10/69)	
D5904	01/69	vb	C	G. Cohen, Kettering	(C08/69)	
D5905	02/71	vb	C	G. Cohen, Kettering	(C10/73)	
D5906	09/68	vb	C	G. Cohen, Kettering	(C11/69)	
D5907	10/68	vb	C	G. Cohen, Kettering	(C07/69)	
D5908	03/69	vb	C	J. Cashmore, Great Bridge	(C01/70)	
D5909	03/71	vb	C	G. Cohen, Kettering	(C10/73)	

CLASS 21   N.B.L./M.A.N./G.E.C. TYPE 2 1000 h.p. DE   Bo-Bo
*Built 1959-1960 (*Re-engined with Paxman 1350 hp engine. Class 29)*

D6100*	10/71	vb	C	B.R. Glasgow Works	(C11/72)	
D6101*	08/71	vb	C	B.R. Glasgow Works	(C10/72)	
D6102*	10/71	vb	C	B.R. Glasgow Works	(C08/72)	
D6103*	10/71	vb	C	B.R. Glasgow Works	(C11/72)	
D6104	12/67	vb	C	Barnes & Bell, Coatbridge	(C04/68)	
D6105	06/68	vb	C	J. McWilliams, Shettleston	(C08/68)	
D6106*	07/71	vb	C	B.R. Glasgow Works	(C07/72)	
D6107*	10/71	vb	C	B.R. Glasgow Works	(C10/72)	
D6108*	05/69	vb	C	J. McWilliams, Shettleston	(C07/71)	
D6109	04/68	vb	C	J. McWilliams, Shettleston	(C01/69)	
D6110	04/68	vb	C	J. McWilliams, Shettleston	(C02/69)	
D6111	08/68	vb	D	Used for carriage heating at Cowlairs	(C09/69)	
D6112*	12/71	vb	C	B.R. Glasgow Works	(C06/72)	
D6113*	10/71	vb	C	B.R. Glasgow Works	(C11/72)	
D6114*	10/71	vb	C	B.R. Glasgow Works	(C09/72)	
D6115	06/68	vb	C	J. McWilliams, Shettleston	(C08/68)	
D6116*	12/71	vb	C	B.R. Glasgow Works	(C06/72)	
D6117	08/68	vb	C	J. McWilliams, Shettleston	(C11/68)	
D6118	12/67	vb	C	J. McWilliams, Shettleston	(C05/68)	

D6119*	12/71	vb	C	B.R. Glasgow Works	(C08/72)	
D6120	12/67	vb	C	J. McWilliams, Shettleston	(C09/68)	
D6121*	10/71	vb	C	B.R. Glasgow Works	(C09/72)	
D6122	12/67	vb	C	D. Woodham, Barry	(C06/80)	
D6123*	09/71	vb	C	B.R. Glasgow Works	(C10/72)	
D6124*	10/71	vb	C	B.R. Glasgow Works	(C09/72)	
D6125	12/67	vb	C	Barnes & Bell, Coatbridge	(C04/68)	
D6126	04/68	vb	C	J. McWilliams, Shettleston	(C02/69)	
D6127	12/67	vb	C	Barnes & Bell, Coatbridge	(C04/68)	
D6128	12/67	vb	C	J. McWilliams, Shettleston	(C09/68)	
D6129*	10/71	vb	C	B.R. Glasgow Works	(C06/72)	
D6130*	10/71	vb	C	B.R. Glasgow Works	(C10/72)	
D6131	12/67	vb	C	J. McWilliams, Shettleston	(C09/68)	
D6132*	10/71	vb	C	B.R. Glasgow Works	(C09/72)	
D6133*	12/71	vb	C	B.R. Glasgow Works	(C07/72)	
D6134	12/67	vb	C	Barnes & Bell, Coatbridge	(C06/68)	
D6135	12/67	vb	C	J. McWilliams, Shettleston	(C05/68)	
D6136	12/67	vb	C	Barnes & Bell, Coatbridge	(C04/68)	
D6137*	08/71	vb	C	B.R. Glasgow Works	(C08/72)	
D6138	12/67	vb	C	J. McWilliams, Shettleston	(C06/68)	
D6139	12/67	vb	C	J. McWilliams, Shettleston	(C06/68)	
D6140	12/67	vb	C	J. McWilliams, Shettleston	(C05/68)	
D6141	12/67	vb	C	J. McWilliams, Shettleston	(C08/68)	
D6142	12/67	vb	C	J. McWilliams, Shettleston	(C09/68)	
D6143	12/67	vb	C	Barnes & Bell, Coatbridge	(C06/68)	
D6144	12/67	vb	C	J. McWilliams, Shettleston	(C08/68)	
D6145	12/67	vb	C	J. McWilliams, Shettleston	(C08/68)	
D6146	12/67	vb	C	J. McWilliams, Shettleston	(C05/68)	
D6147	12/67	vb	C	J. McWilliams, Shettleston	(C07/68)	
D6148	12/67	vb	C	J. McWilliams, Shettleston	(C07/68)	
D6149	12/67	vb	C	J. McWilliams, Shettleston	(C06/68)	
D6150	12/67	vb	C	J. McWilliams, Shettleston	(C08/68)	
D6151	12/67	vb	C	J. McWilliams, Shettleston	(C08/68)	
D6152	08/68	vb	C	J. McWilliams, Shettleston	(C02/69)	
D6153	12/67	vb	C	J. McWilliams, Shettleston	(C05/68)	
D6154	12/67	vb	C	J. McWilliams, Shettleston	(C08/68)	
D6155	12/67	vb	C	J. McWilliams, Shettleston	(C08/68)	
D6156	12/67	vb	C	J. McWilliams, Shettleston	(C05/68)	
D6157	12/67	vb	C	J. McWilliams, Shettleston	(C08/68)	

CLASS 22   N.B.L./M.A.N./VOITH TYPE 2 1100 h.p. DH   Bo-Bo

Built 1959-1962. D6300-D6305 were 1000 h.p.

D6300	05/68	vb	C	J. Cashmore, Newport	(C12/68)	
D6301	12/67	vb	C	G. Cohen, Morriston	(C05/68)	
D6302	05/68	vb	C	J. Cashmore, Newport	(C11/68)	
D6303	05/68	vb	C	J. Cashmore, Newport	(C12/68)	
D6304	05/68	vb	C	J. Cashmore, Newport	(C11/68)	
D6305	05/68	vb	C	J. Cashmore, Newport	(C11/68)	
D6306	12/68	vb	C	J. Cashmore, Newport	(C05/69)	
D6307	03/71	vb	C	B.R. Swindon Works	(C12/71)	
D6308	09/71	vb	C	B.R. Swindon Works	(C05/72)	
D6309	05/71	vb	C	B.R. Swindon Works	(C12/71)	
D6310	03/71	vb	C	B.R. Swindon Works	(C05/72)	
D6311	09/68	vb	C	J. Cashmore, Newport	(C05/69)	
D6312	05/71	vb	C	B.R. Swindon Works	(C01/72)	
D6313	08/68	vb	C	J. Cashmore, Newport	(C11/68)	

D6314		04/69	vb	C	J. Cashmore, Newport	(C07/69)	
D6315		05/71	vb	C	B.R. Swindon Works	(C01/72)	
D6316		03/68	vb	C	J. Cashmore, Newport	(C11/68)	
D6317		09/68	vb	C	J. Cashmore, Newport	(C05/69)	
D6318		05/71	vb	C	B.R. Swindon Works	(C03/72)	
D6319		09/71	vb	C	B.R. Swindon Works	(C11/72)	
D6320		05/71	vb	C	B.R. Swindon Works	(C06/72)	
D6321		08/68	vb	C	J. Cashmore, Newport	(C06/69)	
D6322		10/71	vb	C	B.R. Swindon Works	(C05/72)	
D6323		05/71	vb	C	B.R. Swindon Works	(C08/72)	
D6324		09/68	vb	C	J. Cashmore, Newport	(C05/69)	
D6325		10/68	vb	C	J. Cashmore, Newport	(C05/69)	
D6326		10/71	vb	C	B.R. Swindon Works	(C03/72)	
D6327		05/71	vb	C	B.R. Swindon Works	(C07/72)	
D6328		07/71	vb	C	B.R. Swindon Works	(C05/72)	
D6329		11/68	vb	C	J. Cashmore, Newport	(C05/69)	
D6330		10/71	vb	C	B.R. Swindon Works	(C06/72)	
D6331		03/71	vb	C	B.R. Swindon Works	(C03/72)	
D6332		05/71	vb	C	B.R. Swindon Works	(C12/71)	
D6333		01/72	vb	C	B.R. Swindon Works	(C08/72)	
D6334		10/71	vb	C	B.R. Swindon Works	(C04/72)	
D6335		09/68	vb	C	J. Cashmore, Newport	(C05/69)	
D6336		01/72	vb	C	B.R. Swindon Works	(C06/72)	
D6337		10/71	vb	C	B.R. Swindon Works	(C05/72)	
D6338		01/72	vb	C	B.R. Swindon Works	(C02/72)	
D6339		01/72	vb	C	B.R. Swindon Works	(C06/72)	
D6340		05/71	vb	C	B.R. Swindon Works	(C04/72)	
D6341		11/68	vb	C	J. Cashmore, Newport	(C05/69)	
D6342		12/68	vb	C	J. Cashmore, Newport	(C05/69)	
D6343		10/71	vb	C	B.R. Swindon Works	(C01/72)	
D6344		09/68	vb	C	J. Cashmore, Newport	(C05/69)	
D6345		09/68	vb	C	J. Cashmore, Newport	(C07/69)	
D6346		04/69	vb	C	J. Cashmore, Newport	(C07/69)	
D6347		03/68	vb	C	J. Cashmore, Newport	(C11/68)	
D6348		07/71	vb	C	B.R. Swindon Works	(C05/72)	
D6349		09/68	vb	C	B.R. Swindon Works	(C10/71)	
D6350		09/68	vb	C	J. Cashmore, Newport	(C05/69)	
D6351		11/68	vb	C	J. Cashmore, Newport	(C05/69)	
D6352		05/71	vb	C	B.R. Swindon Works	(C11/71)	
D6353		09/68	vb	C	J. Cashmore, Newport	(C07/69)	
D6354		05/71	vb	C	B.R. Swindon Works	(C02/72)	
D6355		09/68	vb	C	J. Cashmore, Newport	(C05/69)	
D6356		10/71	vb	C	B.R. Swindon Works	(C01/72)	
D6357		12/68	vb	C	J. Cashmore, Newport	(C06/69)	

CLASS 33   B.R.C.W./SULZER/C.P. TYPE 3 1550 h.p. DE   Bo-Bo
Built 1960-1962

D6500	33001		xk				
D6501	33002		xk				
D6502		05/64	xk	C	B.R. Itchingfield Junction	(C07/64)	
D6503	33003		xk				
D6504	33004		xk				
D6505	33005		xk				
D6506	33006		xk				
D6507	33007		xk				
D6508	33008		xk				

D6509	33009		xk			
D6510	33010		xk			
D6511	33101		yk			
D6512	33011		xk			
D6513	33102		yk			
D6514	33103		yk			
D6515	33012		xk			
D6516	33104		yk			
D6517	33105		yk			
D6518	33013		xk			
D6519	33106		yk			
D6520	33107		yk			
D6521	33108		yk			
D6522	33014		xk			
D6523	33015		xk			
D6524	33016		xk			
D6525	33109		yk			
D6526	33017		xk			
D6527	33110		yk			
D6528	33111		yk			
D6529	33112		yk			
D6530	33018		xk			
D6531	33113		yk			
D6532	33114		yk			
D6533	33115		yk			
D6534	33019		xk			
D6535	33116		yk			
D6536	33117		yk			
D6537	33020		xk			
D6538	33118		yk			
D6539	33021		xk			
D6540	33022		xk			
D6541	33023		xk			
D6542	33024		xk			
D6543	33025		xk			
D6544	33026		xk			
D6545	33027		xk			
D6546	33028		xk			
D6547	33029		xk			
D6548	33030		xk			
D6549	33031		xk			
D6550	33032		xk			
D6551	33033		xk			
D6552	33034		xk			
D6553	33035		xk			
D6554	33036	07/79	xk	C	B.R. Hither Green Depot	(C10/78)
D6555	33037		xk			
D6556	33038		xk			
D6557	33039		xk			
D6558	33040		xk			
D6559	33041	11/75	xk	C	B.R. Selhurst Depot	(C06/76)
D6560	33042		xk			
D6561	33043		xk			
D6562	33044		xk			
D6563	33045		xk			
D6564	33046		xk			
D6565	33047		xk			

D6566	33048		xk		
D6567	33049		xk		
D6568	33050		xk		
D6569	33051		xk		
D6570	33052		xk		
D6571	33053		xk		
D6572	33054		xk		
D6573	33055		xk		
D6574	33056		xk		
D6575	33057		xk		
D6576		11/68	xk	C B.R. Eastleigh Works	(C03/69)
D6577	33058		xk		
D6578	33059		xk		
D6579	33060		xk		
D6580	33119		yk		
D6581	33061		xk		
D6582	33062		xk		
D6583	33063		xk		
D6584	33064		xk		
D6585	33065		xk		
D6586	33201		xk		
D6587	33202		xk		
D6588	33203		xk		
D6589	33204		xk		
D6590	33205		xk		
D6591	33206		xk		
D6592	33207		xk		
D6593	33208		xk		
D6594	33209		xk		
D6595	33210		xk		
D6596	33211		xk		
D6597	33212		xk		

Names:
33008   Eastleigh
33025   Sultan
33027   Earl Mountbatten of Burma
33052   Ashford
33056   The Burma Star

CLASS 37   ENGLISH ELECTRIC TYPE 3 1750 h.p. DE   Co-Co
Built 1960-1965

D6600	37300	xq
D6601	37301	xq
D6602	37302	xq
D6603	37303	xq
D6604	37304	xq
D6605	37305	xq
D6606	37306	xq
D6607	37307	xq
D6608	37308	xq
D6700	37119	xr
D6701	37001	xr
D6702	37002	xr
D6703	37003	vr
D6704	37004	xr

D6705	37005	vr
D6706	37006	xr
D6707	37007	xr
D6708	37008	xr
D6709	37009	xr
D6710	37010	xr
D6711	37011	xb
D6712	37012	xb
D6713	37013	vr
D6714	37014	xb
D6715	37015	xr
D6716	37016	xr
D6717	37017	vb
D6718	37018	xr
D6719	37019	xr
D6720	37020	xr
D6721	37021	xb
D6722	37022	xb
D6723	37023	vi
D6724	37024	xr
D6725	37025	xb
D6726	37026	xb
D6727	37027	xb
D6728	37028	vr
D6729	37029	xr
D6730	37030	xr
D6731	37031	xr
D6732	37032	xr
D6733	37033	xb
D6734	37034	xi
D6735	37035	xb
D6736	37036	vb
D6737	37037	xb
D6738	37038	xb
D6739	37039	xb
D6740	37040	vr
D6741	37041	xi
D6742	37042	xr
D6743	37043	xb
D6744	37044	xb
D6745	37045	xr
D6746	37046	xr
D6747	37047	xi
D6748	37048	xr
D6749	37049	xb
D6750	37050	xb
D6751	37051	xb
D6752	37052	xb
D6753	37053	xr
D6754	37054	xb
D6755	37055	xr
D6756	37056	xr
D6757	37057	xr
D6758	37058	vr
D6759	37059	xr
D6760	37060	xr
D6761	37061	vr

D6762	37062	vr
D6763	37063	xr
D6764	37064	xr
D6765	37065	xr
D6766	37066	xr
D6767	37067	xr
D6768	37068	xr
D6769	37069	xr
D6770	37070	xr
D6771	37071	xr
D6772	37072	xr
D6773	37073	xr
D6774	37074	xr
D6775	37075	vb
D6776	37076	xr
D6777	37077	xr
D6778	37078	xr
D6779	37079	xr
D6780	37080	xr
D6781	37081	xb
D6782	37082	vr
D6783	37083	vr
D6784	37084	xb
D6785	37085	xb
D6786	37086	xb
D6787	37087	xb
D6788	37088	xb
D6789	37089	xi
D6790	37090	vb
D6791	37091	xi
D6792	37092	xb
D6793	37093	vr
D6794	37094	xr
D6795	37095	xr
D6796	37096	xr
D6797	37097	vb
D6798	37098	xr
D6799	37099	xb
D6800	37100	vr
D6801	37101	xr
D6802	37102	xb
D6803	37103	xi
D6804	37104	xr
D6805	37105	xr
D6806	37106	xr
D6807	37107	xb
D6808	37108	xb
D6809	37109	xb
D6810	37110	xb
D6811	37111	xb
D6812	37112	xb
D6813	37113	xr
D6814	37114	xb
D6815	37115	xb
D6816	37116	xi
D6817	37117	xr
D6818	37118	xi

D6819	37283	xq
D6820	37120	xq
D6821	37121	xq
D6822	37122	xq
D6823	37123	xq
D6824	37124	xq
D6825	37125	xq
D6826	37126	xq
D6827	37127	xq
D6828	37128	xq
D6829	37129	xq
D6830	37130	xq
D6831	37131	xq
D6832	37132	xq
D6833	37133	xq
D6834	37134	xq
D6835	37135	xq
D6836	37136	xq
D6837	37137	xq
D6838	37138	xq
D6839	37139	xq
D6840	37140	xq
D6841	37141	xq
D6842	37142	xq
D6843	37143	xq
D6844	37144	xq
D6845	37145	xq
D6846	37146	xq
D6847	37147	xq
D6848	37148	xq
D6849	37149	xq
D6850	37150	xq
D6851	37151	xq
D6852	37152	xq
D6853	37153	xq
D6854	37154	xq
D6855	37155	xq
D6856	37156	xq
D6857	37157	xq
D6858	37158	xq
D6859	37159	xq
D6860	37160	xq
D6861	37161	xq
D6862	37162	xq
D6863	37163	xq
D6864	37164	xq
D6865	37165	xq
D6866	37166	xq
D6867	37167	xq
D6868	37168	xq
D6869	37169	xq
D6870	37170	xq
D6871	37171	xq
D6872	37172	xq
D6873	37173	xq
D6874	37174	xq
D6875	37175	xb

D6876	37176	xb
D6877	37177	xb
D6878	37178	xb
D6879	37179	xi
D6880	37180	xb
D6881	37181	xi
D6882	37182	xi
D6883	37183	xb
D6884	37184	xb
D6885	37185	xi
D6886	37186	xb
D6887	37187	xb
D6888	37188	xb
D6889	37189	xb
D6890	37190	xb
D6891	37191	xb
D6892	37192	xb
D6893	37193	xq
D6894	37194	xq
D6895	37195	xq
D6896	37196	vq
D6897	37197	xq
D6898	37198	xq
D6899	37199	xq
D6900	37200	xq
D6901	37201	xq
D6902	37202	xq
D6903	37203	xq
D6904	37204	xq
D6905	37205	xq
D6906	37206	xq
D6907	37207	xq
D6908	37208	xq
D6909	37209	xq
D6910	37210	xq
D6911	37211	xq
D6912	37212	xq
D6913	37213	xq
D6914	37214	xq
D6915	37215	xq
D6916	37216	xq
D6917	37217	vq
D6918	37218	xq
D6919	37219	xq
D6920	37220	xq
D6921	37221	xq
D6922	37222	vq
D6923	37223	xq
D6924	37224	xq
D6925	37225	vq
D6926	37226	xq
D6927	37227	xq
D6928	37228	vq
D6929	37229	xq
D6930	37230	xq
D6931	37231	xq
D6932	37232	xq

D6933	37233		xq		
D6934	37234		xq		
D6935	37235		vq		
D6936	37236		xq		
D6937	37237		xq		
D6938	37238		xq		
D6939	37239		vq		
D6940	37240		xq		
D6941	37241		xq		
D6942	37242		xq		
D6943	37243		xq		
D6944	37244		xq		
D6945	37245		xq		
D6946	37246		xq		
D6947	37247		xq		
D6948	37248		xq		
D6949	37249		xq		
D6950	37250		xq		
D6951	37251		vq		
D6952	37252		xq		
D6953	37253		vq		
D6954	37254		xq		
D6955	37255		xq		
D6956	37256		xq		
D6957	37257		xq		
D6958	37258		xq		
D6959	37259		xq		
D6960	37260		xb		
D6961	37261		xb		
D6962	37262		xb		
D6963	37263		xb		
D6964	37264		xb		
D6965	37265		xi		
D6966	37266		xb		
D6967	37267		xb		
D6968	37268		xi		
D6969	37269		xq		
D6970	37270		xq		
D6971	37271		xq		
D6972	37272		xq		
D6973	37273		xq		
D6974	37274		xq		
D6975	37275		xq		
D6976	37276		xq		
D6977	37277		xq		
D6978	37278		xq		
D6979	37279		xq		
D6980	37280		xq		
D6981	37281		xq		
D6982	37282		xq		
D6983		12/65	vq	C	R.S. Hayes, Bridgend	(C04/66)
D6984	37284		xq		
D6985	37285		xq		
D6986	37286		xq		
D6987	37287		xq		
D6988	37288		xq		
D6989	37289		xq		

D6990	37290	xq
D6991	37291	xq
D6992	37292	xq
D6993	37293	xq
D6994	37294	xq
D6995	37295	xq
D6996	37296	xq
D6997	37297	xq
D6998	37298	xq
D6999	37299	xq

Names:

D6703	THE FIRST EAST ANGLIAN REGIMENT (Removed 9/63)
37012	Loch Rannoch
37026	Loch Awe
37027	Loch Eil
37043	Loch Lomond
37078	Teesside Steelmaster
37081	Loch Long
37180	Sir Dyfed/County of Dyfed
(Reversed opposite side)	
37207	William Cookworthy
37229	The Cardiff Rod Mill
37260	Radio Highland

CLASS 35   BEYER PEACOCK/MAYBACH/MEKYDRO TYPE 3 1700 h.p. DH   B-B

Built 1961-1964

D7000	07/73	vb	C	B.R. Swindon Works	(C10/75)
D7001	03/74	vi	C	G. Cohen, Kettering	(C06/75)
D7002	10/71	vb	C	B.R. Swindon Works	(C06/72)
D7003	01/72	vb	C	B.R. Swindon Works	(C08/72)
D7004	06/72	vb	C	B.R. Swindon Works	(C08/72)
D7005	07/72	vb	C	B.R. Swindon Works	(C10/72)
D7006	09/71	vb	C	B.R. Swindon Works	(C09/72)
D7007	04/72	vb	C	B.R. Swindon Works	(C06/72)
D7008	01/72	vb	C	B.R. Swindon Works	(C09/72)
D7009	05/73	vb	C	B.R. Swindon Works	(C10/74)
D7010	01/72	vb	C	B.R. Swindon Works	(C11/72)
D7011	03/75	vi	C	W. Heselwood, Attercliffe, Sheffield	(C02/77)
D7012	01/72	vb	C	B.R. Swindon Works	(C06/72)
D7013	01/72	vb	C	B.R. Swindon Works	(C10/72)
D7014	01/72	vb	C	B.R. Swindon Works	(C08/72)
D7015	06/72	vb	C	B.R. Swindon Works	(C09/72)
D7016	07/74	vi	C	B.R. Swindon Works	(C06/75)
D7017	03/75	vi	P	West Somerset Railway, Minehead	
D7018	03/75	vi	P	Great Western Society, Didcot	
D7019	09/72	vb	C	B.R. Swindon Works	(C10/72)
D7020	01/72	vb	C	B.R. Swindon Works	(C09/72)
D7021	01/72	vb	C	B.R. Swindon Works	(C06/72)
D7022	03/75	vi	C	G. Cohen, Kettering	(C01/77)
D7023	05/73	vb	C	B.R. Swindon Works	(C05/75)
D7024	01/72	vb	C	B.R. Swindon Works	(C11/72)
D7025	01/72	vb	C	B.R. Swindon Works	(C06/72)
D7026	10/74	vi	C	G. Cohen, Kettering	(C05/75)
D7027	11/71	vb	C	B.R. Swindon Works	(C08/72)
D7028	01/75	vi	C	G. Cohen, Kettering	(C02/77)

D7029	02/75	vi	P	North Yorkshire Moors Railway	
D7030	05/73	vb	C	B.R. Swindon Works	(C03/74)
D7031	05/73	vb	C	B.R. Swindon Works	(C09/75)
D7032	05/73	vb	C	B.R. Swindon Works	(C07/75)
D7033	01/72	vb	C	B.R. Swindon Works	(C11/72)
D7034	01/72	vb	C	B.R. Swindon Works	(C09/72)
D7035	01/72	vb	C	B.R. Swindon Works	(C08/72)
D7036	06/72	vb	C	B.R. Swindon Works	(C10/72)
D7037	09/72	vb	C	B.R. Swindon Works	(C11/72)
D7038	07/72	vb	C	B.R. Swindon Works	(C06/73)
D7039	06/72	vb	C	B.R. Swindon Works	(C08/72)
D7040	01/72	vb	C	B.R. Swindon Works	(C08/72)
D7041	01/72	vb	C	B.R. Swindon Works	(C09/72)
D7042	01/72	vb	C	B.R. Swindon Works	(C07/72)
D7043	01/72	vb	C	B.R. Swindon Works	(C08/72)
D7044	05/73	vb	C	B.R. Swindon Works	(C03/74)
D7045	11/72	vb	C	B.R. Swindon Works	(C08/73)
D7046	01/72	vb	C	B.R. Swindon Works	(C07/72)
D7047	01/72	vb	C	B.R. Swindon Works	(C08/72)
D7048	01/72	vb	C	B.R. Swindon Works	(C08/72)
D7049	01/72	vb	C	B.R. Swindon Works	(C07/72)
D7050	11/72	vb	C	B.R. Swindon Works	(C06/73)
D7051	01/72	vb	C	B.R. Swindon Works	(C06/72)
D7052	11/72	vb	C	B.R. Swindon Works	(C05/73)
D7053	04/73	vb	C	B.R. Swindon Works	(C08/72)
D7054	12/72	vb	C	B.R. Swindon Works	(C04/75)
D7055	04/73	vb	C	B.R. Swindon Works	(C11/75)
D7056	01/72	vb	C	B.R. Swindon Works	(C07/72)
D7057	01/72	vb	C	B.R. Swindon Works	(C10/72)
D7058	10/71	vb	C	B.R. Swindon Works	(C06/72)
D7059	10/71	vb	C	B.R. Swindon Works	(C07/72)
D7060	10/71	vb	C	B.R. Swindon Works	(C10/72)
D7061	01/72	vb	C	B.R. Swindon Works	(C08/72)
D7062	10/71	vb	C	B.R. Swindon Works	(C08/72)
D7063	10/71	vb	C	B.R. Swindon Works	(C11/72)
D7064	10/71	vb	C	B.R. Swindon Works	(C09/72)
D7065	01/72	vb	C	B.R. Swindon Works	(C09/72)
D7066	11/71	vb	C	B.R. Swindon Works	(C09/72)
D7067	10/71	vb	C	B.R. Swindon Works	(C08/72)
D7068	12/72	vb	C	B.R. Swindon Works	(C04/75)
D7069	10/71	vb	C	B.R. Swindon Works	(C08/72)
D7070	09/72	vb	C	B.R. Swindon Works	(C10/72)
D7071	01/72	vb	C	B.R. Swindon Works	(C09/72)
D7072	10/71	vb	C	B.R. Swindon Works	(C09/72)
D7073	12/71	vb	C	B.R. Swindon Works	(C10/72)
D7074	12/72	vb	C	B.R. Swindon Works	(C08/75)
D7075	05/73	vb	C	B.R. Swindon Works	(C02/74)
D7076	05/73	vb	P	Bury Transport Museum	
D7077	07/72	vb	C	B.R. Swindon Works	(C10/72)
D7078	10/71	vb	C	B.R. Swindon Works	(C05/72)
D7079	10/71	vb	C	B.R. Swindon Works	(C08/72)
D7080	11/72	vb	C	B.R. Swindon Works	(C05/73)
D7081	09/71	vb	C	B.R. Swindon Works	(C08/72)
D7082	04/72	vb	C	B.R. Swindon Works	(C10/72)
D7083	10/71	vb	C	B.R. Swindon Works	(C09/72)
D7084	10/72	vb	C	B.R. Swindon Works	(C11/72)
D7085	10/72	vb	C	B.R. Swindon Works	(C11/72)

D7086		01/72	vb	C	B.R. Swindon Works	(C09/72)	
D7087		10/72	vb	C	B.R. Swindon Works	(C09/73)	
D7088		01/72	vb	C	B.R. Swindon Works	(C10/72)	
D7089		05/73	vb	C	T.J. Thompson, Stockton	(C02/76)	
D7090		06/72	vb	C	B.R. Swindon Works	(C09/72)	
D7091		08/72	vb	C	B.R. Swindon Works	(C10/72)	
D7092		06/72	vb	C	B.R. Swindon Works	(C09/72)	
D7093		11/74	vb	C	G. Cohen, Kettering	(C02/77)	
D7094		11/72	vb	C	B.R. Swindon Works	(C07/73)	
D7095		10/72	vb	C	B.R. Swindon Works	(C11/72)	
D7096		12/72	vb	D	Dead Load, R.T.C., Derby		
D7097		12/72	vb	C	B.R. Swindon Works	(C03/75)	
D7098		12/72	vb	C	B.R. Swindon Works	(C03/75)	
D7099		10/72	vb	C	B.R. Swindon Works	(C10/72)	
D7100		11/72	vb	C	B.R. Swindon Works	(C12/74)	

CLASS 25 continued

Note: D7624-D7659 were built by Beyer Peacock.

D7500	25150	06/82	vq				
D7501	25151	09/82	vq				
D7502	25152	01/84	vq				
D7503	25153	04/83	vq				
D7504	25154		xq				
D7505	25155	12/80	xq	C	B.R. Swindon Works	(C09/81)	
D7506	25156	12/81	vq	C	B.R. Swindon Works	(C05/82)	
D7507	25157		vq				
D7508	25158	05/83	vq				
D7509	25159	11/80	vq	C	B.R. Swindon Works	(C03/81)	
D7510	25160	10/82	vq				
D7511	25161		vq				
D7512	25162	05/81	vq	C	B.R. Swindon Works	(C06/82)	
D7513	25163	11/80	vq	C	B.R. Swindon Works	(C03/83)	
D7514	25164	08/83	vq				
D7515	25165	11/78	vq	C	B.R. Derby Works	(C07/81)	
D7516	25166	11/80	vq	C	B.R. Swindon Works	(C06/81)	
D7517	25167	05/83	vq	C	B.R. Swindon Works	(C04/84)	
D7518	25168	05/83	vq	C	B.R. Swindon Works	(C04/84)	
D7519	25169	09/81	vq	C	B.R. Swindon Works	(C02/82)	
D7520	25170	08/82	vq	C	B.R. Derby Works	(C04/83)	
D7521	25171	10/78	vq	C	B.R. at Arbroath	(C01/79)	
D7522	25172	02/81	vq	C	B.R. Swindon Works	(C06/82)	
D7523	25173		xq				
D7524	25174	09/76	vq	C	B.R. Derby Works	(C08/78)	
D7525	25175		xq				
D7526	25176		xq				
D7527	25177	11/82	vq				
D7528	25178		xq				
D7529	25179	11/82	vq				
D7530	25180	11/82	vq				
D7531	25181		xq				
D7532	25182		xq				
D7533	25183	12/80	xq	C	B.R. Swindon Works	(C09/81)	
D7534	25184	08/83	xq	C	B.R. Swindon Works	(C02/84)	
D7535	25185		xq				
D7536	25186	11/82	vq				
D7537	25187	11/82	vq				
D7538	25188	08/82	vq				

D7539	25189		xq			
D7540	25190		xq			
D7541	25191		xq			
D7542	25192		xq			
D7543	25193		xq			
D7544	25194		xq			
D7545	25195		vq			
D7546	25196		xq			
D7547	25197	12/80	xq	C	B.R. Swindon Works	(C05/83)
D7548	25198		xq			
D7549	25199		xq			
D7550	25200		xq			
D7551	25201		xq			
D7552	25202		xq			
D7553	25203	12/80	xq	C	B.R. Swindon Works	(C03/82)
D7554	25204	07/80	xq	C	B.R. Swindon Works	(C10/80)
D7555	25205		xq			
D7556	25206		xq			
D7557	25207		xq			
D7558	25208	05/84	xq			
D7559	25209		xq			
D7560	25210		xq			
D7561	25211		xq			
D7562	25212		xq			
D7563	25212		xq			
D7564	25214	11/82	vq			
D7565	25215	06/83	vq	C	B.R. Swindon Works	(C11/83)
D7566	25216	12/80	vq	C	B.R. Derby Works	(C03/83)
D7567	25217	02/81	vq	C	B.R. Derby Works	(C01/82)
D7568	25218		xb			
D7569	25219	04/83	vb			
D7570	25220	06/82	vb			
D7571	25221	01/84	xb			
D7572	25222	12/80	xb	C	B.R. Swindon Works	(C12/81)
D7573	25223	10/80	vb	C	B.R. Swindon Works	(C11/80)
D7574	25224		vb			
D7575	25225	10/80	vb	C	B.R. Swindon Works	(C11/80)
D7576	25226		xi			
D7577	25227	06/83	xi	C	B.R. Swindon Works	(C12/83)
D7578	25228	03/84	xi			
D7579	25229		xi			
D7580	25230		xi			
D7581	25231		xi			
D7582	25232	12/80	xb	C	B.R. Swindon Works	(C05/83)
D7583	25233	03/83	xi			
D7584	25234		xi			
D7585	25235		xb			
D7586	25236		xb			
D7587	25237		xi			
D7588	25238	10/80	vb	C	B.R. Swindon Works	(C07/83)
D7589	25239		xi			
D7590	25240		xi	C	B.R. Swindon Works	(C12/83)
D7591	25241	05/81	xb	C	B.R. Swindon Works	(C09/81)
D7592	25242	05/84	xo			
D7593	25243	09/83	xb	C	B.R. Swindon Works	(C01/84)
D7594	25244		xi			
D7595	25245		xb			

D7596	25246	10/81	xb	C	B.R. Swindon Works	(C03/83)	
D7597	25247	07/83	xi	C	B.R. Swindon Works	(C12/83)	
D7598	25248	11/82	vq				
D7599	25249		xq				
D7600	25250	05/84	xq				
D7601	25251		xq				
D7602	25252	03/80	vq	C	B.R. Swindon Works	(C09/80)	
D7603	25253	09/83	vq				
D7604	25254		xq				
D7605		03/72	vq	C	B.R. Derby Works	(C06/72)	
D7606	25256		xq				
D7607	25257		xq				
D7608	25258		xq				
D7609	25259		xq				
D7610	25260	12/82	vq				
D7611	25261	01/81	vq				
D7612	25262		xq				
D7613	25263	11/80	vq	C	B.R. Swindon Works	(C05/83)	
D7614	25264	12/80	vq	C	B.R. Swindon Works	(C06/83)	
D7615	25265		xq				
D7616	25266		xq				
D7617	25267	02/81	vq	C	B.R. Swindon Works	(C03/82)	
D7618	25268		xq				
D7619	25269		xq				
D7620	25270	11/82	vq				
D7621	25271	10/81	vq	C	B.R. Derby Works	(C09/82)	
D7622	25272	07/81	vq	C	B.R. Derby Works	(C08/82)	
D7623	25273	02/81	vq	C	B.R. Swindon Works	(C04/82)	
D7624	25274	05/82	vq				
D7625	25275	04/82	vq				
D7626	25276		xq				
D7627	25277	04/84	xq				
D7628	25278		xq				
D7629	25279		xq				
D7630	25280	11/81	vq	C	B.R. Swindon Works	(C07/83)	
D7631	25281	02/81	vq	C	B.R. Swindon Works	(C05/81)	
D7632	25282		xq				
D7633	25283		xq				
D7634	25284		xq				
D7635	25285		xq				
D7636	25286		xq				
D7637	25287		xq				
D7638	25288		xq				
D7639	25289	01/84	xq				
D7640	25290	10/81	vq	C	B.R. Derby Works	(C05/83)	
D7641	25291	05/81	vq	C	B.R. Swindon Works	(C11/82)	
D7642	25292	10/81	vq	C	B.R. Swindon Works	(C04/83)	
D7643	25293	02/81	vq	C	B.R. Swindon Works	(C08/81)	
D7644	25294	10/82	vq				
D7645	25295	06/78	xq	C	B.R. Derby Works	(C10/81)	
D7646	25296		xq				
D7647	25297		xq				
D7648	25298		xq				
D7649	25299	10/81	vq				
D7650	25300		xq				
D7651	25301	12/82	xq	C	B.R. Swindon Works	(C09/84)	
D7652	25302		vq				

D7653	25303		xq			
D7654	25304	11/82	vq			
D7655	25305	07/83	xq	F	ADB97251 Mobile train heating unit	
D7656	25306		vq			
D7657	25307		xq			
D7658	25308	10/83	xq			
D7659	25309		xq			
D7660	25310	10/82	xq	F	ADB97250 Mobile train heating unit	
D7661	25311		xq			
D7662	25312	06/82	xq			
D7663	25313		xq			
D7664	25314	03/83	xq	F	ADB97252 Mobile train heating unit	
D7665	25315		xq			
D7666	25316		xq			
D7667	25317	04/83	xq			
D7668	25318	07/82	xq			
D7669	25319	03/83	xq			
D7670	25320	12/83	xq			
D7671	25321		xq			
D7672	25322		xq			
D7673	25323		xq			
D7674	25324		xq			
D7675	25325		xq			
D7676	25326		xq			
D7677	25327	02/84	xq			

Note: 25322 carried an official painted name TAMWORTH CASTLE

CLASS 20   ENGLISH ELECTRIC TYPE 2 1000 h.p. DE   Bo-Bo
Built 1957-1968

D8000	20050	12/80	vq	P	National Railway Museum, York	
D8001	20001		vq			
D8002	20002		xq			
D8003	20003	12/82	vq	C	B.R. Crewe Works	(C02/84)
D8004	20004		xq			
D8005	20005		xq			
D8006	20006		vq			
D8007	20007		vq			
D8008	20008		xq			
D8009	20009		xq			
D8010	20010		vq			
D8011	20011		xq			
D8012	20012	03/76	vq	C	B.R. Glasgow Works	(C01/77)
D8013	20013		vq			
D8014	20014	03/76	vq	C	B.R. Glasgow Works	(C01/77)
D8015	20015		xq			
D8016	20016		xq			
D8017	20017	12/82	vq	C	B.R. Crewe Works	(C02/84)
D8018	20018	12/76	vq	C	B.R. Glasgow Works	(C05/78)
D8019	20019		xq			
D8020	20020		vq			
D8021	20021		vq			
D8022	20022		xq			
D8023	20023		vq			
D8024	20024	05/77	vq	C	B.R. Glasgow Works	(C03/78)
D8025	20025		xq			

D8026	20026		xq				
D8027	20027	12/82	vq				
D8028	20028		vq				
D8029	20029		xq				
D8030	20030		xq				
D8031	20031		xq				
D8032	20032		xq				
D8033	20033	11/77	vq	C	B.R. Crewe Works	(C12/79)	
D8034	20034		vq				
D8035	20035		xq				
D8036	20036	06/84	xq				
D8037	20037		xq				
D8038	20038	03/76	vq	C	B.R. Glasgow Works	(C06/77)	
D8039	20039		xq				
D8040	20040		vq				
D8041	20041		xq				
D8042	20042		xq				
D8043	20043		xq				
D8044	20044		xq				
D8045	20045		xq				
D8046	20046		xq				
D8047	20047		vq				
D8048	20048		xq				
D8049	20049		xq				
D8050	20128		vq				
D8051	20051		vq				
D8052	20052		vq				
D8053	20053		vq				
D8054	20054		xq				
D8055	20055		xq				
D8056	20056		vq				
D8057	20057		vq				
D8058	20058		vq				
D8059	20059		vq				
D8060	20060		vq				
D8061	20061		xq				
D8062	20062	09/76	xq	C	B.R. Derby Loco Works	(C06/79)	
D8063	20063		xq				
D8064	20064		xq				
D8065	20065		xq				
D8066	20066		xq				
D8067	20067		xq				
D8068	20068		xq				
D8069	20069		xq				
D8070	20070		xq				
D8071	20071		vq				
D8072	20072		xq				
D8073	20073		vq				
D8074	20074	01/76	vq	C	B.R. Glasgow Works	(C11/76)	
D8075	20075		vq				
D8076	20076		xq				
D8077	20077		vq				
D8078	20078		vq				
D8079	20079	04/77	vq	C	B.R. Derby Loco Works	(C11/78)	
D8080	20080		xq				
D8081	20081		xq				
D8082	20082		vq				

D8083	20083		xq			
D8084	20084		vq			
D8085	20085		xq			
D8086	20086		xq			
D8087	20087		xq			
D8088	20088		xq			
D8089	20089		xq			
D8090	20090		vq			
D8091	20091	09/78	vq	C	B.R. Glasgow Works	(C01/79)
D8092	20092		xq			
D8093	20093		xq			
D8094	20094		xq			
D8095	20095		xq			
D8096	20096		xq			
D8097	20097		xq			
D8098	20098		xq			
D8099	20099		vq			
D8100	20100		xq			
D8101	20101		vq			
D8102	20102		xq			
D8103	20103		xq			
D8104	20104		vq			
D8105	20105		xq			
D8106	20106		xq			
D8107	20107		xq			
D8108	20108		vq			
D8109	20109	02/82	vq	C	B.R. Glasgow Works	(C04/82)
D8110	20110		xq			
D8111	20111		xq			
D8112	20112		xq			
D8113	20113		xq			
D8114	20114		xq			
D8115	20115		xq			
D8116	20116		xq			
D8117	20117		vq			
D8118	20118		xq			
D8119	20119		xq			
D8120	20120		vq			
D8121	20121		xq			
D8122	20122		xq			
D8123	20123		xq			
D8124	20124		xq			
D8125	20125		xq			
D8126	20126		xq			
D8127	20127		xq			
D8128	20128		xo			
D8129	20129		xo			
D8130	20130		xo			
D8131	20131		vo			
D8132	20132		vo			
D8133	20133		xo			
D8134	20134		vo			
D8135	20135		vo			
D8136	20136		vo			
D8137	20137		xo			
D8138	20138		xo			
D8139	20139		xo			

D8140	20140	xo
D8141	20141	vo
D8142	20142	xo
D8143	20143	xo
D8144	20144	xo
D8145	20145	xo
D8146	20146	xo
D8147	20147	vo
D8148	20148	xo
D8149	20149	xo
D8150	20150	xo
D8151	20151	xo
D8152	20152	xo
D8153	20153	xo
D8154	20154	xo
D8155	20155	xo
D8156	20156	xo
D8157	20157	vo
D8158	20158	vo
D8159	20159	vo
D8160	20160	xo
D8161	20161	vo
D8162	20162	xo
D8163	20163	vo
D8164	20164	xo
D8165	20165	xo
D8166	20166	xo
D8167	20167	xo
D8168	20168	vo
D8169	20169	vo
D8170	20170	vo
D8171	20171	xo
D8172	20172	vo
D8173	20173	vo
D8174	20174	xo
D8175	20175	xo
D8176	20176	xo
D8177	20177	vo
D8178	20178	vo
D8179	20179	xo
D8180	20180	vo
D8181	20181	xo
D8182	20182	xo
D8183	20183	vo
D8184	20184	xo
D8185	20185	vo
D8186	20186	vo
D8187	20187	vo
D8188	20188	vo
D8189	20189	xo
D8190	20190	xo
D8191	20191	xo
D8192	20192	xo
D8193	20193	xo
D8194	20194	vo
D8195	20195	vo
D8196	20196	vo

D8187	20197	xo
D8198	20198	xo
D8199	20199	xo

Class continued with D8300

CLASS 15 CLAYTON*/PAXMAN/B.T.H. TYPE 1 800 h.p. DE Bo-Bo
*Built 1957-1961 (*D8200-9 were built by Yorkshire Engine Co)*

D8200	03/71	vq	C	B.R. Crewe Works	(C02/72)
D8201	03/71	vq	C	B.R. Crewe Works	(C02/72)
D8202	09/68	vq	C	G. Cohen, Kettering	(C10/69)
D8203	03/69	vq	D	ADB968003 Carriage Heating Unit	(C10/81)
D8204	03/71	vq	C	B.R. Crewe Works	(C04/72)
D8205	09/68	vq	C	G. Cohen, Kettering	(C04/69)
D8206	09/68	vq	C	D. Woodham, Barry	(C02/76)
D8207	03/71	vq	C	B.R. Crewe Works	(C04/72)
D8208	09/68	vq	C	G. Cohen, Kettering	(C04/69)
D8209	03/71	vq	C	B.R. Crewe Works	(C03/72)
D8210	03/71	vq	C	B.R. Crewe Works	(C03/72)
D8211	03/71	vq	C	B.R. Crewe Works	(C12/71)
D8212	09/68	vq	C	G. Cohen, Kettering	(C04/69)
D8213	12/68	vq	C	G. Cohen, Kettering	(C10/69)
D8214	12/70	vq	C	B.R. Crewe Works	(C12/71)
D8215	12/70	vq	C	B.R. Crewe Works	(C11/71)
D8216	03/71	vq	C	B.R. Crewe Works	(C01/72)
D8217	03/68	vq	C	G. Cohen, Kettering	(C01/69)
D8218	03/71	vq	C	B.R. Crewe Works	(C11/71)
D8219	09/68	vq	C	G. Cohen, Kettering	(C04/69)
D8220	03/71	vq	C	B.R. Crewe Works	(C11/71)
D8221	03/71	vq	C	B.R. Crewe Works	(C12/71)
D8222	03/71	vq	C	B.R. Crewe Works	(C12/71)
D8223	12/68	vq	C	G. Cohen, Kettering	(C10/69)
D8224	03/71	vq	C	B.R. Crewe Works	(C12/71)
D8225	03/71	vq	C	B.R. Crewe Works	(C12/71)
D8226	03/71	vq	C	B.R. Crewe Works	(C12/71)
D8227	09/68	vq	C	G. Cohen, Kettering	(C11/69)
D8228	03/71	vq	C	B.R. Crewe Works	(C12/71)
D8229	03/71	vq	C	B.R. Crewe Works	(C01/72)
D8230	03/71	vq	C	B.R. Crewe Works	(C11/71)
D8231	03/71	vq	C	B.R. Crewe Works	(C01/72)
D8232	03/71	vq	C	B.R. Crewe Works	(C11/71)
D8233	02/69	vq	P	Sold for preservation, but still at HM	
D8234	03/71	vq	C	B.R. Crewe Works	(C11/71)
D8235	10/68	vq	C	G. Cohen, Kettering	(C07/69)
D8236	10/68	vq	C	G. Cohen, Kettering	(C07/69)
D8237	03/69	vq	D	ADB968002 Carriage Heating Unit at TO	
D8238	09/68	vq	C	G. Cohen, Kettering	(C06/69)
D8239	03/71	vq	C	B.R. Crewe Works	(C01/72)
D8240	10/68	vq	C	G. Cohen, Kettering	(C07/69)
D8241	04/68	vq	C	J. Cashmore, Great Bridge	(C12/68)
D8242	03/71	vq	C	B.R. Crewe Works	(C11/71)
D8243	02/69	vq	D	ADB968000 Carriage Heating Unit at BR	

CLASS 20 continued

| D8300 | 20200 | 08/79 | xo | C | B.R. Glasgow Works | (C10/79) |
| D8301 | 20201 | | xo | | | |

D8302	20202		xo				
D8303	20203		xo				
D8304	20204		xo				
D8305	20205		xo				
D8306	20206		xo				
D8307	20207	07/83	xo				
D8308	20208		xo				
D8309	20209		vo				
D8310	20210		vo				
D8311	20211		xo				
D8312	20212		xo				
D8313	20213		xo				
D8314	20214		vo				
D8315	20215		vo				
D8316	20216		xo				
D8317	20217		xo				
D8318	20218		xo				
D8319	20219		xo				
D8320	20220		xo				
D8321	20221		xo				
D8322	20222		xo				
D8323	20223		xo				
D8324	20224		xo				
D8325	20225		xo				
D8326	20226		xo				
D8327	20227		xo				

CLASS 16   N.B.L./PAXMAN/G.E.C. TYPE 1 800 h.p. DE   Bo-Bo
Built 1958

D8400	07/68	vq	C	G. Cohen, Kettering	(C11/69)	
D8401	09/68	vq	C	G. Cohen, Kettering	(C09/69)	
D8402	07/68	vq	C	G. Cohen, Kettering	(C11/69)	
D8403	07/68	vq	C	G. Cohen, Kettering	(C04/69)	
D8404	02/68	vq	C	Cox & Danks, North Acton	(C07/68)	
D8405	09/68	vq	C	G. Cohen, Kettering	(C12/69)	
D8406	09/68	vq	C	Birds Comm. Motors, Long Marston	(C07/69)	
D8407	09/68	vq	C	G. Cohen, Kettering	(C12/69)	
D8408	09/68	vq	C	G. Cohen, Kettering	(C04/69)	
D8409	09/68	vq	C	G. Cohen, Kettering	(C04/69)	

CLASS 17   CLAYTON*/PAXMAN+/G.E.C.§ TYPE 1 900 h.p. DE   Bo-Bo
Built 1962-1965.
*D8588-D8616 Beyer Peacock. +D8586-7 Rolls Royce. §D8588-D8616 Crompton Parkinson.

D8500	03/71	vq	C	B.R. Glasgow Works	(C11/71)	
D8501	10/68	vq	C	B.R. Glasgow Works	(C12/71)	
D8502	10/71	vq	C	B.R. Glasgow Works	(C04/73)	
D8503	10/71	vq	C	B.R. Glasgow Works	(C06/72)	
D8504	11/71	vq	C	J. Cashmore, Great Bridge	(C09/75)	
D8505	10/71	vq	C	B.R. Glasgow Works	(C04/74)	
D8506	09/71	vq	C	B.R. Glasgow Works	(C12/71)	
D8507	12/71	vq	C	R.A. King, Norwich	(C09/75)	
D8508	12/71	vq	C	R.A. King, Norwich	(C09/75)	
D8509	10/68	vq	C	B.R. Glasgow Works	(C01/72)	
D8510	03/71	vq	C	B.R. Glasgow Works	(C11/71)	
D8511	10/68	vq	C	J. McWilliams, Shettleston	(C08/70)	

D8512	12/68	vq	F	Used by G.E.C. Stafford as a generator	(C01/73)
D8513	09/71	vq	C	B.R. Glasgow Works	(C12/71)
D8514	10/68	vq	C	B.R. Glasgow Works	(C12/71)
D8515	10/71	vq	C	B.R. Glasgow Works	(C12/72)
D8516	10/71	vq	C	R.A. King, Norwich	(C09/75)
D8517	10/68	vq	C	J. McWilliams, Shettleston	(C09/70)
D8518	10/68	vq	C	B.R. Glasgow Works	(C02/72)
D8519	10/68	vq	C	B.R. Glasgow Works	(C05/72)
D8520	10/68	vq	C	B.R. Glasgow Works	(C05/72)
D8521	10/68	vq	D	S18521	(C04/79)
D8522	10/68	vq	C	B.R. Glasgow Works	(C05/72)
D8523	10/68	vq	C	B.R. Glasgow Works	(C06/72)
D8524	10/68	vq	C	J. McWilliams, Shettleston	(C09/70)
D8525	10/71	vq	C	R.A. King, Norwich	(C09/75)
D8526	10/68	vq	C	B.R. Glasgow Works	(C05/72)
D8527	12/68	vq	C	B.R. Glasgow Works	(C06/72)
D8528	10/71	vq	C	B.R. Glasgow Works	(C07/73)
D8529	12/71	vq	C	R.A. King, Norwich	(C09/75)
D8530	03/71	vq	C	B.R. Glasgow Works	(C10/71)
D8531	09/71	vq	C	R.A. King, Norwich	(C09/75)
D8532	12/68	vq	C	B.R. Glasgow Works	(C06/72)
D8533	10/68	vq	C	B.R. Glasgow Works	(C01/72)
D8534	10/68	vq	C	B.R. Glasgow Works	(C02/73)
D8535	03/71	vq	C	B.R. Glasgow Works	(C11/71)
D8536	12/71	vq	C	R.A. King, Norwich	(C09/75)
D8537	07/68	vq	C	J. McWilliams, Shettleston	(C01/69)
D8538	10/71	vq	C	B.R. Glasgow Works	(C12/72)
D8539	10/71	vq	C	R.A. King, Norwich	(C12/75)
D8540	10/71	vq	C	B.R. Glasgow Works	(C01/73)
D8541	10/71	vq	C	B.R. Glasgow Works	(C02/73)
D8542	10/71	vq	C	J. Cashmore, Great Bridge	(C09/75)
D8543	09/71	vq	C	B.R. Glasgow Works	(C06/72)
D8544	05/69	vq	C	J. McWilliams, Shettleston	(C01/71)
D8545	10/71	vq	F	Used by G.E.C. Stafford as a generator	(C11/73)
D8546	10/71	vq	C	J. Cashmore, Great Bridge	(C09/75)
D8547	02/69	vq	C	Birds Comm. Motors, Long Marston	(C03/70)
D8548	12/71	vq	C	J. Cashmore, Great Bridge	(C09/75)
D8549	09/71	vq	C	B.R. Glasgow Works	(C06/72)
D8550	10/71	vq	C	J. Cashmore, Great Bridge	(C09/75)
D8551	10/71	vq	C	J. Cashmore, Great Bridge	(C09/75)
D8552	12/71	vq	C	R.A. King, Norwich	(C09/75)
D8553	12/68	vq	C	J. McWilliams, Shettleston	(C02/69)
D8554	05/69	vq	C	J. McWilliams, Shettleston	(C01/71)
D8555	09/71	vq	C	B.R. Glasgow Works	(C05/72)
D8556	02/69	vq	C	Birds Comm. Motors, Long Marston	(C03/70)
D8557	09/71	vq	C	J. McWilliams, Shettleston	(C08/75)
D8558	12/71	vq	C	B.R. Glasgow Works	(C02/73)
D8559	10/71	vq	C	B.R. Glasgow Works	(C04/74)
D8560	02/69	vq	C	Birds Comm. Motors, Long Marston	(C12/69)
D8561	11/71	vq	C	B.R. Glasgow Works	(C07/73)
D8562	10/71	vq	C	B.R. Glasgow Works	(C06/73)
D8563	12/71	vq	C	J. Cashmore, Great Bridge	(C09/75)
D8564	02/69	vq	C	Birds Comm. Motors, Long Marston	(C03/70)
D8565	11/71	vq	C	B.R. Glasgow Works	(C07/73)
D8566	12/68	vq	C	J. McWilliams, Shettleston	(C04/69)
D8567	10/71	vq	F	Used by G.E.C. Stafford as a generator	(C01/73)
D8568	10/71	vq	P	North Yorkshire Moors Railway	

D8569		12/68	vq	C	J. McWilliams, Shettleston	(C05/69)
D8570		11/68	vq	C	Birds Comm. Motors, Long Marston	(C07/69)
D8571		05/69	vq	C	J. McWilliams, Shettleston	(C07/71)
D8572		05/69	vq	C	J. Cashmore, Great Bridge	(C08/70)
D8573		10/71	vq	C	J. McWilliams, Shettleston	(C08/75)
D8574		12/71	vq	C	R.A. King, Norwich	(C09/75)
D8575		10/68	vq	C	J. McWilliams, Shettleston	(C04/69)
D8576		03/69	vq	C	Birds Comm. Motors, Long Marston	(C03/70)
D8577		02/69	vq	C	Birds Comm. Motors, Long Marston	(C03/70)
D8578		05/69	vq	C	J. McWilliams, Shettleston	(C08/71)
D8579		10/71	vq	C	B.R. Glasgow Works	(C11/73)
D8580		10/71	vq	C	R.A. King, Norwich	(C09/75)
D8581		10/71	vq	C	B.R. Glasgow Works	(C10/73)
D8582		01/69	vq	C	J. McWilliams, Shettleston	(C06/69)
D8583		09/71	vq	C	B.R. Glasgow Works	(C08/73)
D8584		10/68	vq	C	J. McWilliams, Shettleston	(C05/69)
D8585		10/68	vq	C	J. McWilliams, Shettlestoñ	(C06/69)
D8586		09/71	vq	C	B.R. Glasgow Works	(C07/73)
D8587		10/71	vq	C	B.R. Glasgow Works	(C02/74)
D8588		10/71	vq	C	B.R. Glasgow Works	(C07/73)
D8589		07/70	vq	C	W. Willoughby at Gateshead Depot	(C11/70)
D8590		03/71	vq	C	J. McWilliams, Shettleston	(C05/72)
D8591		12/68	vq	C	J. McWilliams, Shettleston	(C06/69)
D8592		09/71	vq	C	B.R. Glasgow Works	(C03/72)
D8593		10/71	vq	C	B.R. Glasgow Works	(C09/73)
D8594		09/71	vq	C	B.R. Glasgow Works	(C03/72)
D8595		12/68	vq	C	J. McWilliams, Shettleston	(C05/69)
D8596		12/68	vq	C	J. McWilliams, Shettleston	(C05/69)
D8597		10/71	vq	C	B.R. Glasgow Works	(C07/73)
D8598		12/71	vq	D	S18598	(C)
D8599		10/71	vq	C	B.R. Glasgow Works	(C11/71)
D8600		10/71	vq	C	B.R. Glasgow Works	(C04/73)
D8601		10/71	vq	C	B.R. Glasgow Works	(C02/74)
D8602		10/71	vq	C	B.R. Glasgow Works	(C04/72)
D8603		10/71	vq	C	B.R. Glasgow Works	(C04/72)
D8604		10/71	vq	C	B.R. Glasgow Works	(C04/72)
D8605		10/68	vq	C	A. Draper, Hull	(C06/70)
D8606		03/71	vq	C	B.R. Glasgow Works	(C04/72)
D8607		10/71	vq	C	J. McWilliams, Shettleston	(C08/75)
D8608		10/71	vq	C	J. McWilliams, Shettleston	(C08/75)
D8609		10/68	vq	C	J. McWilliams, Shettleston	(C05/69)
D8610		10/71	vq	C	B.R. Glasgow Works	(C08/73)
D8611		10/68	vq	C	J. McWilliams, Shettleston	(C08/69)
D8612		10/71	vq	C	J. McWilliams, Shettleston	(C08/75)
D8613		10/71	vq	C	J. McWilliams, Shettleston	(C08/75)
D8614		10/71	vq	C	B.R. Glasgow Works	(C12/72)
D8615		10/71	vq	C	B.R. Glasgow Works	(C12/73)
D8616		10/71	vq	C	J. McWilliams, Shettleston	(C08/75)

CLASS 55   E.E./NAPIER/E.E. TYPE 5 3300 h.p. DE   Co-Co
Built 1961-1962 "Deltics"

D9000	55022	01/82	xd	P	Nene Valley Railway	
D9001	55001	01/80	xd	C	B.R. Doncaster Works	(C02/80)
D9002	55002	01/82	xd	P	National Railway Museum, York	
D9003	55003	12/80	xd	C	B.R. Doncaster Works	(C03/81)
D9004	55004	11/81	xd	C	B.R. Doncaster Works	(C07/83)

D9005	55005	02/81	xd	C	B.R. Doncaster Works	(C02/83)	
D9006	55006	02/81	xd	C	B.R. Doncaster Works	(C07/81)	
D9007	55007	12/81	xd	C	B.R. Doncaster Works	(C08/82)	
D9008	55008	12/81	xd	C	B.R. Doncaster Works	(C08/82)	
D9009	55009	01/82	xd	P	North Yorkshire Moors Railway		
D9010	55010	12/81	xd	C	B.R. Doncaster Works	(C05/82)	
D9011	55011	11/81	xd	C	B.R. Doncaster Works	(C12/82)	
D9012	55012	05/81	xd	C	B.R. Doncaster Works	(C09/81)	
D9013	55013	12/81	xd	C	B.R. Doncaster Works	(C12/82)	
D9014	55014	11/81	xd	C	B.R. Doncaster Works	(C02/82)	
D9015	55015	01/82	xd	P	Midland Railway Centre, Butterley		
D9016	55016	12/81	xd	P	Nene Valley Railway		
D9017	55017	12/81	xd	C	B.R. Doncaster Works	(C01/83)	
D9018	55018	10/81	xd	C	B.R. Doncaster Works	(C01/82)	
D9019	55019	12/81	xd	P	North Yorkshire Moors Railway		
D9020	55020	01/80	xd	C	B.R. Doncaster Works	(C01/81)	
D9021	55021	12/81	xd	C	B.R. Doncaster Works	(C09/82)	

Names:
55001	ST. PADDY
55002	THE KING'S OWN YORKSHIRE LIGHT INFANTRY
55003	MELD
55004	QUEEN'S OWN HIGHLANDER
55005	THE PRINCE OF WALES'S OWN REGIMENT OF YORKSHIRE
55006	THE FIFE AND FORFAR YEOMANRY
55007	PINZA
55008	THE GREEN HOWARDS
55009	ALYCIDON
55010	THE KING'S OWN SCOTTISH BORDERER
55011	THE ROYAL NORTHUMBERLAND FUSILIERS
55012	CREPELLO
55013	THE BLACK WATCH
55014	THE DUKE OF WELLINGTON'S REGIMENT
55015	TULYAR
55016	GORDON HIGHLANDER
55017	THE DURHAM LIGHT INFANTRY
55018	BALLYMOSS
55019	ROYAL HIGHLAND FUSILIER
55020	NIMBUS
55021	ARGYLL AND SUTHERLAND HIGHLANDER
55022	ROYAL SCOTS GREY

CLASS 14   B.R./PAXMAN/VOITH TYPE 1 650 h.p. DH   0-6-0
Built 1964-1965

D9500	04/69	vo	F	N.C.B., Ashington Colliery		
D9501	03/68	vo	C	C.F. Booth, Rotherham	(C07/68)	
D9502	04/69	vo	F	N.C.B., Ashington Colliery		
D9503	04/68	vo	F	B.S.C., Corby Quarries	(C09/80)	
D9504	04/68	vo	F	N.C.B., Ashington Colliery		
D9505	04/68	vo	F	Maldegen, Belgium	(E05/75)	
D9506	03/68	vo	C	A. Young, Park Gate, Rotherham	(C03/70)	
D9507	04/68	vo	F	B.S.C., Steelworks Disposal Site, Corby	(C)	
D9508	10/68	vo	F	N.C.B., Ashington Colliery	(C01/84)	
D9509	10/68	vo	C	G. Cohen, Kettering	(C02/71)	
D9510	04/68	vo	F	B.S.C., Tube Works, Corby	(C)	
D9511	04/68	vo	F	N.C.B., Ashington Colliery	(C07/79)	

D9512	04/68	vo	F	B.S.C., Steelworks Disposal Site, Corby	(C02/82)
D9513	03/68	vo	F	N.C.B., Ashington Colliery	
D9514	04/69	vo	F	N.C.B., Ashington Colliery	
D9515	04/68	vo	F	Zarragossa, Spain	(E06/82)
D9516	04/68	vo	P	Main Line Steam Trust, Loughborough	
D9517	10/68	vo	F	N.C.B., Ashington Colliery	(C01/84)
D9518	04/69	vo	F	N.C.B., Ashington Colliery	
D9519	10/68	vo	C	G. Cohen, Kettering	(C01/71)
D9520	04/68	vo	P	Rutland Railway Museum	
D9521	04/69	vo	F	N.C.B., Ashington Colliery	
D9522	12/67	vo	C	A. Young, Park Gate, Rotherham	(C08/68)
D9523	04/68	vo	P	Main Line Steam Trust, Loughborough	
D9524	04/69	vo	P	Scottish Railway Pres. Society, Falkirk	
D9525	04/68	vo	F	N.C.B., Philadelphia Loco. Depot	
D9526	11/68	vo	P	West Somerset Railway, Minehead	
D9527	04/69	vo	F	N.C.B., Ashington Colliery	(C01/84)
D9528	03/69	vo	F	N.C.B., Ashington Colliery	(C05/79)
D9529	04/68	vo	P	North Yorkshire Moors Railway	
D9530	10/68	vo	F	N.C.B., Tower Colliery	
D9531	12/67	vo	F	N.C.B., Ashington Colliery	
D9532	04/68	vo	F	B.S.C., Steelworks Disposal Site, Corby	(C)
D9533	04/68	vo	F	N.C.B., Steelworks Disposal Site, Corby	(C)
D9534	04/68	vo	F	Maldegen, Belgium	(E05/75)
D9535	12/68	vo	F	N.C.B., Ashington Colliery	(C01/84)
D9536	04/69	vo	F	N.C.B., Ashington Colliery	
D9537	04/68	vo	P	Gloucester & Warwickshire Railway	
D9538	04/69	vo	F	B.S.C., Corby Quarries	(C)
D9539	04/68	vo	P	Gloucester & Warwickshire Railway	
D9540	04/68	vo	F	N.C.B., Ashington Colliery	(C01/84)
D9541	04/68	vo	F	B.S.C., Steelworks Disposal Site, Corby	(C)
D9542	04/68	vo	F	B.S.C., Steelworks Disposal Site, Corby	(C)
D9543	04/68	vo	C	C.F. Booth, Rotherham	(C11/68)
D9544	04/68	vo	F	B.S.C., Corby Quarries	(C09/80)
D9545	04/68	vo	F	N.C.B., Ashington Colliery	(C07/79)
D9546	04/68	vo	C	C.F. Booth, Rotherham	(C11/68)
D9547	04/68	vo	F	B.S.C., Steelworks Disposal Site, Corby	(C)
D9548	04/68	vo	F	Zarragossa, Spain	(E05/82)
D9549	04/68	vo	F	Zarragossa, Spain	(E05/82)
D9550	04/68	vo	C	C.F. Booth, Rotherham	(C11/68)
D9551	04/68	vo	P	West Somerset Railway, Minehead	
D9552	04/68	vo	F	B.S.C., Corby Quarries	(C09/80)
D9553	04/68	vo	P	Gloucester & Warwickshire Railway	
D9554	04/68	vo	F	B.S.C., Steelworks Disposal Site, Corby	(C)
D9555	04/69	vo	F	N.C.B., Ashington Colliery	

CLASS 56   B.R./PAXMAX/BRUSH TYPE 5 3250 h.p. DE   Co-Co
Built 1977-1984 (56001-30 built by Electroputere, Rumania)

56001	ao
56002	ao
56003	ao
56004	ao
56005	ao
56006	ao
56007	ao
56008	ao
56009	ao

56010	ao
56011	ao
56012	ao
56013	ao
56014	ao
56015	ao
56016	ao
56017	ao
56018	ao
56019	ao
56020	ao
56021	ao
56022	ao
56023	ao
56024	ao
56025	ao
56026	ao
56027	ao
56028	ao
56029	ao
56030	ao
56031	ao
56032	ao
56033	ao
56034	ao
56035	ao
56036	ao
56037	ao
56038	ao
56039	ao
56040	ao
56041	ao
56042	ao
56043	ao
56044	ao
56045	ao
56046	ao
56047	ao
56048	ao
56049	ao
56050	ao
56051	ao
56052	ao
56053	ao
56054	ao
56055	ao
56056	ao
56057	ao
56058	ao
56059	ao
56060	ao
56061	ao
56062	ao
56063	ao
56064	ao
56065	ao
56066	ao

56067	ao	
56068	ao	
56069	ao	
56070	ao	
56071	ao	
56072	ao	
56073	ao	
56074	ao	
56075	ao	
56076	ao	
56077	ao	
56078	ao	
56079	ao	
56080	ao	
56081	ao	
56082	ao	
56083	ao	
56084	ao	
56085	ao	
56086	ao	
56087	ao	
56088	ao	
56089	ao	
56090	ao	
56091	ao	
56092	ao	
56093	ao	
56094	ao	
56095	ao	
56096	ao	
56097	ao	
56098	ao	
56099	ao	
56100	ao	
56101	ao	
56102	ao	
56103	ao	
56104	ao	
56105	ao	
56106	ao	
56107	ao	
56108	ao	
56109	ao	
56110	ao	
56111	ao	
56112	ao	
56113	ao	
56114	ao	
56115	ao	
56116	ao	
56117	ao	
56118	ao	
56119	ao	
56120	ao	
56121	ao	
56122	ao	
56123	ao	

56124	ao	
56125	ao	
56126	ao	
56127	ao	
56128	ao	
56129	ao	
56130	ao	
56131	ao	
56132	ao	
56133	ao	
56134	ao	
56135	ao	

Names:

56031	Merehead
56032	Sir De Morgannwg-County of South Glamorgan (Reversed opposite side)
56035	Taff Merthyr
56037	Richard Trevithick
56038	Western Mail
56040	Oystermouth
56074	Kellingley Colliery
56076	Blyth Power
56124	Blue Circle Cement
56133	Crewe Locomotive Works

CLASS 58   B.R./RUSTON/BRUSH TYPE 5 3300 h.p. DE   Co-Co
Built 1983-

58001	ao	
58002	ao	
58003	ao	
58004	ao	
58005	ao	
58006	ao	
58007	ao	
58008	ao	
58009	ao	
58010	ao	
58011	ao	
58012	ao	
58013	ao	
58014	ao	
58015	ao	
58016	ao	
58017	ao	
58018	ao	
58019	ao	
58020	ao	
58021	ao	
58022	ao	
58023	ao	
58024	ao	
58025	ao	
58026	ao	
58027	ao	

58028	ao
58029	ao
58030	ao
58031	ao
58032	ao
58033	ao
58034	ao
58035	ao
58036	ao
58037	ao
58038	ao
58039	ao
58040	ao
58041	ao
58042	ao
58043	ao
58044	ao
58045	ao
58046	ao
58047	ao
58048	ao
58049	ao
58050	ao

6. EXPERIMENTAL DIESEL LOCOMOTIVES

MAIN LINE LOCOS

ARMSTRONG WHITWORTH/SULZER/C.P. 800 h.p. DE **1 Co 1**
Built 1933
Unnumbered (C) [   ]

B.R.C. & W./SULZER/A.E.I. 2750 h.p. DE **Co-Co**
Built 1962
D0260 LION 09/63 vf C B.R.C. & W. (C03/65) [   ]

BRUSH/MAYBACH/BRUSH 2800 h.p. DE **Co-Co**
Built 1961
D0280 FALCON 12/70 vb F To operating stock D1200 (class 53) [   ]

ENGLISH ELECTRIC/NAPIER/ENGLISH ELECTRIC 3300 h.p. DE **Co-Co**
Built 1955
      DELTIC 05/60 vb P Science Museum, London [   ]

ENGLISH ELECTRIC 2700 h.p. DE **Co-Co**
Built 1962. Prototype for class 50.
DP2 07/67 vb C English Electric, Vulcan Foundry (C05/68) [   ]

BRUSH/SULZER/BRUSH 3946 h.p. DE **Co-Co**
Built 1968
HS4000 KESTREL 04/71 xk E Sold to U.S.S.R. (C /75) [   ]

SHUNTERS

BRUSH 200 h.p. DE **0-4-0**
Built 1958
D9998 (C) [   ]

VULCAN/FRICHS/WILSON 275 h.p. DM **0-6-0**
Built 1939
      VULCAN (C) [   ]

R.S. & H./GARDNER/WILSON 204 h.p. DM **0-6-0**
Built 1948
Unnumbered F To departmental stock as DS1173 [   ]

ENGLISH ELECTRIC 500 h.p. DE **0-6-0**
Built 1957
D0226 09/57 v P Keighley & Worth Valley Railway [   ]

ENGLISH ELECTRIC/ENGLISH ELECTRIC/KRUPP 500 h.p. DH **0-6-0**
Built 1957
D0227 09/57 v (C) [   ]

YORKSHIRE ENGINE Co./ROLLS ROYCE 600 h.p. DM **0-8-0**
Built 1961
      TAURUS 03/64 C Yorkshire Engine Co. (C /64) [   ]

YORKSHIRE ENGINE Co./ROLLS ROYCE 400 h.p. DM **0-6-0**
Built 1956
      JANUS n [   ]

NORTH BRITISH LOCOMOTIVE Co. 400 h.p. DH   0-6-0
Built 1954

Unnumbered		P	Flint & Deeside Railway

NORTH BRITISH LOCOMOTIVE Co. 300 h.p. DH   0-4-0
Built 1954

Unnumbered		P	Telford Horsehay Steam Trust
Unnumbered		P	Isle of Wight Steam Railway

7. GAS TURBINE LOCOMOTIVES

BROWN BOVERI 2450 h.p. GE   A1A-A1A
Built 1950 for W.R.

18000	12/60	vb	F	O.R.E., Vienna Arsenal

METROPOLITAN VICKERS 3000 h.p. GE   Co-Co
Built 1952 for W.R.

18100	01/58	vb	R	Rebuilt to electric loco E1000	(R)

ENGLISH ELECTRIC 2750 h.p. GM   4-6-0
Built 1961. Experimental loco on standard class 5MT 4-6-0 chassis.

GT3	02/63	vb	C	T.W. Ward, Brindle Heath, Manchester	(C03/66)

8. ELECTRIC LOCOMOTIVES
LANCASHIRE & YORKSHIRE RAILWAY

LANCASHIRE & YORKSHIRE RAILWAY 600 h.p. EE   **2-4-2**
Built 1912
No. 1   /22   n   C   L.&Y.R. Horwich Works   (C /22)

SOUTHERN RAILWAY

CLASS 70   **S.R./ENGLISH ELECTRIC 1470 h.p. RE/OE**   **Co-Co**
Built 1941, 1945, 1948

CC1	20001	01/69	vb	C	J. Cashmore, Newport	(C08/69)
CC2	20002	12/68	vb	C	J. Cashmore, Newport	(C09/69)
	20003	10/68	vb	C	G. Cohen, Kettering	(C11/69)

LONDON & NORTH EASTERN RAILWAY
Also includes locos of the North Eastern Railway & L.N.E.R. designed locos.

CLASS EM1 (LATER CLASS 76)   **B.R./MET.VIC. 1868 h.p. OE**   **Bo + Bo**
Built 1950-53 (26000 built by L.N.E.R. 1941)

26000	**		03/70	vb	C	B.R. Crewe Works	(C10/72)
26001	76001		11/80	vo	C	C.F. Booth, Rotherham	(C04/83)
26002	76002		06/78	vo	C	C.F. Booth, Rotherham	(C02/84)
26003	76003	76036	07/81	ao	C	C.F. Booth, Rotherham	(C06/83)
26004	76004		06/78	vo	C	C.F. Booth, Rotherham	(C02/84)
26005			03/70	vo	C	B.R. Crewe Works	(C08/71)
26006	76006		07/81	xo	C	C.F. Booth, Rotherham	(C05/83)
26007	76007		07/81	xo	C	C.F. Booth, Rotherham	(C /83)
26008	76008		07/81	xo	C	C.F. Booth, Rotherham	(C06/83)
26009	76009		07/81	xo	C	C.F. Booth, Rotherham	(C /83)
26010	76010		07/81	xo	C	C.F. Booth, Rotherham	(C06/83)
26011	76011		07/81	xo	C	C.F. Booth, Rotherham	(C06/83)
26012	76012		07/81	xo	C	C.F. Booth, Rotherham	(C /)
26013	76013		07/81	xo	C	C.F. Booth, Rotherham	(C05/83)
26014	76014		07/81	xo	C	C.F. Booth, Rotherham	(C05/83)
26015	76015		07/81	xo	C	C.F. Booth, Rotherham	(C03/83)
26016	76016		07/81	xo	C	C.F. Booth, Rotherham	(C04/83)
26017			03/70	vo	C	J. Cashmore at Reddish Depot	(C10/71)
26018	76018	76035	07/81	ao	C	C.F. Booth, Rotherham	(C /)
26019			09/71	vo	C	B.R. Crewe Works	(C05/72)
26020	76020		08/77	vr	P	National Railway Museum	
26021	76021		07/81	xo	C	C.F. Booth, Rotherham	(C04/83)
26022	76022		07/81	xo	C	C.F. Booth, Rotherham	(C06/83)
26023	76023		07/81	xo	C	C.F. Booth, Rotherham	(C /)
26024	76024		07/81	xo	C	C.F. Booth, Rotherham	(C /)

26025	76025		07/81	xo	C	C.F. Booth, Rotherham	(C03/83)	
26026	76026		07/81	xo	C	C.F. Booth, Rotherham	(C /)	
26027	76027		07/81	xo	C	C.F. Booth, Rotherham	(C04/83)	
26028	76028		07/81	xo	C	C.F. Booth, Rotherham	(C06/83)	
26029	76029		07/81	xo	C	Coopers Metals, Brightside, Sheffield	(C04/83)	
26030	76030		07/81	xo	C	C.F. Booth, Rotherham	(C04/83)	
26031			09/71		vo	C	B.R. Crewe Works	(C05/72)
26032	76032		07/81	ao	C	Coopers Metals, Brightside, Sheffield	(C04/83)	
26033	76033		07/81	ao	C	Coopers Metals, Brightside, Sheffield	(C04/83)	
26034	76034		07/81	ao	C	C.F. Booth, Rotherham	(C03/83)	
26035			03/70	vo	C	J. Cashmore at Reddish Depot	(C10/71)	
26036	76036	76003	07/81	vo	C	F. Berry, Leicester	( )	
26037	76037		07/81	ao	C	F. Berry, Leicester	( )	
26038	76038	76050	02/77	vo	C	C.F. Booth, Rotherham	( )	
26039	76039	76048	02/77	vo	C	C.F. Booth, Rotherham	( )	
26040	76040		07/81	vo	C	F. Berry, Leicester	( )	
26041	76041		11/80	vo	C	C.F. Booth, Rotherham	(C03/83)	
26042			02/70	vo	C	J. Cashmore at Reddish Depot	(C10/71)	
26043	76043	76043	06/78	vo	C	C.F. Booth, Rotherham	(C02/84)	
26044	76044	76031	07/81	ao	C	Coopers Metals, Brightside, Sheffield	(C01/84)	
26045			11/71	vo	C	B.R. Crewe Works	(C04/72)	
26046	76046		11/80	vr	C	C.F. Booth, Rotherham	(C03/83)	
26047	76047		11/80	vr	C	C.F. Booth, Rotherham	( )	
26048	76048	76039	11/81	ar	C	C.F. Booth, Rotherham	( )	
26049	76049		11/80	vr	C	C.F. Booth, Rotherham	(C03/83)	
26050	76050	76038	11/81	ar	C	C.F. Booth, Rotherham	(C05/83)	
26051	76051		07/81	vr	C	C.F. Booth, Rotherham	(C04/83)	
26052	76052		06/78	vr	C	C.F. Booth, Rotherham	(C02/84)	
26053	76053		11/80	vr	C	C.F. Booth, Rotherham	(C03/83)	
26054	76054		07/81	vr	C	C.F. Booth, Rotherham	(C05/83)	
26055	76055		02/77	vr	C	C.F. Booth, Rotherham	(C02/84)	
26056	76056		06/78	vr	C	C.F. Booth, Rotherham	(C02/83)	
26057	76057		02/77	vr	C	C.F. Booth, Rotherham	(C02/83)	

**26000 built as L.N.E.R. 6700 then 6000. Loaned to the Netherlands Railways 9/47-3/52.

Names:

26000	TOMMY		26052	NESTOR
26046	ARCHIMEDES		26053	PERSEUS
26047	DIOMEDES		26054	PLUTO
26048	HECTOR		26055	PROMETHEUS
26049	JASON		26056	TRITON
26050	STENTOR		26057	ULYSSES
26051	MENTOR			

CLASS ES1 NORTH EASTERN RAILWAY/B.T.H. 640 h.p. RE/OE Bo-Bo
Built 1905

NER	LNER	BR				
1	6480*	26500	02/64	P	National Railway Museum, York	
2	6481	26501	02/64	C	W. Willoughby, Choppington	(C10/66)

*—Also carried 4075

CLASS EB1 NORTH EASTERN RAILWAY/E.E. 1100 h.p. OE Bo-Bo

Built 1914

NER	LNER	BR						
3	6490	26502	08/50	C	W. Wanty, Sheffield	(C06/51)	
4	6491	26503	08/50	C	W. Wanty, Sheffield	(C04/51)	
5	6492	26504	08/50	C		(C /51)	
6	6493	26505	08/50	C	W. Wanty, Sheffield	(C08/51)	
7	6494	26506	08/50	C	W. Wanty, Sheffield	(C05/51)	
8	6495	26507	08/50	C	W. Wanty, Sheffield	(C07/51)	
9	6496	26508	08/50	C	W. Wanty, Sheffield	(C04/51)	
10	6497	26509	08/50	C	W. Wanty, Sheffield	(C08/51)	
11	6498	26510		D	Departmental use see 100	( )	
12	6499	26511	08/50	C	W. Wanty, Sheffield	(C04/51)	

CLASS EE1 NORTH EASTERN RAILWAY/MET.VIC. 1800 h.p. OE 2-C-2

Built 1922

NER	LNER	BR					
13	6999	26600	08/50	C	W. Wanty, Sheffield	(C07/51)	

CLASS EM2 B.R./MET.VIC. 2490 h.p. OE Co-Co

Built 1953-55. Allocated TOPS class 77, but never ran in service as that class.

27000	10/68	vb	E	Netherlands Railway 1502	
27001	10/68	vb	E	Netherlands Railway 1505	
27002	10/68	vb	E	Netherlands Railway 1506 (condemned)	
27003	10/68	vb	E	Netherlands Railway 1501	
27004	10/68	vb	E	Netherlands Railway 1503	
27005	10/68	vb	E	Netherlands Railway	(C11/69)
27006	10/68	vb	E	Netherlands Railway 1504	

Names:

27000	ELECTRA		27004	JUNO
27001	ARIADNE		27005	MINERVA
27002	AURORA		27006	PANDORA
27003	DIANA			

BRITISH RAILWAYS

UNCLASSIFIED METROPOLITAN VICKERS 2500 h.p. OE A1A-A1A

Rebuilt 1958 from Gas Turbine Loco. 18100.

E1000	E2000	/68	ve	C	J. Cashmore, Great Bridge	( )

CLASS 81 B.R.C. & W./B.T.H. 3200 h.p. OE Bo-Bo

Built 1959-64. Formerly Class AL1.

E3001	81001		xe			
E3002		11/68	ve	C	B.R. Crewe Works	(C01/69)
E3003	81002		xe			
E3004	81003		xe			
E3005	81004		xe			
E3006	81005		xe			
E3007	81006		xe			
E3008	81007		xe			
E3009		09/68	ve	C	B.R. Crewe Works	(C09/68)

E3010	81008		xe					
E3011	81009		xe					
E3012	81010		xe					
E3013	81011		xe					
E3014	81012		xe					
E3015	81013		xe					
E3016	81014		xe					
E3017	81015		xe					
E3018	81016	07/83	xe					
E3019		07/71	ve	C	B.R. Crewe Works	(C10/71)		
E3020	81017		xe					
E3021	81018		xe					
E3022	81019		xe					
E3023	81020		xe					

Class continued with E3096

CLASS 83   ENGLISH ELECTRIC 2950 h.p. OE   Bo-Bo
Built 1960-61

E3024	83001	07/83	xe	C	F. Berry, Leicester	(	)	
E3025	83002	07/83	xe	C	F. Berry, Leicester	(	)	
E3026	83003	05/75	xe	C	B.R. Crewe Works	(C07/75)		
E3027	83004	01/78	xe	C	B.R. Willesden Depot	(C02/78)		
E3028	83005	07/83	xe	C	F. Berry, Leicester	(	)	
E3029	83006	07/83	xe	C	F. Berry, Leicester	(	)	
E3030	83007	07/83	xe	C	F. Berry, Leicester	(	)	
E3031	83008	07/83	xe	C	F. Berry, Leicester	(	)	
E3032	83009	07/83	xe					
E3033	83010	07/83	xe	C	F. Berry, Leicester	(	)	
E3034	83011	07/83	xe	C	F. Berry, Leicester	(	)	
E3035	83012		xe					

Class continued with E3098

CLASS 84   N.B.L./G.E.C. 3300 h.p. OE   Bo-Bo
Built 1960-61

E3036	84001	01/79	xe	P	National Railway Museum, York		
E3037	84002	09/80	xe	F	G.E.C., Manchester		
E3038	84003	10/80	xe	D	Railway Technical Centre, Derby		
E3039	84004	11/77	xe				
E3040	84005	04/77	xe				
E3041	84006	01/78	xe	C	J. Cashmore at Gresty Road, Crewe	(C10/79)	
E3042	84007	04/77	xe	C	J. Cashmore at Gresty Road, Crewe	(C10/79)	
E3043	84008	10/79	xe				
E3044	84009	08/78	xe	D	ADB968021 Load test unit for 506 at LG		
E3045	84010	10/80	xe	F	G.E.C., Manchester		

CLASS 82   METROPOLITAN VICKERS 3300 h.p. OE   Bo-Bo
Built 1960-62

E3046		01/71	ve	C	B.R. Crewe Works	(C06/71)		
E3047	82001	07/83	xe					
E3048	82002	07/83	xe	C	F. Berry, Leicester	(	)	
E3049	82003	07/83	xe					
E3050	82004	10/83	xe	C	F. Berry, Leicester	(	)	
E3051	82005							
E3052	82006	07/83	xe	C	F. Berry, Leicester	(	)	

E3053	82007	07/83	xe	C	F. Berry, Leicester	(	)
E3054	82008		xe				
E3055		09/69	ve	C	B.R. Crewe Works	(C08/70)	

CLASS 85   B.R./E.E. 3200 h.p. OE   Bo-Bo
Built 1961-64

E3056	85001		xe
E3057	85002		xe
E3058	85003		xe
E3059	85004		xe
E3060	85005		xe
E3061	85006		xe
E3062	85007		xe
E3063	85008		xe
E3064	85009		xe
E3065	85010		xe
E3066	85011		xe
E3067	85012		xe
E3068	85013		xe
E3069	85014		xe
E3070	85015		xe
E3071	85016		xe
E3072	85017		xe
E3073	85018		xe
E3074	85019		xe
E3075	85020		xe
E3076	85021		xe
E3077	85022		xe
E3078	85023		xe
E3079	85024		xe
E3080	85025		xe
E3081	85026		xe
E3082	85027	07/83	xe
E3083	85028		xe
E3084	85029		xe
E3085	85030		xe
E3086	85031		xe
E3087	85032		xe
E3088	85033	07/84	xe
E3089	85034		xe
E3090	85035		xe
E3091	85036		xe
E3092	85037		xe
E3093	85038		xe
E3094	85039		xe
E3095	85040		xe

CLASS 81 continued

E3096	81021		xe
E3097	81022		xe

CLASS 83 continued

E3098*	83013	07/83	xe	C	F. Berry, Leicester	(	)
E3099*	83014	07/83	xe	C	F. Berry, Leicester	(	)
E3100	83015		xe				

—Originally E3303/4.

CLASS 86　　　B.R. & E.E./E.E. 4040 h.p. OE　　　**Bo-Bo**

Built 1965-66

E3101	86252		xe
E3102	86009		xe
E3103	86004		xe
E3104	86010		xe
E3105	86030		xe
E3106	86214		xe
E3107	86248		xe
E3108	86038		xe
E3109	86016	86316	xe
E3110	86027	86327	xe
E3111	86024	86324	xe
E3112	86006		xe
E3113	86232		xe
E3114	86030	86320	xe
E3115	86003		xe
E3116	86238		xe
E3117	86227		xe
E3118	86041	86261	xe
E3119	86229		xe
E3120	86019	86319	xe
E3121	86241		xe
E3122	86012	86312	xe
E3123	86015	86315	xe
E3124	86035		xe
E3125	86209		xe
E3126	86231		xe
E3127	86240		xe
E3128	86013	86313	xe
E3129	86205		xe
E3130	86037		xe
E3131	86222		xe
E3132	86221		xe
E3133	86236		xe
E3134	86224		xe
E3135	86040	86256	xe
E3136	86044	86253	xe
E3137	86045	86259	xe
E3138	86242		xe
E3139	86043	86257	xe
E3140	86046	86258	xe
E3141	86208		xe
E3142	86047	86254	xe
E3143	86203	86103	xe
E3144	86048	86260	xe
E3145	86014	86314	xe
E3146	86017	86317	xe
E3147	86211		xe
E3148	86032		xe
E3149	86246		xe
E3150	86202	86102	xe
E3151	86212		xe
E3152	86023	86323	xe
E3153	86039		xe
E3154	86042	86255	xe

E3155	86234		xe
E3156	86220		xe
E3157	86021	86321	xe
E3158	86223		xe
E3159	86028	86328	xe
E3160	86036		xe
E3161	86249		xe
E3162	86226		xe
E3163	86018	86318	xe
E3164	86225		xe
E3165	86215		xe
E3166	86216		xe
E3167	86228		xe
E3168	86230		xe
E3169	86239		xe
E3170	86002		xe
E3171	86011	86311	xe
E3172	86233		xe
E3173	86204		xe
E3174	86022	86322	xe
E3175	86218		xe
E3176	86007		xe
E3177	86217		xe
E3178	86244		xe
E3179	86207		xe
E3180	86008		xe
E3181	86243		xe
E3182	86245		xe
E3183	86251		xe
E3184	86206		xe
E3185	86005		xe
E3186	86025	86325	xe
E3187	86034		xe
E3188	86031		xe
E3189	86250		xe
E3190	86210		xe
E3191	86201		xe
E3192	86247		xe
E3193	86213		xe
E3194	86235		xe
E3195	86036	86326	xe
E3196	86219		xe
E3197	86237		xe
E3198	86033		xe
E3199	86001		xe
E3200	86029	86329	xe

Names:

86101	Sir William A Stanier FRS	86210	City of Edinburgh
86102	Robert A Riddles	86211	City of Milton Keynes
86103	André Chapelon	86212	Preston Guild
86204	City of Carlisle	86213	Lancashire Witch
86205	City of Lancaster	86214	Sans Pareil
86206	City of Stoke on Trent	86215	Joseph Chamberlain
86207	City of Lichfield	86216	Meteor
86208	City of Chester	86217	Comet
86209	City of Coventry	86218	Planet

86219	Phoenix	
86220	Goliath	
86221	Vesta	
86222	Fury	
86223	Hector	
86224	Caledonian	
86225	Hardwicke	
86226	Mail	
86227	Sir Henry Johnson	
86228	Vulcan Heritage	
86229	Sir John Betjeman	
86230	The Duke of Wellington	
86231	Starlight Express	
86232	Harold Macmillan	
86233	Laurence Olivier	
86234	J B Priestley O M	
86235	Novelty	
86236	Josiah Wedgwood	
86237	Sir Charles Halle	
86238		
86239	L S Lowry	
86240	Bishop Eric Treacy	
86241	Glenfiddich	
86242	John Kennedy G.C.	
86243	The Boys Brigade	
86244	The Royal British Legion	
86245	Dudley Castle	
86246		
86247	Abraham Derby	
86248	Sir Clwyd-County of Clwyd	
86249	County of Merseyside	
86250	The Glasgow Herald	
86251	The Birmingham Post	
86252	The Liverpool Daily Post	
86253	The Manchester Guardian	
86254	William Webb Ellis	
86255	Penrith Beacon	
86256	Pebble Mill	
86257	Snowdon	
86258	Talyllyn The First Preserved Railway	
86259	Peter Pan	
86260	Driver Wallace Oaks G.C.	
86261	Driver John Oxon G.C.	
86311	Airey Neave	
86312	Elizabeth Garrett Anderson	
86315	Rotary International	
86316	Wigan Pier	
86328	Aldaniti	

CLASS 71

Built 1959-60

B.R./E.E. 2500 h.p. RE/OE

Bo-Bo

E5000	E5024			xe	R	Rebuilt see E6104	
E5001		71001	11/77	xe	P	National Railway Museum, York	
E5002		71002	11/77	xe	C	J. Cashmore, Newport (C01/79)	
E5003				xe	R	Rebuilt see E6107	
E5004		71004	11/77	xe	C	B.R. Doncaster Works (C01/80)	
E5005				xe	R	Rebuilt see E6108	
E5006				xe	R	Rebuilt see E6103	
E5007		71007	11/77	xe	C	J. Cashmore, Newport (C11/78)	
E5008		71008	11/77	xe	C	J. Cashmore, Newport (C11/78)	
E5009		71009	11/77	xe	C	B.R. Doncaster Works (C09/79)	
E5010		71010	11/77	xe	C	B.R. Doncaster Works (C08/79)	
E5011		71011	11/77	xe	C	B.R. Doncaster Works (C11/79)	
E5012		71012	11/77	xe	C	J. Cashmore, Newport (C11/78)	
E5013		71013	11/77	xe	C	B.R. Doncaster Works (C11/79)	
E5014		71014	11/77	xe	C	B.R. Doncaster Works (C09/79)	
E5015				xe	R	Rebuilt see E6101	
E5016				xe	R	Rebuilt see E6102	
E5017				xe	R	Rebuilt see E6109	
E5018	E5003	71003	11/77	xe	C	B.R. Doncaster Works (C03/80)	
E5019				xe	R	Rebuilt see E6105	
E5020	E5005	71005	11/77	xe	C	J. Cashmore, Newport (C11/78)	
E5021				xe	R	Rebuilt see E6110	
E5022	E5006	71006	11/77	xe	C	J. Cashmore, Newport (C11/78)	
E5023				xe	R	Rebuilt see E6106	

E6001	73001		ye		
E6002	73002		ye		
E6003	73003		ye		
E6004	73004		ye		
E6005	73005		ye		
E6006	73006		ye		
E6007	73101		ye		
E6008	73102		ye		
E6009	73103		ye		
E6010	73104		ye		
E6011	73105		ye		
E6012	73106		ye		
E6013	73107		ye		
E6014	73108		ye		
E6015	73109		ye		
E6016	73110		ye		
E6017	73111		ye		
E6018	73112		ye		
E6019	73113		ye		
E6020	73114		ye		
E6021	73115	04/82	yr	C B.R. Selhurst Depot	(C06/82)
E6022	73116		ye		
E6023	73117		ye		
E6024	73118		ye		
E6025	73119		ye		
E6026	73120		ye		
E6027		07/72	ye	C B.R., Slade Green Depot	(C02/73)
E6028	73121		ye		
E6029	73122		ye		
E6030	73123		ye		
E6031	73124		ye		
E6032	73125		ye		
E6033	73126		ye		
E6034	73127		ye		
E6035	73128		ye		
E6036	73129		ye		
E6037	73130		ye		
E6038	73131		ye		
E6039	73132		ye		
E6040	73133		ye		
E6041	73134		ye		
E6042	73135		ye		
E6043	73136		ye		
E6044	73137		ye		
E6045	73138		ye		
E6046	73139		ye		
E6047	73140		ye		
E6048	73141		ye		
E6049	73142		ye		

Names:

73101	Brighton Evening Argus	73129	City of Winchester
73121	Croydon 1883-1983	73142	Broadlands
73123	Gatwick Express		

CLASS 74   B.R./PAXMAN/E.E. 2552 h.p. ED   Bo-Bo
Rebuilt 1967-68 Class 71

E6101	74001	12/77	ye	C	Birds Comml. Motors, Long Marston	(C09/78)	
E6102	74002	06/77	ye	C	J. Cashmore, Newport	(C12/77)	
E6103	74003	12/77	ye	C	J. Cashmore, Newport	(C12/77)	
E6104	74004	12/77	ye	C	Birds Comml. Motors, Long Marston	(C01/81)	
E6105	74005	12/77	ye	C	Pounds Ltd., Havent at Fratton Depot	(C01/81)	
E6106	74006	06/76	ye	C	G. Cohen, Kettering	(C07/77)	
E6107	74007	12/77	ye	C	Birds Comml. Motors, Long Marston	(C09/78)	
E6108	74008	12/77	ye	C	Birds Comml. Motors, Long Marston	(C09/78)	
E6109	74009	12/77	ye	C	Birds Comml. Motors, Long Marston	(C09/78)	
E6110	74010	12/77	ye	C	B.R. Doncaster Works	(C10/79)	

CLASS 87   B.R./G.E.C. 4850 h.p. OE   Bo-Bo
Built 1973-75

87001		ae	
87002		ae	
87003		ae	
87004		ae	
87005		ae	
87006		ae	
87007		ae	
87008		ae	
87009		ae	
87010		ae	
87011		ae	
87012		ae	
87013		ae	
87014		ae	
87015		ae	
87016		ae	
87017		ae	
87018		ae	
87019		ae	
87020		ae	
87021		ae	
87022		ae	
87023		ae	
87024		ae	
87025		ae	
87026		ae	
87027		ae	
87028		ae	
87029		ae	
87030		ae	
87031		ae	
87032		ae	
87033		ae	
87034		ae	
87035		ae	
87036	87101	ae	

Names:

87001	Royal Scot (formerly STEPHENSON)		87021	Robert the Bruce
87002	Royal Sovereign		87022	Cock o' the North
87003	Patriot		87023	Highland Chieftain (to 5/84)
87004	Britannia			
87005	City of London		87024	Lord of the Isles
87006	City of Glasgow		87025	Borderer (to 11/82)
87007	City of Manchester			County of Cheshire (from 11/82)
87008	City of Liverpool		87026	Redgauntlet (to 11/82)
87009	City of Birmingham			Sir Richard Arkwright (from 11/82)
87010	King Arthur		87027	Wolf of Badenoch
87011	The Black Prince		87028	Lord President
87012	Coeur-de-Lion		87029	Earl Marischal
87013	John o' Gaunt		87030	Black Douglas
87014	Knight of the Thistle		87031	Hal o' the Wynd
87015	Howard of Effingham		87032	Kenilworth
87016	Sir Francis Drake		87033	Thane of Fife
87017	Iron Duke		87034	William Shakespeare
87018	Lord Nelson		87035	Robert Burns
87019	Sir Winston Churchill		87101	STEPHENSON
87020	North Briton			

9. DEPARTMENTAL LOCOMOTIVES

The following lists standard gauge locos in departmental/service use with the four Pre-Nationalisation and constituent companies and B.R. Where no heading is given reference should be made to the respective sections of the book for details.

L.M.S.R. & CONSTITUENT COMPANIES

LYR/DICK KERR 600 h.p. OE/RE   2-4-2
Built 1912 on frames of intended steam loco
1   /20   n   C   B.R. Horwich Works   (C   /22)

MIDLAND RAILWAY/DICK KERR 88 h.p. BE   4W
Built 1914 for Poplar/West India Docks, London
41550   BEL 1   09/64   n   C   Poplar Docks by R.A.King, Norwich   (C11/64)

LANCASHIRE & YORKSHIRE RAILWAY/BTH 36 h.p. BE   4W
Built 1916/7 for Clifton Jct Power Station
2   03/64   v   C   L.M.S. Derby Loco Works   (C05/46)

NORTH STAFFORDSHIRE RAILWAY/BTH 82 h.p. BE   4W
Built 1917 for Oakamoor Copper Works
BEL 2   06/63   n   P   National Railway Museum   (C   /   )

'SIMPLEX'/DORMAN 40 h.p. PM   4W
Built 1917 & 1920 for LYR
LYR1   11/30   n   P   Chasewater Light Railway
LYR2   11/30   n   C   Arnott Young   (C   /63)
LYR3   11/30   n   C   Sythite, Mold   (C   /65)

MERCURY TRUCK & TRACTOR Co. PM   4W
Built 1927 for Wolverton Works
1311   1311G   n   P   Midland Railway Centre, Butterley

J. FOWLER/RUSTON & HORNSBY 88 h.p. DM   0-4-0

Built 1935. Also carried ED2 before ED1.

2	ED1	06/62	n	C	Derby Locomotive Works	(C06/62)	

FOWLER 88 h.p. DM   0-4-0

Built 1949

ED2	06/65	n	C	B.R. Derby Works	(C09/67)	
ED3	09/67	n	C	G. Cohen, Kettering	(C03/68)	
ED4	02/64	n	C	J. Cashmore, Great Bridge	( )	
ED5	06/65	n	C	J. Cashmore, Kettering	( )	
ED6	09/67	n	C	G. Cohen, Kettering	( )	

FOWLER/SANDERS 150 h.p. DM   0-4-0

Built 1940. Into B.R. stock 1955.

ED7	02/64	n			(C04/64)	

Note: LMS nos. 7056/5, 1831 were converted to Mobile Power Units in 1939/40 (MPU1/2/3)

L.N.E.R. & CONSTITUENT COMPANIES

DICK KERR 100 h.p. OE   1A-A1

Built 1925, converted to Works Car (formerly Gateshead & District Tramways No. 17)

DE320224	07/61	C	(C)	

G.W.R. & CONSTITUENT COMPANIES

MR 'SIMPLEX'/DORMAN 40 h.p. PM   4W

Built 1923/1927

15	02/51	n	C	B.R. Swindon Works	(C03/51)	
23	07/60	n	C	B.R. Swindon Works	(C10/60)	
24	11/60	n	C	B.R. Swindon Works	(C11/60)	
26	07/60	n	C	B.R. Swindon Works	(C10/60)	
27	07/60	n	C	B.R. Swindon Works	(C10/60)	

J. FOWLER/M.A.N. 70 h.p. DM   0-4-0

Built 1933 as Demonstrator, sold to GWR

1	03/40	n	P	Chasewater Light Railway	( )	

S.R. & CONSTITUENT COMPANIES

S.R./'SIMPLEX'/DORMAN 40 h.p. PM   4W

Built c1940, Exmouth Junction C&W Depot

49s	DS49	09/59	n	C	T.W. Ward, Briton Ferry	(C /)	

LSWR/DICK KERR 240 h.p. RE   Bo-Bo

Built 1899 for LSWR (Waterloo & City Section)

74s	DS74	07/65	n	C	Cox & Danks, Park Royal	(C07/65)	

SIEMENS 120 h.p. RE   Bo

Built 1898 for LSWR (Waterloo & City Section)

75s	DS75	05/68	n	P	National Railway Museum	

PM TYPE TRACTOR   4W

Built for Ashford Works

112s	details unknown	

HARDY RAILMOTORS/HARRIER 45 h.p. PM   **4W**
Built 1930 for Eastleigh Works

343s   DS343   02/52 n C   (C /)

DICK KERR
Built/Converted 1908, 1911 & 1916 as Maintenance Vehicles

342s   n C   (C12/31)
344s   n C   (C06/23)
345s   n C   (C08/31)

DREWRY/BAGULEY 20 h.p. PM   **4W**
Built 1915, Inspection Vehicle

346s   DS346   /49 n C   (C /)

J. FOWLER/SANDERS, 420 CLASS 150 h.p. DM   **0-4-0**
Built 1941 & 1943

400s   DS400   /57 n C   Pounds Shipbreakers, Fratton
600s   DS600   01/63 n C   Birds Comml. Motors, Long Marston   (C08/69)

S.R./THORNEYCROFT PM   **4W**
Built c1935, Lancing Works Machine No. 199

499s   DS499   03/65 n C   Lancing Works   (C /)

RUSTON & HORNSBY TYPE 48DS 48 h.p. DM   **4W**
Built 1945/6 (later sold 1948 to B.R.)

                      /59 n C   E.L. Pitt, Brackley, Coventry   (C /)
DS1169   08/67 n C   G. Cohen, Kettering   (C07/73)

Built 1947
DS1173   04/67 v   transferred to Capital Stock as DS2341

BRITISH RAILWAYS

HIBBERD/ENGLISH NATIONAL GAS 'PLANET' 52 h.p. DM   **4W**
Built 1950, carrying Capital Stock No. Series 11104

52   03/67 n C   J. Cashmore, Newport   (C   )

RUSTON & HORNSBY/WILSON 88 h.p. DM   **4W**

56   /76 n C   T.J. Thomson, Stockton   (   )

Built 1958
81   07/67 v F   To Capital Stock D2956

RUSTON & HORNSBY 150 h.p. DM   **4W**
Built 1958-61

82   05/70 n C   T.J. Thomson, Stockton   (   )
83   /69 n C   W. Heselwood, Sheffield   (C   )
84   /76 n C   A. Young, Parkgate   (C   )
85   /76 n C   A. Young, Parkgate   (C   )
86   /76 n C   A. Young, Parkgate   (C   )
87   /70 n C   T.J. Thomson, Stockton   (   )

Built 1961. Formerly capital stock D2612/5

88		09/67	v	C	(	)
89		11/67	v	C	(	)

Built 1958

91		08/67	v	F	To Capital Stock D2370
92		08/67	v	F	To Capital Stock D2371

SECMAFER/PERKINS 210 h.p. DH   4W
Built 1965, on trial 1966-8, then returned.
DS209   Formerly SNCF 233.5.2

STRACHAN & HENSHAW DM   4W
Built 1969 for Crewe Works
7042

'SIMPLEX'/PETTER 20 h.p. DM   4W
Built 1978 for Wolverton Works
9125

NOORD NEDERLANDSCHE MACHINENFABRIEK DH   4W
Built 1977 as road/rail vehicle converted 1980, Crewe Works.
7158

The following is a list of locos, allocated for departmental work at some stage in their careers but never actually allocated Departmental/Service numbers.

D812	Spares for D832 and static display
D832	Possible use for APT development (never actually used)
D844	Train Pre-Heating Unit, 1971/2
D1033	Train Pre-Heating Unit, 1976/7
D1034	Train Pre-Heating Unit, 1975/6
D2115	Hookagate Rail Welding Depot Shunting Loco
D2133	Taunton CCE Depot Shunting Loco
D2991	Eastleigh Works Generator
08173	Internal use, Polmadie Depot (as PO1)
08247	Internal use, Polmadie Depot (as PO1), returned to Capital Stock
D3509	Meldon Quarry Shunting Loco
D3510	Hookagate Rail Welding Depot Shunting Loco
D5901	Dead Load Vehicle, Railway Technical Centre, Derby 1969-1975
D7076	Dead Load Vehicle, Railway Technical Centre, Derby
D7096	Dead Load Vehicle, Railway Technical Centre, Derby
D8512	Test Loco,, 1969-1972
D8521	Generator Loco (as S18521), then spares for D8598
74010	Earmarked for use as Departmental Loco, but condemned 1979

The following departmental locos are lised in the current departmental number series order and, again, reference shoulder be made to the respective sections for details of those without headings. Former numbers are in brackets.

RUSTON & HORNSBY TYPE 88DS 88 h.p. DM   4W
Built 1957 for Reading Signal Works

97020	20		n	C

Converted 1972/5 as Test Locos

| 97101 | (D8598) | Departmental number never carried | (C |) |
| 97201* | (24061) | Also carried RDB 968007 | | |

Converted 1983/4 as Electric Train Heating Units ("ETHEL 1/2/3")

97250   (25310)
97251   (25305)
97252   (25314)

Converted 1984 as Test Locos, Departmental numbers not yet carried.

97401   (46009)
97402   (46023)

RUSTON & HORNSBY/BTH 165 h.p. DE   0-6-0
Built 1952 (97659) & 1959 (remainder)

97650   (PWM650) o
97651   (PWM651) v
97652   (PWM652) v
97653   (PWM653) v
97654   (PWM654) v

Converted 1973 (97701/2), 1975 (97707-10) & 1980 (97703-6) from Class 501 Watford-Euston 1957 - cars.

97701	(M61136)	also carried LDB975178
97702	(M61139)	also carried LDB975179
97703	(M61182)	
97704	(M61185)	
97705	(M61184)	
97706	(M61189)	
97707	(M61166)	also carried LDB975407
97708	(M61173)	also carried LDB975408
97709	(M61172)	also carried LDB975409
97710	(M61175)	also carried LDB975410

VARIOUS SHUNTERS
Transferred/converted 1978/9/81 + /84§*

97800*	(08600)	also carried 97880
97801	(86267)	also carried RDB968020 'Pluto'
97802	(08070)	
97803+	(05001)	
97804+	(06003)	
97805§	(03079)	

TRAIN PRE-HEATING UNITS & LOAD BANK*

The followng is a list of such conversions:

ADB 968000	(D8243)	TDB 968004	(D7055)	ADB 968013	(31013)
ADB 968001	(D8233)	TDB 968005	(D7089)	ADB 968014	(31002)
ADB 968002	(D8237)	TDB 968006+	(D5705)	ADB 968015	(31014)
ADB 968003	(D8203)	ADB 968008	(24054)	ADB 968016	(31008)
—	(D8234)	ADB 968009	(24142)	ADB 968021*	(84009)

+ *Also carried S15705*